URBAN LIFE AND URBAN LANDSCAPE SERIES

MAKING SENSE OF THE CITY

LOCAL GOVERNMENT,
CIVIC CULTURE,
AND COMMUNITY LIFE
IN URBAN AMERICA

EDITED BY

ROBERT B. FAIRBANKS

AND

PATRICIA MOONEY-MELVIN

THE OHIO STATE UNIVERSITY PRESS

COLUMBUS

Library of Congress Cataloging-in-Publication Data

Making sense of the city : local government, civic culture, and
community life in urban America / Edited by Robert B. Fairbanks and
Patricia Mooney-Melvin.
p. cm. — (Urban life and urban landscape series)
Festschrift in honor of Zane L. Miller.
ISBN 0-8142-0881-9
1. Cities and towns—United States—History. 2. Municipal
government—United States—History.   3. City planning—United
States—History.   4. Miller, Zane L. I. Fairbanks, Robert B. (Robert
Bruce), 1950–   II. Mooney-Melvin, Patricia.   III. Miller, Zane L.
IV. Series.
HT123 .M287 2001
307.76'0973—dc21   2001002155

Paper (ISBN: 978-0-8142-5719-7)

Jacket design by David Drummond.
Text Design by Nighthawk Design.
Type set in 10 pt. Palatino by Bookcomp, Inc.

For Zane L. Miller,
scholar, mentor, and friend

Contents

Preface

Seated at his desk—pipe clenched between his teeth in days gone by—surrounded by city maps and overflowing bookcases and file drawers, with piles of books and papers on the floor, Zane L. Miller appears to be the quintessential absentminded professor, immersed in his own world. Appearances can be deceiving, and in Zane's case they definitely are. Instead of retreating into the world of the past, he has embraced it, communicated his enthusiasm for making sense of it, and energetically shared his insights as well as his questions with both scholarly and broader public audiences. He is as comfortable sitting in the mayor's office, talking with a community group, or working with planners as he is at an academic conference. With his feet planted firmly, and contemporaneously, within and outside the university, Zane typifies the historian at his or her best: a professional who demands a high level of scholarship that is as accessible to a broad reading public as it is to academic colleagues, and who is ever mindful of his or her responsibilities as both citizen and scholar.

Toward that end Miller founded and codirected with Henry D. Shapiro the University of Cincinnati Center for Neighborhood and Community Studies and has participated in endless civic activities, including holding positions on the steering committee of Hamilton County's Democratic Party, Cincinnati's Historic Conservation Board, and the Ohio Historic Site Preservation Advisory Board. He has consulted with a variety of organizations in regard to school integration, public housing, and urban renewal. Miller also founded and codirected the Cincinnati Seminar on the City, which provided a forum for public discourse of urban historians with anyone interested in the life and history of cities. In a recent interview Miller explained his commitment to the broader community when he said, "Civic activity makes democracy tick" and "Scholarship, history, and public service all help improve society." For Miller, history offers "useful lessons about human imagination and human capacities but nothing of immediately practical use for our period, for people in past periods shared our humanity but thought and acted differently than we do because they lived in different conceptual and perceptual worlds." But he goes on to argue that understanding that the past was created by people who shaped their worlds by making choices within the constraints of their time clears the way for those living in the present to make informed, and historically constrained, choices about the future. Such an approach is clearly controversial and differs from the advocacy history promoted by so many historians today.

Nothing about Zane's approach to the past has been conventional, although central to his examination of the past has been the attempt to understand the efforts of people to comprehend and make sense of their environment. In *Boss Cox's Cincinnati*, Zane's exploration of the political response of Cincinnatians to the impact of rapid urbanization at the end of the nineteenth century moved beyond the battle between the forces of "good" and "evil" for control of the city. He found that the way contemporaries perceived the spatial arrangement of the city and then used it in their attempts to solve governance problems helped explain the political world of turn-of-the-century Cincinnati. Unlike many historians during the late 1960s, Miller saw the urban environment as an arena where the spatial dynamics of the urban landscape were as important to understanding urban order and disorder as class, ethnicity, or race.

Later, influenced by his close association with intellectual historian Henry D. Shapiro, Zane explored with greater intensity the role of human perception of reality as the key to understanding the urban past. For their graduate students, the Miller-Shapiro collaboration provided a model of collegiality. They taught an innovative undergraduate seminar together, coedited the Ohio State University Press's Urban Life and Urban Landscape series, codirected the Center for Neighborhood and Community Studies, and made contributions that enhanced and advanced the work of each other. Graduate students who worked with Miller benefited enormously from this collaboration and adopted some of its practices in creating a nourishing community where graduate students read and commented on each other's work and prepared sessions for conferences far outside of the formal seminar setting.

Under the Miller-Shapiro approach, we came to understand history as problem solving. Our job as budding historians was to identify how problems were defined during the era we studied and to examine the consequences of those social constructs. Although our topics, time periods, and locales differ, central to our collective approach to history is an emphasis on the impact of ideas and perception rather than events, and a concern with process rather than with cause and effect.

For his students, Zane has been more than a good historian and active citizen. He has been a mentor, someone who, according to *Webster's Ninth New Collegiate Dictionary*, is "a wise and trusted teacher, guide, and friend." Regardless of gender, class, race, age, or background, he accepted us as students who would grow into historians as we transformed knowledge into professional understanding. Miller has been a generous teacher and colleague, patient but demanding, sharing ideas and information, guiding and chiding (when necessary), and always supportive. Wherever we have landed, whatever the topics upon which we have ultimately focused, Zane's approach to life and scholarship has left an indelible mark on our careers.

The sense of community Zane promoted among us has survived as we have gone our separate ways professionally. One of the pleasures of editing this volume has been working together in a cooperative enterprise that yielded this tangible evidence of his legacy. We have had the opportunity to work with both our own colleagues in graduate school and those we met later as Zane's "new students." We thank all our collaborators for their ideas, enthusiasm, and relative timeliness.

We would like to thank our respective universities, the University of Texas at Arlington (UTA) and Loyola University Chicago, for their support of this endeavor. Among other things, this support has included costs to defray photocopying and postage by the UTA history department and, through the support of a Loyola University Support Grant, the preparation of the index.

We also benefited from the help and encouragement of past and present members of The Ohio State University Press staff. Barbara Hanrahan, former director, enthusiastically supported our proposal. Former acquisitions editors Emily Rogers and Darrin Pratt also provided needed advice and support. Current manuscript editors Ruth Melville and Beth Ina, along with Lynne Bonenberger, who copyedited the text, have been encouraging and helpful throughout the process. Finally we wish to thank the two manuscript referees. Henry D. Shapiro, a supporter of this venture from the beginning, provided valuable suggestions for improving the manuscript. So did the other, anonymous, reader, who reminded us of Zane's humanity and openness to different perspectives, and of what festschrifts are really about.

Introduction

Robert B. Fairbanks and
Patricia Mooney-Melvin

Zane L. Miller has argued that the main theme of the history of the city, as well as what goes on inside it, is not continuity but flux.[1] The same can be said of the scholarly examination of the urban environment. Those who study cities have subjected them to different questions and modes of analysis in their quest to understand the urban environment. The amount of documentation available, historians' individual interests, contemporary approaches to writing history, and influential historians have all shaped the topics covered and the approaches selected to unlock the mysteries inherent in the past. As a result, shifting paradigms, new insights, and differing issues of concern have characterized the study of America's urban history.

Making Sense of the City examines various responses to the challenges of urban life in nineteenth- and twentieth-century America. What distinguishes this collection of essays from a number of other studies of the urban community is the assumption that the interaction between definition and action provided both a basis for understanding this community and a prescription for initiatives to improve its environment. This orientation suggests that a relationship exists between the definition of urban needs, the public responses to those needs, and the ways urbanites made sense of the city over time. Accordingly, the authors explore the process of urban problem solving and argue that how problems were defined and redefined at different periods is critical to understanding the nature of action in the urban environment.

The authors of this volume argue that whenever city dwellers found that their beliefs about urban life failed to correspond to the perceived actualities of the world around them, they resolved the disjunction through the world of ideas. Their ideas, poised between consciousness and reality, gave meaning to their world through a process of definition and action.[2] Based on the assumption that at any given time a broad and fundamental agreement exists about the nature of the city that allows contemporaries to

1

engage in dialogues about needs and actions on the local level, the chronology of urban history that results in these essays emphasizes that ideas of what cities were or ought to have been are locked in time and not place.[3] Ideas, organizations, strategies, or programs, for example, may seem to transcend time when in fact they possess different meanings in different historical contexts, regardless of their geographic location. As a result, the authors focus closely on the words and actions of various individuals, institutions, and organizations who participated in the public discourse about what the city was, or could be, and who defined urban needs and acted upon them within this context.

The following essays about local government, civic culture, and community life reflect the influence of Professor Zane L. Miller, the man whom this volume honors. Curiosity about the dynamic between definition and redefinition typifies Miller's approach to the study of the past and animates the issues he explores. Over the course of his career, Miller has taken a penetrating look at the relationship between ideas and action; urban definition and its impact on neighborhood life, city planning, and local government; and the changing nature of civic culture. During his tenure at the University of Cincinnati (1965–99), he supervised seventeen Ph.D. dissertations[4] and helped mentor numerous graduate students working with other professors, as well as a number of postdoctoral students. While his former students all have selected topics that reflect their own interests, what distinguishes their work is a concern with definition and the impact that the process of redefinition has had on understanding what goes on inside the urban environment.

Working with Professor Henry D. Shapiro, Miller developed an approach to urban history that he called *symptomatic history*. The focus of such history is the exploration of specific events, places, or individuals to demonstrate general patterns of thought and action during a particular era of time. As Miller defined it in the introduction to *Suburb: Neighborhood and Community in Forest Park, Ohio, 1935–1976*, "the past is really past, and it breaks into a series of discrete and discontinuous chronological periods separated by shifts in the way people characterize reality." This approach centers its attention on structure since, as Miller argues, "the way people organized reality usually manifests itself in a general disposition to change old institutions or create new ones." Hence, the way in which they see reality affects what they believe and how they act upon it. At its most basic level, according to Miller, symptomatic history examines how "people created their institutional and territorial milieus within which experience and ideas flow" and explores how they operated within the world as they understood it.[5] For Miller, as well as many of his students, the key to unlocking urban history is understanding the changing conceptions of cities over time and the consequences of those changes primarily, although not exclusively, on the local level.

This approach distinguishes Miller's work from the vast amount of historical scholarship since 1980[6] that focuses on the impact of social or economic forces and argues that these larger, impersonal forces shaped the city itself as well as the response to the city; that examines the urban experience through the use of a categorical analysis such as race, gender, or ethnicity; or that uses culture as an interpretive tool. For instance, much of the current work in urban history emphasizes the role of racism in molding the response to a variety of twentieth-century problems, while other studies emphasize the destructive impact of capitalism in creating humane cities.[7] Other recent urban history has been driven by themes emphasizing ethnic, class, and gender conflict.[8] Finally, Miller's approach to urban history, although sharing some broad methodological similarities, differs from recent studies that employ a group-based "application of 'culture' as an interpretive paradigm." According to Timothy J. Gilfoyle, contemporary urban historians have drawn upon "cultural methodologies and questions" in their analyses of social, economic, and ethnic or racial groups as well as the "built environment, regionalism, and suburbanization." Gilfoyle argues that historians, embracing theories of anthropologist Clifford Geertz and sociologist Claude S. Fischer with their focus on language to illustrate how subcultural groups conceptualized the city and civic identity, have produced an urban history that emphasizes fragmentation and provides a "plurality of microtheories" rather than a "totalizing theory, hegemonic interpretation, or universal paradigm."[9] Miller's approach differs from this by emphasizing basic cultural assumptions about city and society shared by all members of the population at different periods in United States history.

All the contributors to this volume have been influenced by this emphasis and also have been affected by another characteristic of Miller's work, a penchant for bringing a new perspective to whatever historical event is studied. For instance, in his first book, *Boss Cox's Cincinnati: Urban Politics in the Progressive Era,* Miller explored the urban political machine not from the dominant biographical or social approach, but rather by placing the conflict between political machines and reforms in the spatial context of core, zone, and periphery. Nineteenth-century urban growth altered virtually every relationship possible in urban areas, and urbanites struggled to come to terms with the new metropolitan community that confronted them as the nineteenth century became the twentieth. Miller's exploration of the political response of Cincinnatians to the impact of rapid urbanization and the apparent chaos generated in its wake suggested that more was going on than just a contest between "evil" bosses and "good" reformers. Instead, the spatial dynamics of the modern city demanded a new type of politician able to connect different segments of the city, defined by place more than by ethnicity and class, and thus able to create a viable governing coalition. Readers went to the volume in search of insights about politics and the urban version of the battle between good and evil, which they found, but came away as well with a clearer understanding of the nature of the "new" city of turn-of-the-century America.[10]

Likewise, Miller's examination of suburban development that resulted in *Suburb: Neighborhood and Community in Forest Park* was quite different from the social science literature that mainly critiqued suburbia. Nor was it an attempt to build on the history literature that emphasized the forces and actions that shaped suburbia. Rather, Miller used Forest Park to examine the ways Americans had defined their society and structured their territorial communities during the mid-twentieth century. He developed a new chronology crafted around shifts in prevailing modes of thought to understand the changing nature of Forest Park. His narrative begins in the 1930s during the era of the metropolitan mode of thought and continues into the 1950s and the period characterized by the community of limited liability. His study concludes in the era of the community of advocacy that commenced, according to Miller, during the mid-1960s.[11]

Miller's more recent book on urban redevelopment, *Changing Plans for America's Inner Cities: Cincinnati's Over-the-Rhine and Twentieth-Century Urbanism,* coauthored with Bruce Tucker, also brings a fresh perspective to an older discussion. Unlike the bulk of recent scholarship that uses urban redevelopment to expose racism and condemn the actions of civic leaders, Miller and Tucker use the efforts to improve the Over-the-Rhine section of Cincinnati to illustrate some of the consequences of changing "modes of thought about American cities and their neighborhoods."[12] *Changing Plans for America's Inner Cities* provides a detailed examination of public policy that started out as redevelopment and was transformed into conservation as a function of the changing ways Americans thought about their society. The shift from one mode of thought to another affected not only the web of beliefs that motivated urban planners but also the arsenal of weapons used by all parties involved in the battle for the future of Over-the-Rhine.[13] As with Miller's other books, this one reframed the questions about urban development and provided an entirely different way of approaching and understanding the subject matter.

Making Sense of the City, then, follows the Miller emphasis of looking at the process of urban problem solving during specific periods of the past and examining well-studied areas such as political and social reform in innovative or informative ways. In addition, some contributors apply this approach to the investigation of more overlooked aspects of the urban experience to deepen our understanding of cities and their civic and community life. All the authors attempt to make sense of a variety of developments in American cities at a given point in time. The authors subscribe to the argument that at different times shared assumptions about what the city is or could be exist, and that these assumptions provide the basis for the debate about city needs and actions. Like Miller, the authors believe that the perception of the city and the broad civic culture it provokes, or fails to provoke, represents an important key to understanding the public and private responses to the city during specific historical eras.

Judith Spraul-Schmidt explores the invention of the municipal corporation during the mid-nineteenth century in chapter 1, "Reconstituting City Government: Midcentury State Constitution Making, Defining the Municipal Corporation, and the Public Welfare." Through a close examination of the action of state constitutional conventions held in Louisiana, New York, and Ohio during the 1840s and 1850s, Spraul-Schmidt observes that revisions in those state constitutions explicitly redefined the role and status of each state's cities as a special type of corporation. This reformulation of city government by the state, she argues, should not be construed as an effort to limit city government but rather as a redefinition of the city's role as a much more activist and service-providing entity. Accordingly, Spraul-Schmidt offers new insight into the real meaning of John F. Dillon's *Treatise on the Law of Municipal Corporations*.

Alan I Marcus, in "The Medieval Image in the Modern Mind: History, Democracy, and Turn-of-the-Century American Municipal Governance," explores urban government reform through an analysis of the use of the past in contemporary discussions and critiques of the prevailing approaches to city governance. He focuses particularly on the discourse of what he describes as the idea of the medieval origins of modern cities and the problems caused by those roots. He demonstrates how the concern with the past shaped the discussion about urban government structure, democracy, and citizenship. Taking the past on its own terms seriously, Marcus examines how contemporaries defined urban problems. He suggests that the way reformers and educators conceptualized the problems exerted a profound impact on their responses to specific concerns.

In "Advocating City Planning in the Public Schools: The Chicago and Dallas Experiences, 1911–1928," Robert B. Fairbanks also explores changing perceptions of cities and city problems and continues the discussion of civics and citizen making that Marcus initiated. Fairbanks centers his chapter around the publication of *Wacker's Manual of the Plan of Chicago* (1911) and *Our City—Dallas: A Community Civics* (1927). He starts by asking how these two books written for grammar school civics classes to promote planning can be so different, even though similar types of planning associations sponsored both. He concludes by suggesting that the difference reflects changing notions of both planning and the city, changes that are echoed in the texts of the two books. He also places his discussion against the broader transformation of civic education throughout the United States. Once again, the emphasis is on taking seriously what those in the past assumed and said about their world and exploring how different perceptions of reality are linked to actions.

In chapter 4, "The Boss Becomes a Manager: Executive Authority and City Charter Reform, 1880–1929," Robert A. Burnham uses a similar type of urban history approach to provide a clearer understanding of the changing conceptions of executive authority in early-twentieth-century urban government reform. Burnham rejects the notion that the alterations were evolutionary; rather, he relates them to changing notions about the city. Moreover, he shows how transformations in business administrative practices paralleled those in government. Burnham pays attention to the structure of those changes and the rhetoric about them in his provocative interpretation of urban reform during the first quarter of the twentieth century.

Patricia Mooney-Melvin follows in chapter 5 with an analysis of the relationship between urban definition and urban action and connects this interaction to the neighborhood organization movement of the twentieth century. In "Before the Neighborhood Organization Revolution: Cincinnati's Neighborhood Improvement Associations, 1890–1940," Mooney-Melvin traces the changing nature of neighborhood organizations and ties them to altered beliefs about neighborhoods and their role in the city. She starts with the emergence of a turn-of-the-century neighborhood movement that used an organic metaphor to describe the relationship between the city and its constituent parts. She investigates the role neighborhood organizations played during this era and explores the interwar period when the neighborhood and its relationship to the city was redefined. Through an examination of the relatively understudied neighborhood improvement associations, Mooney-Melvin rejects the suggestion that neighborhoods as well as neighborhood organizing ceased to be important points of local identification and action between 1920 and 1940 and evaluates the dynamics of neighborhood organizational activity before the explosion of neighborhood action that dates from the 1950s.

In chapter 6, "Playing with Democracy: Municipal Recreation, Community Organizing, and Citizenship," Andrea Tuttle Kornbluh analyzes the little studied public recreation movement and discovers a chronology and emphasis consistent with some of the other chapters. In her examination of the municipal recreation initiatives of the 1920s, 1930s, and 1940s, Kornbluh finds that urban recreation programming promoted not only a range of individual leisure activities but also a type of community organization focused on participatory democracy designed to empower citizens to shape their communities. With special attention to the efforts of local recreational leaders to organize blacks and women during this period, she scrutinizes the words and actions of local and national recreation leaders.

Bradley D. Cross explores the effort of a Cincinnati suburb to create a new identity in chapter 7, "Making History: The Search for Civic and Cultural Identity in an American New Town, 1940–1980." Faced with the threat of annexation from Cincinnati, Mariemont incorporated as a village and created a new civic identity. Cross investigates the process by which the community developed its new identity based not so much on its past as an American town built in the 1920s but rather as on a constructed past as an English village, complete with English-style architecture, a town crier, and a double-decker bus. The reinvention of Mariemont, Cross argues, reflected a new conception of culture as a set of lifestyle choices in which the physical environment served as a platform in an individual's search for cultural identity.

In chapter 8, "Giving Meaning to Democracy: The Development of the Fair Housing Movement in Cincinnati, 1945–1970," Charles F. Casey-Leininger provides a careful study of the fair housing movement in Cincinnati that developed after World War II. He documents the efforts of private organizations and government to promote choice for Cincinnati blacks and offers insight into an often ignored topic in the history of twentieth-century race relations. Despite the actions of groups such as the Mayor's Friendly Relations Committee, the Greater Cincinnati Committee on Equal Opportunity in Housing, and several neighborhood associations, the story is one of failed attempts. While Casey-Leininger acknowledges that several reasons may be responsible for this failure, he stresses changes in social thought in the mid-1950s that emphasized individual choice and the need for self-determinism among the many groups in American society. This chapter follows the pattern of its predecessors and explores the fair housing movement in Cincinnati within the broader context of ideas, and focuses on the words and deeds of proponents and opponents engaged in the battle.

Roger W. Lotchin concludes the volume with "The Queen City and Its Historian," a discussion of Miller and the importance of his work in urban history. Lotchin locates Miller's scholarship within its historiographical context and discusses how it has informed our understanding of various aspects of the urban world and of the city as a whole. In addition, he points to another salient feature of Miller's work: studying the past is not just intriguing for its own sake; it is also civically responsible. The vision that Miller shared with his students and colleagues was that historians are citizens as well as scholars. Not surprisingly, as Lotchin points out, Miller intended his work to be of use to professionals and activists engaged in meeting the challenges of the urban environment as well as to members of the scholarly community.

The result of Miller's approach to urban history is not only new insights into well-studied topics and an incentive to examine little-studied events or movements to understand larger issues in urban history. It also possesses the potential to use history in the service of society. By taking the past seriously—that is, by examining the rhetoric and actions of historical actors in the past for what they meant to their contemporaries rather than what they mean to urban scholars today—we increase the understanding of what historical periods were really about. If the uniqueness of past eras stems from the thoughts and actions of historical actors in any given time period rather than "inevitable emanations of objective reality," and if those thoughts and actions reflect radically different shared taxonomies of reality over time, it could be argued that few historical lessons seem applicable today and history may not be as utilitarian as some historians claim. However, what such an approach to history does provide is a lesson in the central role of choice in the past. History, in this context, demonstrates the wide range of possibilities in problem solving and "encourages us to employ or reject past ideas or create new ones to serve our own purposes."[14] Recently called "'liberation' history"[15] by Miller, it suggests as well that initiatives, programs, or strategies, for example, that failed at one point in time might not at another because the historical context—the meanings and intents—have changed.

Making Sense of the City represents a tribute to Zane L. Miller's fresh and provocative approach to urban history. It is also a measure of the impact he has had on our development as historians. The issues we write about, such as government, planning, reform, neighborhoods, suburbia, and race, can be found among his many interests. The methodology we employ reflects his influence. We look at how our historical actors defined problems, and then we search "for patterns in what they said and did not say and in what they did and did not do as they attempt to solve their problems." Additionally, we place "these patterns of talk, action, and inaction in the context of contemporary discussions of American civilization that might have informed their thinking and activities."[16]

It is our hope that this volume reflects Zane Miller's influence on us as scholars and provides new insight on the relationship between changing definitions of the urban community and the corresponding civic culture that produced various responses to perceived urban needs. This book also attempts to bring some order to the field of urban history by focusing on an approach that ties actions to shared assumptions about the city and that creates a new chronology based on different conceptions of the city over time. Finally, this compilation of essays also hopes to promote and encourage a dialogue among scholars about the city and its importance in our lives.

Notes

1. Zane L. Miller, "Queensgate II: A History of a Neighborhood," in Zane L. Miller and Thomas H. Jenkins, eds., *The Planning Partnership: Participants' Views of Urban Renewal* (Beverly Hills: Sage Publications, 1982), pp. 51–79.

2. Henry D. Shapiro has argued that the need to understand the world "functions in a problem solving" manner. People "acknowledge a dilemma explicitly, or more often implicitly," by attempting to restore the lack of harmony they perceive between the way the world is and the way they believe it should be. Henry D. Shapiro, *Appalachia on Our Mind: The Southern Mountains and Mountaineers in the American Consciousness, 1870–1920* (Chapel Hill: Univ. of North Carolina Press, 1978), pp. xvi–xviii. See also Leon Festinger, *A Theory of Cognitive Dissonance* (Stanford: Stanford University Press, 1957), pp. 11–18;

Patricia Mooney-Melvin, *The Organic City: Urban Definition and Community Organization, 1880–1920* (Lexington: University Press of Kentucky, 1987), pp. 12–14; and Thomas Bender, "The Culture of Intellectual Life: The City and the Professions," in John Higham and Paul K. Conkin, eds., *New Directions in Intellectual History* (Baltimore: Johns Hopkins University Press, 1979), p. 191.

3. Alan Marcus has discussed the assumptions that differentiate this approach to the social and cultural/intellectual process in "Back to the Present: Historians' Treatment of the City as a Social System during the Reign of the Idea of Community," in Howard Gillette Jr. and Zane L. Miller, eds., *American Urbanism: A Historiographical Review* (New York: Greenwood Press, 1987), p. 9.

4. The following is the list of dissertations under Miller's direction: Harry A. A. Jebsen, "Blue Island, Illinois: The History of a Working Class Suburb" (1971); Louis R. Thomas, "A History of the Cincinnati Symphony Orchestra to 1931" (1972); Wilbert J. Cameron Jr., "Community Control of Education in Cincinnati, 1900–1921" (1977); Gary P. Kocolowksi, "Louisville at Large: Industrial-Urban Organization, Inter-City Migration, and Occupational Mobility in the Central United States, 1865–1906" (1978); Patricia Mooney-Melvin, "Neighborhood in the 'Organic' City: The Social Unit Plan and the First Community Organization Movement, 1900–1920" (1978); Alan I Marcus, "In Sickness and in Health: The Marriage of the Municipal Corporation to the Public Interest and the Problem of Public Health, 1820–1870, the Case of Cincinnati" (1979); James H. Campbell, "New Parochialism: Change and Conflict in the Archdiocese of Cincinnati, 1878–1925" (1981); Robert B. Fairbanks, "Better Housing Movements and the City: Definitions of and Responses to Cincinnati's Low Cost Housing Problem, 1910–1954" (1981); Carol J. Blum, "Women's Culture and Urban Culture: Cincinnati's Benevolent Women's Activities and the Invention of the 'New Woman,' 1815–1895" (1987); Andrea Tuttle Kornbluh, "The Bowl of Promise: Cincinnati Social Welfare Planners, Cultural Pluralism and the Metropolitan Community, 1911–1952" (1988); Paul A. Tenkotte, "Rival Cities to Suburb: Covington and Newport Kentucky, 1790–1890" (1988); Robert A. Burnham, "'Pulling Together for Pluralism': Politics, Planning, and Government in Cincinnati, 1924–1959" (1990); Judith Spraul-Schmidt, "The Origins of Modern City Government: From Corporate Regulation to Municipal Corporation in New York, New Orleans, and Cincinnati, 1785–1870" (1990); Charles F. Casey-Leininger, "Creating Democracy in Housing: Civil Rights and Housing Policy in Cincinnati, 1945–1980" (1993); Douglas G. Knerr, "'The house America has been waiting for': The Lustron Experiment in Factory Made Housing, 1946–1954" (1996); Bradley D. Cross, "New Jerusalems for a New World: The Garden City Idea in Modern Planning Thought and Practice in Britain, Canada, and the United States, 1900–1970" (1997); and Roger C. Hansen, "Invitation to Annexation: Metropolitan Fragmentation and Community in Cincinnati and Houston, 1920–1980" (1998).

5. Zane L. Miller, *Suburb: Neighborhood and Community in Forest Park, Ohio, 1935–1976* (Knoxville: University of Tennessee Press, 1981), pp. xv–xvi.

6. In "White Cities, Linguistic Turns, and Disneylands: The New Paradigms of Urban History," *Reviews in American History* 26 (March 1998): 176–204, Timothy J. Gilfoyle reviewed the state of the field since 1980. For a review of the literature on urban history that reaches further into the past, consult Howard Gillette Jr. and Zane L. Miller, eds., *American Urbanism: A Historiographical Review* (Westport, CT: Greenwood Press, 1987).

7. See, for example, Thomas J. Sugrue, *The Origins of the Urban Crisis: Race and Inequality in Postwar Detroit* (Princeton: Princeton University Press, 1996); Arnold R. Hirsch, *Making the Second Ghetto: Race and Housing in Chicago, 1940–1960* (Cambridge: Cambridge Univ. Press, 1983); and Ronald H. Bayor, *Race and the Shaping of Twentieth-Century Atlanta* (Chapel Hill: University of North Carolina Press, 1996).

8. See, for example, Christine Stansell, *City of Women: Sex and Class in New York, 1790–1860* (New York: Knopf, 1986); Earl Lewis, *In Their Own Interests: Race, Class and Power in Twentieth-Century Norfolk, Virginia* (Berkeley: Univ. of California Press, 1991); George J. Sanchez, *Becoming Mexican American: Ethnicity, Culture, and Identity in Chicano Los Angeles, 1900–1945* (New York: Oxford Univ. Press, 1993); Eileen McMahon, *Which Parish Are You From? A Chicago Irish Community and Race Relations* (Lexington: University Press of Kentucky, 1995); Matthew Edel, Elliott D. Sclar, and Daniel Luria, *Shaky Palaces: Homeownership and Social Mobility in Boston's Suburbanization* (New York: Columbia University Press, 1984); Elizabeth Blackmar, *Manhattan for Rent, 1785–1850* (Ithaca: Cornell Univ. Press, 1989); John Fairfield, *The Mysteries of the Great City: The Politics of Urban Design, 1877–1937* (Columbus: The Ohio State University Press, 1993); and Joe R. Feagin, *Free Enterprise City: Houston in Political and Economic Perspectives* (New Brunswick: Rutgers University Press, 1988).

9. Gilfoyle, "White Cities," pp. 176, 191.

10. Zane L. Miller, *Boss Cox's Cincinnati: Urban Politics in the Progressive Era* (New York: Oxford University Press, 1968).

11. Miller, *Suburb: Neighborhood and Community in Forest Park.*

12. Zane L. Miller and Bruce Tucker, *Changing Plans for America's Inner Cities: Cincinnati's Over-the-Rhine and Twentieth-Century Urbanism* (Columbus: The Ohio State University Press, 1998), p. xix.

13. Patricia Mooney-Melvin, review of *Changing Plans for America's Inner Cities: Cincinnati's Over-the-Rhine and Twentieth-Century Urbanism,* by Zane L. Miller and Bruce Tucker, *Ohio History* 108 (Summer/Autumn 1999): 201–2.

14. John D. Fairfield, "Democracy in Cincinnati: Civic Virtue and Three Generations of Urban History," *Urban History* 24:2 (1997): 216.

15. Zane L. Miller, Appendix A, "Methodological Note on 'Liberation' History," unpublished manuscript, 1999, in the possession of Robert Fairbanks.

16. Miller, *Changing Plans for America's Inner Cities,* p. xvii.

Chapter One

Reconstituting City Government: Midcentury State Constitution Making, Defining the Municipal Corporation, and the Public Welfare

JUDITH SPRAUL-SCHMIDT

In the 1840s and 1850s American city governments took on new responsibilities to serve directly the public interest of the communities they represented. This moved them well beyond their traditional practice of regulating trade and establishing orderly settings for commerce through the passage of ordinances as empowered by specific acts of their state legislatures. American cities in the mid-nineteenth century moved consistently from providing services such as fire fighting on an emergency basis and began to build police forces that transcended the old watch and lighting forces. At the same time incorporated cities and villages became a special class of corporations in the laws of their states and in national practice were consistently called "municipal" corporations. This classification occurred in a series of state constitutional conventions in the 1840s and 1850s that reevaluated the roles of counties and townships, the initial local agents of state government, and the roles of all corporations, those special bodies that had been created to share in the sovereignty of the state for particular purposes.[1]

The formulation of this first systematic law of municipal corporations involved the creation of a separate category of corporations designated "private" corporations, from which explicitly public, or governmental, corporations were sorted out. Under the private corporation heading, lawmakers grouped together eleemosynary corporations (for charitable, educational, and religious purposes) and corporations for profit. The for-profit category included business corporations, such as manufacturing and insurance companies; public interest improvement companies, such as railroads, bridges, and turnpikes; and banks.[2] In effect, the new state

constitutions differentiated private corporations as a distinct, nongovern-
mental category that would later be subdivided and revised. The state constitutional conventions of the 1840s and 1850s also institutionalized the
growing practice of replacing the traditional, individual legislative charter
passed as a separate law with incorporation under the terms of general acts
for private corporations.

This new distinction between public and private corporations provided
a key element in forging a new direction for city governments. It left
municipal corporations explicitly in the public domain and therefore subject to state regulations not exercised over private corporations. But the
definition of municipal corporations as specifically governmental—as promoters of the public welfare of a unit of citizens—gave them a position
from which to acquire unprecedented responsibilities and powers. In
effect, it laid the groundwork for the explosion of municipal services and
of city government that occurred in the late nineteenth century, more than
a decade before the Civil War. This study will focus on three of the many
states that reconstituted themselves in the 1840s and 1850s: Louisiana,
New York, and Ohio. Each of these states was dominated by one of the
nation's largest and fastest growing cities—New Orleans, the third-largest
city in 1840 and fifth in 1850; New York, first in both decades; and Cincinnati, sixth in both decades—and each of these cities dominated the state
discourse on municipal government. These states varied enormously in
history and location. Louisiana was founded as an outpost of the French
empire, shifted to Spain and back to France, and for less than half a century had been an American Southern state and home to one of the world's
most important ports. New York's principal city was entrenched as the
commercial and financial center of the nation in the old Northeast. Ohio,
the first state in the Northwest Territory, boasted Cincinnati, the young
queen of the western cities. All of them, nonetheless, addressed the issue
of municipal government at their midcentury constitutional conventions
and came to the strikingly similar conclusions adopted by other states
throughout the nation at the same time.

Louisiana's constitutional conventions met in 1844–45 and 1852. The first
occurred in August 1844 in Jackson but adjourned at the end of the month
and reconvened in New Orleans from January 14 to March 12, 1845.[3]
Louisiana's first constitution, framed in 1812, made no specific references
to corporations of any kind but did provide for some degree of local government in New Orleans, which had been incorporated as a city by the territorial Louisiana assembly. Under that law the citizens of New Orleans had
the right to appoint public officers for the administration and the policing
of the city.[4] The new constitution of 1845 retained that provision, but added
prohibitions against either the mayor or the recorder serving in the general

assembly. It also named the mayor, recorder, and aldermen as justices of the peace with such criminal jurisdiction as the legislature found necessary to vest in them for "the police and good order" of the city.[5]

Nonetheless, the Louisiana convention of 1844–45 distinguished public municipal corporations from the private category, which explicitly included charitable as well as business corporations. Convention debates about private corporations ranged over the appropriate role of the state for each kind of corporation in the private category, and the specific relation of each kind of private corporation to state government. These discussions led to new perceptions. For example, the new constitution prohibited the state from subscribing to the stock of any business corporation, a reversal of the practice of the previous decade, when both the state and the city of New Orleans made such subscriptions in reaction to the financial disasters of the second quarter of the nineteenth century.[6] For the same reasons, delegates first proposed harsh restrictions on bank corporations, then banned them altogether.[7]

The Louisiana constitution of 1845 permitted the establishment of other "private corporations," but only under the terms of general laws passed by the legislature. The prevailing view held that incorporation under general provisions was warranted by the success of prior experiments with that system, by the drain on legislative time of considering separate enabling acts, and by the inherent fairness of making the benefits of incorporation available to all qualified applicants. A minority argued that the new constitution ought to leave open the possibility of incorporation by special charter and of excepting institutions "for scientific, religious, or benevolent purposes" from limitations on the term of their corporate grant. The majority responded that the legislature would retain full discretion to set the terms of incorporation in its passage of the general statutes, including allowances for the renewal of corporate privileges.[8]

By these steps, the convention implicitly acknowledged that the proliferation of corporations that had occurred in the previous two decades would continue and would be facilitated under the new system of incorporation by general legislation. The terms of that proliferation, however, would be systematically controlled by the legislature in its role as guardian of the "public interest" of the state. The device of incorporation by general legislation that allowed for the creation of any number of private corporations—whether churches, colleges, manufacturing companies, or railroads—removed their offensive monopoly status. Carrying this a step further, the Louisiana constitution limited private corporations to an existence of twenty-five years and permitted the state legislature to revoke any previously granted charters in the year 1890.[9] This assertion of the revocability of private corporation charters enabled corporations to play an important role in the development of the state but separated that role from the governmental responsibility of sharing in the sovereignty of the state.

This new legal understanding of private corporations helped define public corporations as well. Thus the public or governmental functions of municipal corporations—such as levying taxes, passing ordinances, and issuing bonds—took on new prominence. The delegation from the parish of Orleans, which contained the city of New Orleans, wanted to authorize the Louisiana legislature to permit "political corporations" to pass local ordinances so long as those corporations were prohibited from borrowing money or issuing bonds "except for purposes strictly relative to municipal affairs." Such measures, the delegates contended, should "prevent an abuse of the taxing power by municipal corporations."[10] The convention rejected the proposal, however, and merely excluded municipal corporations from the requirement for organization under general acts for all other, or private, corporations.[11] The convention thus chose to confine its pronouncements on city matters to recognizing the right of New Orleans to pass ordinances.

But the convention returned repeatedly to the issue of New Orleans's role as the only important city in the state. When the Louisiana convention assembled in Jackson in 1844, New Orleans representatives moved for its adjournment to "the city" and for the designation of a New Orleans newspaper as official convention printer. Despite the objections of "country" interests, city proponents succeeded in reassembling the convention in New Orleans by arguing that the city, as the home of the legislature, was accustomed to handling and disseminating official business. Accordingly, New Orleans won the printer's contract as well, despite the lament that this was "left to the city to be monopolized as well as everything else."[12]

Affirmation of the reality that "New Orleans was the centre of all information" in the state strengthened the resolve of those who held that "large cities were not the appropriate places for the functions of popular governments." Self-proclaimed spokesmen for the "country" interests argued that the concentrated and compact city population of New Orleans lent itself so readily to organization for lobbying purposes that it could not fairly be countered by the opposite but unequal interests of the country. The specific evil against which they warned was the tendency of the commercial city to favor large state government expense.[13]

Those wary of the city sought to hold its influence in check by limiting New Orleans's representation in the new state legislature and by removing its designation as state capital. Despite estimates that New Orleans held as much as one-third of the state's population, the city was limited to one-fifth of the seats in the state senate in the reapportionment of legislative seats in the new constitution.[14] While the delegates expressed great pride in New Orleans's standing as an important American city, they pointedly objected to its position as the state capital, which made it a true metropolis, the political as well as commercial and cultural center of Louisiana. Tensions between "the city" and "the country" prompted the convention resolution to mandate the establishment after 1848 of a new capital "at some place not less than sixty miles from the city of New Orleans, by the nearest travelling route."[15] As a result, the 1848 session of the Louisiana legislature moved the state capital upriver to Baton Rouge.[16]

Consideration of the structure of state government and the place of New Orleans in it continued into the 1850s, and in 1852 another convention in the new capital of Baton Rouge produced a new constitution subsequently ratified by the electorate. Once more, the "country" interests sought to restrain New Orleans from exercising undue legislative influence. This time it resulted in senatorial apportionment that counted the city separately from the rest of the state and gave its citizens proportionately fewer representatives. The new constitution retained a provision empowering the citizens of New Orleans to appoint officers "for the administration of the police of said city" but contained no general commentary on municipal corporations.[17]

The Louisiana convention of 1852, while reaffirming the 1845 constitutional provisions for the state's principal municipal corporation, the city of New Orleans, lifted the ban on banking corporations put into place by the 1845 constitution. Under the constitution of 1852, banking corporations could be created through either general laws or special acts, with the stipulation that the legislature should "provide for the registry of all bills or notes issued or put into circulation as money, and shall require ample security for the redemption of the same in specie."[18] Thus in 1852 Louisianians agreed with their counterparts in other states that banks, with proper regulation, not only should continue as an important part of the American scene but should continue to multiply. The key was to use the device of general corporate regulation to strip them of their most opprobrious former characteristic of monopoly privilege.

In summary, the Louisiana constitutional conventions of 1844–45 and 1852 separated private from public corporations and defined their places in the restructured state government. While the delegates distinguished several different types of private corporations, they agreed that all but municipal corporations should be chartered under general incorporation acts. The 1845 constitution banned banking corporations outright, but its successor permitted even banks to be chartered under general laws. Both documents allowed for the individual chartering of municipal corporations, in specifically exempting them from the prohibition against separately chartering private corporations.

New Yorkers met in Albany on June 1, 1846, to revise their state constitution. Like their predecessors in Louisiana and other states, they specifically addressed the place of the city in a new scheme of state government and in doing so defined the municipal corporation in a way that distinguished it from other kinds of corporations. The New York convention also confronted the issue of distinguishing between different kinds of corporations in the

establishment of its standing committees. One considered private corporations; a second, banks; a third, the organization and powers of cities and
incorporated villages. A fourth examined "the power of counties, towns, and
other municipal corporations, except cities and incorporated villages."[19]

The convention discussed the categorization of corporations most
directly in its debates on the report of the committee on "corporations other
than banking and municipal." Admitting the "necessity" of corporations,
the committee chair argued that the question was "how they should be regulated so as to produce all necessary good and prevent unjust inequali-
ties." The committee's proposed solution was to allow private companies
to incorporate only under the terms of general acts of the legislature,
thereby saving legislative time and encouraging the proliferation of corporations while establishing uniform standards for their activities. Yet the
convention delegates reserved to the legislature the right to pass separate
acts of incorporation—individual charters—"in cases where in the judgment of the Legislature, the objects of the corporation cannot be obtained
under general laws."[20] As the assemblage saw it, this exception allowed for
the grants of right of way to internal improvements corporations, such singular but potentially advantageous enterprises as railroads, bridges, or
telegraphic companies.[21] Despite this debate, the text of the constitution
did not restrict this exception to internal improvement corporations.

The New York convention representatives recognized as well a distinction between private corporations for charitable or religious purposes and
corporations for "private gain"—business corporations. They pointed out
that not-for-profit corporations had flourished under general incorporation acts in the years since the passage of New York's last constitution in
1821 and should continue to do so. Availability of corporate rights without
the necessity of obtaining passage of an individual legislative bill, they
argued, would be equally successful for profit-making corporations.[22]

The New York constitutional convention of 1846 dealt separately with
those business corporations created for banking. While banks posed historic problems of monopoly privilege and undue influence, the demand
for the credit they offered outweighed these drawbacks. The delegates
resolved to meet both problems by allowing for the organization of banks
solely under the terms of general acts, specifically prohibiting the state legislature from issuing any special charter for banking privileges. By directing the legislature to organize all banks in the state under clearly defined
statutes, the convention intended to democratize them and to realize the
potential of banks, like internal improvement corporations, to serve the
interests of the state and its people.[23] Like Louisiana before it, the state of
New York also officially accepted the desirability of the proliferation of private corporations and directed the terms under which it would proceed.
The new constitution empowered the legislature to determine the qualifications for incorporation and ordered that they be made universally avail-

able. The principle of incorporation under general laws made incorporation available to any group of persons desiring it, without regard to political influence, and so was no longer a monopoly privilege. As they no longer obtained special privileges, corporations were then clearly private, formally removed from their prior role as sharers in the ruling sovereignty of the state. Corporations fulfilled purposes newly defined as private, serving the legitimate interests of the state by advancing the prosperity of its individual citizens and increasing its collective wealth. Within the category of private corporations, the convention recognized distinctions between those organized for charitable or religious purposes and those organized for private gain, the business corporations. New York's new constitution directed the establishment of all these private corporations under the terms of general laws, but reserved to the legislature the right to grant special charters as it deemed necessary for any corporations other than banks.[24]

As in Louisiana, the convention specifically exempted "[c]orporations . . . for municipal purposes" from the requirement that corporations ordinarily be organized under general incorporation statutes. Settling for municipal incorporation under the prior system of separate legislative enactment of charters, the New York convention's committee on cities and villages, like the committee on corporations, addressed the problem of municipal corporations in the new scheme of state government. The problematic municipal corporations, the debaters agreed, were the cities and incorporated villages that traditionally had been chartered under separate legislative acts, not counties, towns, or other geographic subdivisions of state government (which would soon be identified as quasicorporations). The convention agreed at the outset that those governmental subdivisions had always been different from the chartered cities and should continue to be treated separately from them.[25]

In addition, the committee on cities and villages asserted the case for organizing separately chartered public corporations, like all other corporations, under the terms of general laws. Advocates of this view argued for the inherent justness of generally applicable laws and contended that passage of such laws would engage the collective wisdom of the whole legislature on the general welfare while individual ("local") acts commanded the attention only of the representatives of the affected locality. "State government," explained one delegate, "should concentrate the experience and wisdom of a greater number of persons for the common benefit. . . . Special legislation defeats this design."[26] These advocates reminded their colleagues that their state's municipal corporations included the large cities of New York, Brooklyn, Albany, Rochester, and Buffalo as well as their smaller village counterparts. The convention declined the committee's recommendation to end the system of city incorporation by special charter, but agreed that cities and their smaller counterparts—incorporated villages—could be regulated under the terms of a general law *after* they received their separate charters. Thus the convention kept this counsel in directing the legislature to provide for the organization of municipal corporations, like private corporations, under the terms of general acts. Cities and villages, however, would continue to incorporate under the terms of separate charters in the form of individual acts of the legislature.[27]

Two important assumptions were implicit in the convention's requirement that the New York legislature enact general legislation outlining the powers and responsibilities of municipal corporations. The first was that these governmental corporations, like their private counterparts, would continue to proliferate and to expand their scope. The second was that the individually chartered cities constituted an organic group, so that it was most appropriate for the legislature to draw generally applicable outlines for their activities.

The convention directed the legislature in drafting laws for the general regulation of municipal corporations, "to restrict their power of taxation, assessment, borrowing money, contracting debts and loaning their credit, so as to prevent abuses in assessments, and in contracting debt."[28] The convention placed ceilings on state as well as municipal investments. Both the state and the cities had invested extensively in canal and railroad projects in the 1820s and 1830s, and the convention took very seriously its charge to avoid future government indebtedness on that scale.[29]

The convention also called for setting limitations on municipal expenditures consistent with similar restrictions on state government, but did not challenge or ban new municipal financing arrangements for taxation, assessments, and issuing bonds to provide for the new services the cities were beginning to offer. This freed the cities from the old necessity of making separate application to the legislature for each new levy or loan and, like the establishment of general laws for organizing corporations, acknowledged that such practices had become normative. Indeed, such regulation encouraged the new fiscal arrangements by providing standard guidelines for their use.[30]

Just as the Louisiana constitutional conventions revealed an ambivalent attitude toward "the city" (New Orleans) on the part of self-defined "country" interests, so the New York assemblage also had its "anti-urban" contingent. However, the prime spokesman for this point of view hailed not from an upstate, rural district, but from another large city—Brooklyn. The growing importance of New York City comprised his main target.[31] While much has been made of the "hostility" to the city, most notably in the ongoing attempts to trace the evolution of American city powerlessness, the convention settled the involved New York City issues fairly easily and in a manner that was not anti-urban. As in the case of the decisions on city finance, which set taxing and bonding limits within which cities had more autonomy than before, these New York City issues were resolved in ways consistent with the establishment of the new municipal corporation serving the public welfare in a new scheme of state government.

Unlike its counterparts in Ohio and Louisiana, the New York convention faced a colonial legacy that included royal grants of land and charter rights to both Albany and New York. The convention handled these questions by concluding that such grants did not constrain the state legislature from taking action in the middle of the nineteenth century. The convention reached this conclusion by redefining New York City as both a political (municipal) corporation and, in its capacity as a large landholder, a private corporation; it then made its status as a municipal corporation superior to its status as a private corporation. The delegates characterized New York City "first, as a large political corporation exercising rights of political government; and next, as a large private corporation, exercising the rights of a private corporation."[32] While the legislature could not take away private property rights without just recompense and compelling reasons of public necessity, the delegates believed that the legislature remained always in a position to change the internal political structure of local government. The laws of New York in the mid-nineteenth century, like those in other states, provided that the legislature could alter city charters, whether they originated with the legislature or the royal governors.[33]

The 1846 New York constitution institutionalized the replacement of the older commercial role of the city by the new public welfare role. Before the convention, New York City had come to the forefront of municipal innovation in a move that demonstrated that new city government role. It no longer seemed an adequate fulfillment of a government's function for it to define the public good but to leave its obtainment to private initiative. As Edward Spann has noted, citizens of New York in the 1840s began to relinquish their old role as primary enforcers of city ordinances and insist that the city government take up that task. Such demands prompted the passage by the legislature of a new police law for the city in 1844, and its approval by the New York City common council in 1845. This law created a salaried, regularly constituted day and night police force, and vested policing responsibilities in the city in a force of not more than eight hundred men, serving in patrol districts coinciding with the political wards. Unlike the old night watchmen, all policemen acquired the power to make arrests in the name of the city without fear of being sued. Appointment and removal powers were the mayor's, but supervision of the force, viewed as a full-time job, rested with the chief of police.[34] The force also coordinated existing corporation policing authorities, including inspection of public conveyances and the night watch. The new law abolished the old fee system of payments for particular services as rendered and put in its place a largely tax-supported system drawing revenues from all the city's inhabitants.

The constitution that emerged from the 1846 New York convention and gained the acceptance of the state electorate ratified a system of local government that included geographic administrative subdivisions (counties and towns) and municipal corporations (cities and villages). It recognized a separate role for private corporations, whether for profit, charity, or public service, and directed that they be organized and chartered under the terms of general legislation. This system would open their advantages to all in the state who qualified and relieve the legislature of the work of enacting individual charters. Municipal corporations, distinguished from private corporations, would also be organized under the terms of general legislation, although the convention decided to continue the practice of chartering them individually. While some delegates, like their counterparts in Louisiana, expressed apprehensions about the power of their principal city in securing what it wanted from the legislature, they did not challenge the general role defined for the new municipal corporation. The convention did not question the city's new police law, nor did it challenge the far-reaching Croton waterworks project initiated in the 1830s to provide the city with a safe and adequate water supply. While it did call for limitations on municipal expenditures, it acknowledged the regular use of municipal taxation to support such citywide agencies as the police and the issuance of municipal bonds to finance ongoing projects such as the waterworks. Within these limits, cities were given new authority to raise and disburse revenues without making separate legislative appeals, while that avenue remained open to them in cases where they needed to go beyond those limits.

When Ohioans convened to redraft their constitution in 1850, they did so well aware of the precedents of recent years in other states. In Ohio, too, delegates sought to assign to corporations and to local governments a "proper" place in the mid-nineteenth-century scheme of state governance. The Ohio convention, like its New York counterpart, appointed many (sixteen) standing committees. Among those that touched on the corporate issue were the "committee on Corporations, other than corporations for banking," and the "committee on Banking and Currency."[35]

In its initial report to the convention, the committee on corporations recommended that "the Legislature shall pass no special act conferring corporate powers." This position, although not held unanimously, represented a majority belief that general incorporating laws could and should be framed without excepting either municipal corporations or such special cases as the public-serving turnpike and railroad corporations. Delegates supporting the proposal to include even municipal corporations in state prohibitions against special charters specifically cited the New York example; some concluded that the New York constitution of 1846 did not go far enough. At least one such delegate complaining of New York's "conservative influence" argued that subjecting all corporations to general laws would not only do much to free the corporation from its "bad repute" but would also simplify the task of the legislature and of judicial review as well. "If corporations, municipal and private, were formed and regulated by general laws," he maintained, "then a mooted point in any locality, instead of being a special and temporary case, would immediately become a practical and useful matter of reference in all quarters of the State."[36] Although this position eventually won out, it did so only after the same kind of consideration given the issue at previous conventions in other states.

At the same time, the committee endorsed the position that municipal corporations, and especially cities and villages, formed a distinct classification. The committee recommended that "it shall be the duty of the Legislature to provide for the organization of cities and incorporated villages, by general laws, and to restrict their power of taxation, assessment, borrowing money, contracting debts and loaning their credit, so as to prevent abuses in assessment to contracting debts by such municipal corporations."[37]

Debate on these provisions centered on whether or not it would prove practical to organize all corporations, even cities and villages, under general laws. Counties and townships, the other "municipal corporations," were not discussed in this regard, for they had always been organized solely under general terms. The constitution maintained their status as administrative subunits of the state, whether incorporated or not. It provided for cities and villages as part of another statewide system of local governance.[38] While incorporated townships and counties, too, were identified as municipal corporations, or corporations operating for internal governmental purposes, cities and incorporated villages continued to be classified together, separately from them.[39]

Municipal corporations were also, and now explicitly, distinguished from private corporations, which fell under the headings of eleemosynary (or charitable), educational, and religious, and corporations for profit, including manufacturing, insurance, and the special case of banking, as well as public-interest companies such as those that built roads or railroads. "Now there are these different classes of corporations," concluded one delegate, "and different rules ought to be applied to them."[40] The convention devoted much attention to corporate classification. Implicit in the discussion was the assumption that not only could cities or different kinds of corporate entities be classed together for legislative convenience, but in fact they formed such classes by their very nature and therefore ought to be classified together in the interest of fairness and equality.[41] Thus when the Ohio convention met in 1850–51 the grouping together of cities for legislative action was no longer a matter of question. The delegates turned their attention to the practicality of eliminating all separate charters for cities and organizing the state's municipal corporations under such general terms as the newer western states such as California and Iowa.

At least one champion of eliminating special charters based his argument in part on the workability of devising a scheme of classifications according to city size. He argued as well for the particular advantages of using such a system to regulate the operation of the new kinds of powers that the cities were beginning to seek and to exercise, powers to serve a singular public interest rather than traditional corporate city goals. Specifically, he cited the example of Cincinnati's requests for the authority to create and operate a fire department that went beyond the older concept of a volunteer force organized under the auspices of city government. Subsequent to the passage of new fire department authorization for Cincinnati, "that law . . . had been passed for eleven other cities of this State, and each of them containing some improvement." Now Cincinnati sought a new fire law, which, as he saw, it might have proved unnecessary if the initial bill had not been "a mere local measure, passed without that scrutiny which the importance of the subject deserved and which a general law would have received." Like his counterparts in New York in 1846, he credited the assembly as a whole with a particular wisdom and experience, or at least care in consideration, that would not obtain in reference to purely local measures. "And if we have a good law," he concluded, "let us all enjoy the benefit of it; and if there is anything wrong in it, let all be interested in its rectification." Such a system, as he saw it, could only improve city regulations.[42]

The Ohio convention, then, barred the legislature from granting any special charters, including those for municipal purposes, although delegates insisted that this measure would not bar the passage of laws defining, for example, new city boundaries. The new constitution carried the requirement as well that "all laws of a general nature shall have a uniform operation throughout the state."[43] In Ohio, corporations, whether operating privately for such purposes as business profit, charity, or the public convenience of access, or publicly for municipal purposes, would continue to flourish under the terms of general laws calculated to regulate them without the harm to the public good that monopoly grants could permit.

Ohio voters ratified the document framed by their convention delegates in 1851, and the general assembly met its responsibility to draw its "Act to Provide for the organization of cities and incorporated villages" in May 1852. Although the term "municipal corporation" was avoided in the title of the act, it was used throughout the lengthy provisions, reflecting its now common usage as a term for a city and, in the case of the Ohio act, for the other designated but lesser urban corporations.[44]

The Ohio act of 1852 showed no ambiguity about the kinds and degrees of municipal corporations encompassed within the categories of cities and incorporated villages, and no difficulty with enunciating their respective powers and responsibilities. Cities with populations of more than twenty thousand, which in 1852 meant only Cincinnati, became cities of the first class. Those with populations between five thousand and twenty thousand constituted cities of the second class. To avoid any possible confusion with townships, all lesser municipal incorporations, including places formerly designated towns, boroughs, or villages, became incorporated villages, and the special road district, a district incorporated for the single purpose of road construction, became an "incorporated village for special purpose."[45] All of the categories allowed for later expansion, whether into such further subdivisions as cities of the first grade of the first class, or into additional kinds of incorporated villages for special purposes, such as fire or water districts, as those kinds of services came to be standard local governmental fare. In 1852, however, the categories allowed the organization of cities and villages into classifications that reflected their population demands while creating a uniform system of local corporate government throughout the state of Ohio. This system of classification proved sufficiently flexible to permit the dramatic expansion of municipal government that occurred in the second half of the nineteenth century.

Louisiana, New York, and Ohio each revised their constitutions in the mid-nineteenth century and in the process explicitly reconsidered the role and status of their cities as municipal corporations. The specific manner in which each of these states distinguished this entity as a particular kind of corporation with a directly governmental function differed, but their actions demonstrated an agreement on fundamental principles evidenced throughout the country at that time.

Historians have long debated the relative powers and liberties of private and public corporations, pointing to the formation of a laissez-faire attitude toward the private bodies and a growing restrictiveness toward public ones.[46] Such a reading overlooks the changing roles of both kinds of corporations over time. Too often students have accepted as given the distinction between public and private corporations, not recognizing that it was the problem of drawing this distinction that underlay much of the midcentury debate about corporations in states including Louisiana, New York, and Ohio. In addition, any discussion of nineteenth-century corporations must take into account the increasingly active roles played by city governments as they came to be defined as municipal corporations. Early state constitutions—before the mid-nineteenth century—did not carry specific limitations on city expenditures, especially through taxation and the issuance of bonds, because they generally were unnecessary. Only after the midcentury, when the cities began to make regular and extensive use of these devices for raising money and financing public services and works, did states establish limitations. Within the terms of those limitations the cities could raise funds without the passage of separate enabling acts by state legislatures. In addition the state legislatures remained generally responsive to the petitions of individual local constituencies, especially from their largest cities, whether in framing flexible general laws or special laws.[47] State legislatures also provided for the expansion of municipal governments as such into new areas of very broad and direct responsibility for public action in the decades after the passage of the new midcentury constitutions.

The flurry of midcentury state constitution making set the stage for the growth of urban responsibility in the next two decades. New York, New Orleans, and Cincinnati all took on new public duties in this period: public schools, fire protection, and water and sewerage service joined gridded street plans as standard features of city life.[48] Providing these services on a regular basis required unprecedented expenditures. The cities met the challenge, with state approval, through the new devices of regular municipal taxation and bond issues. As they pursued new activities, these cities and their representatives in the state legislatures continued to define their role as municipal corporations. Each, of course, followed its own path in instituting public services and in approaching its state government for the authority to do so, but each shared with the others and with other American cities a "remarkable degree of commonality, though not complete uniformity" of municipal law.[49] John F. Dillon codified this newly developing municipal law in the first "American work on this branch of the law," his 1872 *Treatise on the Law of Municipal Corporations*.[50] The warm welcome the *Treatise* received suggests that Dillon effectively identified a national, American law of municipal corporations from the separate laws of the thirty-seven states. An examination of his citations—and more particularly the dates of each—supports the contention that Dillon was dealing with a recent aspect of American law, one that emerged after 1850.[51]

In the state of Ohio, where the state constitution proscribed enacting special corporation legislation, all laws pertaining to the powers of cities took the form of amendments to the 1852 City Organizing Act. That body of law was revised in 1869 into what was officially termed for the first time in any state a "Municipal Code."[52] The code classified all municipal corporations in the state into four categories, each with a minimum population requirement: cities of the first class (twenty thousand), cities of the second class (five thousand), villages (five hundred), and villages for special purposes (one thousand for any future municipal incorporation). The only villages incorporated for special purposes at the passage of the code were special road districts, but the classification scheme allowed for the creation of other such special-purpose municipal corporations. The scheme explicitly provided for the "advancement" of each of these kinds of municipal corporations into the next grade, and established all municipal rights and duties on the basis of their classification. In sixty-one chapters, the municipal code laid out the law of municipal corporations in operation in Ohio.

Three years after the passage of this first formal state municipal code, Dillon compiled his *Treatise on the Law of Municipal Corporations*. Dillon wrote that as an Iowa jurist he felt the "necessity for a work upon Municipal Corporations" because "questions relating to the powers, duties, and liabilities of municipalities" appeared at nearly every term of the court in his state and others. He continued: "Although the subject is one of unsurpassed practical importance, since nearly every considerable city and town in the United States is incorporated, no American work upon it has ever appeared."[53] Dillon presented this 1872 volume as a manual of practice on the subject so that lawyers and judges would have ready access to rulings in other states.[54]

The *Treatise* consisted of twenty-three chapters providing a comprehensive discussion of the law of municipal corporations. Chapter 1 gave an introductory historical overview of "Municipal Institutions" from ancient times to the present. This overview continued in chapters 2, "Corporations Defined and Classified," and 3, "Creation of Several Kinds of Municipal Corporations." Dillon followed with "Public and Private Corporations Distinguished" before going on to consider "Municipal Charters" in two separate chapters. The first considered their general nature. In this discussion, the author set forth "Dillon's Rule": "It is a general and undisputed proposition of law that a municipal corporation possesses, and can exercise, the following powers, and no others: First, those granted in *express words*; second, those *necessarily or fairly implied* in or *incident* to, the powers expressly granted; third, those *essential* to the declared objects and purposes of the corporation—not simply convenient, but indispensable" (101). Municipal corporations were required to seek specific authorizations of their actions, but once granted, the city councils retained "a discretion as to the manner in which the power shall be used" that "cannot be controlled by the courts"(107–8).

Dillon proceeded from his general principles of municipal law in chapter 5 to enumerate the usual powers of the municipal corporation as enunciated by state laws and courts. Chapter 6 cataloged the "Special Powers and Special Limitations" created by municipal charters, ranging from authority over wharves, ferries, fire, police, and health responsibilities to borrowing money, limitations on power to become indebted, and aid to railway companies.[55] Later chapters returned to some of these topics, to all the subjects addressed in general municipal acts, and to issues that had arisen in the courts as the cities used their new powers. Dillon's discussion of the power of the municipality to borrow money, for example, rested almost entirely on cases from midcentury, before the general power to borrow without the need to appeal to the legislature for each occasion became institutionalized. Even where formal limitations were set on indebtedness, Dillon described ways to circumvent those limits legitimately.

Dillon discussed at length the issue of municipal control of property and the limits on its rights. He cited cases affirming municipal rights such as eminent domain and taxation but pointed also to the state's paramount position. Thus, as in the case in which Dillon promulgated his "Rule," the state could allow a railroad corporation the use of the city streets for construction of its tracks without the consent of the city.[56] The municipal corporation did not hold the same private property rights as an individual.

The *Treatise* illuminated not only the actual practice of municipal corporation activity in the two decades after midcentury but also its interpretation by state courts. Although the significance of Dillon's work is usually seen as its promulgation of the "Rule" and the limitations on municipal power that it points to, it is possible to see its significance in a very different and untraditional way. Thus, what the *Treatise* achieves is the exposition of a national movement, the development of a new understanding of the municipal corporation pieced together from the common problems and assumptions of numerous cities. This alternative understanding of Dillon acknowledges his conclusion that the municipal corporation of the latter nineteenth century was a creature of the state. It does not concur with the conclusion that the *Treatise* and the legal developments of the period that it chronicles set new limitations on municipal corporations or fostered a new dependence on state government. Any reading of Dillon's *Treatise* must take into account the extent of the new activities on which cities embarked as they assumed their newly defined public role. To accomplish their ends, cities appealed to the state legislatures for the increased authority they needed. These proliferating appeals of cities to the legislatures in this period are not necessarily signs of weakness. Rather, they can be seen as signs of the energetic way cities were tackling their new role. So, too, the flurry of judicial activity that Dillon points to in the two decades after mid-century reflects an increase in city activities as the new municipal corporations experimented with their new powers and bureaucracies and with the terms of their revised relationships with their state legislatures.[57]

Dillon's *Treatise* and its wide acceptance highlighted the reality of the new and exclusive definition of cities as municipal corporations. No longer were cities the limited corporations of the early nineteenth century when city governments were not expected to be social service providers. Those earlier corporate entities operated in very much the same way as other corporations to maintain an orderly setting for the individual pursuit of commerce and civilization. By the middle of the nineteenth century, public and private corporations had been distinguished from each other and their separate roles articulated. Private corporations were specifically removed from the public role that had formerly inhered in all corporations. Municipal corporations remained in the public domain, imbued with direct responsibility for promoting the public welfare within their boundaries.

After midcentury cities no longer limited themselves to the old pattern of regulating activities within the corporation limits to maintain the public order. At least in the cases of New York, New Orleans, and Cincinnati, city governments now came to assume responsibility for providing public social services. The old pragmatic responses to particular emergencies, such as creating volunteer fire departments and boards of health for the duration of an epidemic, no longer seemed adequate. In city after city in the 1840s, local residents came to demand that their city governments become responsible not only for elucidating but for enforcing the terms of the public order and for providing new services. In their petitions, in their participation in city charter and state constitutional conventions, as well as in their ratification of legislative pronouncements, citizens joined with their elected officials and their representatives in the legislatures who passed the enabling laws to define a new role for city government. They created what was in effect a new institution, characterized as an explicitly public, governmental body providing a series of regular, ongoing services to whole city populations on a daily basis, supported largely by taxation and bond issues and administered by a salaried bureaucracy for the promotion of the public welfare: the American municipal corporation.

Notes

1. Not surprisingly, Zane L. Miller identified this phenomenon of the shift in the practices of city government in the mid-nineteenth century. He discusses it in a variety of places, including "The Rise of the City," *Hayes Historical Journal* 3 (Spring/Fall 1980): 73–84. See also Miller, "Scarcity, Abundance, and American Urban History," *Journal of Urban History* 4 (1978): 131–56. Alan I Marcus, *Plague of Strangers: Social Groups and the Origins of City Services in Cincinnati* (Columbus: The Ohio State University Press, 1991), explores this issue in an important way. See also Leonard P. Curry, *The Corporate City: The American City as a Political Entity, 1800–1850* (Westport, CT: Greenwood Press, 1997). In an age in which the term "municipal" applied to any matters relating to internal government and not exclusively to cities, incorporated counties and other incorporated political subdivisions fell under the new municipal rubric as well. For additional writings that address the issue of changing city government from a different perspective, but notice the phenomenon of mid-century change, see Philip J. Ethington, *The Public City: The Political Construction of Urban Life in San Francisco, 1850–1900* (Cambridge: Cambridge University Press, 1994), and Amy S. Greenberg, *Cause for Alarm: The Volunteer Fire Department in the Nineteenth-Century City* (Princeton: Princeton University Press, 1998).

2. James Willard Hurst, the foremost student of the place of business corporations in American law, points out that while by the end of the century they would come to be the dominant corporate form, very few of them existed before the 1780s and the formation of the new nation. Between 1780 and 1830, Hurst observed, most of what would later be called business corporations "were chartered for activities of some community interest—supplying transportation, water, insurance, or banking facilities." In Hurst's evaluation, "such public-interest undertakings practically monopolized the corporate form." More important in number and impact among corporate bodies, however, were the charitable incorporations and such bodies as the corporate cities. Only in the 1830s was there a "rather rapid relative increase in charters for a general range of business, especially for manufacturing." These businesses did not obtain the kind of exclusive monopoly privileges that were formerly a corporate hallmark,

and they were fairly regularly organized under new general incorporation laws. *The Legitimacy of the Business Corporation in the Laws of the United States, 1780–1970* (Charlottesville: University of Virginia Press, 1970), pp. 15, 18.

3. Division of the sessions between the two sites resulted from a series of confrontations between what delegates referred to as "the city" and "the country." These recurring confrontations involved matters as diverse as a proposal to move the convention from Jackson to New Orleans, the selection of the appropriate official printer, proposals to move the seat of government from the city to "the country," and the issue of representation in the houses of the general assembly. The constitution that emerged from these disputes reflected both the special place of New Orleans in the revised scheme of state and local government and jealousy toward the city's particular influence in Louisiana decision making.

4. *Constitution of Louisiana, 1812.* All of the state constitutions are printed in Francis Newton Thorpe, *The Federal and State Constitutions, Colonial Charters and other Organic Laws of the States, Territories, and Colonies now or heretofore forming the United States of America* (Washington, DC: Government Printing Office, 1909); see also Bayrd Still, "State Constitutional Development in the United States, 1829–1851" (Ph.D. dissertation, University of Wisconsin, 1933); John Alexander Jameson, *A Treatise on Constitutional Conventions* (New York: Charles Scribner and Sons, 1867).

5. The convention considered organizing a category of municipal corporations, but instead made special provisions for New Orleans, the only substantial city in the state. *Proceedings and Debates of the Convention of Louisiana, and Constitution of the State of Louisiana adopted in Convention,* Robert J. Ker, reporter (New Orleans, 1845), pp. 856ff.

6. Ibid.; see also *Official Report of Debates in the Louisiana Convention* (New Orleans, 1845).

7. *Proceedings and Debates, Louisiana Constitutional Convention of 1852* (Baton Rouge, 1852), p. 81. The first committee proposal on banking allowed for the issuance of bank charters under certain conditions. Such application should be preceded by six months' public notice. The grant should be limited to a term of twenty years, bear specific affirmation of the right of the legislature to make alterations at any time, and bind the incorporators "individually and in solido" for the acts and liabilities of the corporation. While the passage of such a provision would have allowed the creation of banking corporations, its strictures, especially individual liability for corporate debts, made it unpalatable to the bank supporters to whom it was offered as a compromise. The new constitution ultimately resolved that in Louisiana "no new corporate body shall hereafter be created, renewed, or extended, with banking or discounting privileges."

8. *Proceedings and Debates,* pp. 931–33, 856–63; *Louisiana Constitution, 1845,* Art. 123: "Corporations shall not be created in this State by special laws, except for political or municipal purposes: but the Legislature shall provide, by general laws, for the organization of all other corporations, except corporations with banking or discounting privileges, the creation of which is prohibited."

9. *Laws of Louisiana, 1848*, p. 70: "An Act to provide for the organization of corporations in this State" (3–16–48).

10. *Proceedings and Debates*, pp. 382, 387, 392.

11. In contrast to such states as Ohio and New York, Louisiana had only one important city, New Orleans, and only one other place, the adjacent suburb of LaFayette, held a city charter.

12. *Proceedings and Debates*, p. 94.

13. Ibid., pp. 94ff., 388, 394, 397, 838, 906.

14. *Constitution of Louisiana, 1845*, Arts. 16, 112.

15. Ibid., Art. 112.

16. *Laws of Louisiana, 1848*, p. 70.

17. *Proceedings and Debates*; Leon Cyprian Soule, *The Know Nothing Party in New Orleans: A Reappraisal* (Baton Rouge: Louisiana Historical Association, 1961), pp. 18–26. Debates in the course of the Louisiana convention of 1852 typified the tendency for local politicians to take their differences over city affairs into the state arena. Most notably, New Orleans "Creoles"—generally affiliated with the Democratic party—sought to move elections from July to September when many "American" Whigs left the city to escape the scourge of yellow fever. In doing this, the Creole Democrats proposed changes not in the structure or function of city government but in its control. And they used the state political arena to fight an essentially partisan battle because it seemed to be the battleground most likely to prove favorable to their cause.

In New Orleans, as in other cities, the activities of city government increased at the same time that political parties increased their role in the cities. These two developments created what has been characterized as a new urban politics; Miller, "Rise of the City," pp. 73–84. Like city governments themselves, partisan organizations in New Orleans and other mid-nineteenth-century cities established regular ongoing institutions to replace the ad hoc, narrowly focused groups mobilized only at campaign times. These new parties also forged regular relationships with both national and state political parties.

18. *Constitution of Louisiana, 1852*, Art. 2, s. 16, Art. 6, s. 124.

19. *Debates and Proceedings in the New York State Convention, for the Revision of the Constitution*, S. Croswell and R. Sutton, reporters (Albany, 1846); see *Documents of the Convention of the State of New York* (Albany, 1846), 2 vols., for the complete listing of committees and all committee reports.

20. *Debates and Proceedings*, pp. 736ff.

21. In practice, the New York legislature continued to pass special incorporating acts for corporations other than banks after the ratification of the 1846 constitution. The legislature took several years to pass the general incorporation statutes for different kinds of corporations and even after their passage continued to respond to requests for special charters. Ronald Seavoy argues that "it was not until 1848 that the constitutional policy of enacting general incorporation statutes for business corporations was actively pursued, a policy that became the norm after 1856." See Seavoy, *Origins of the American Business Corporation,*

1784–1855. Broadening the Concept of Public Service during Industrialization (Westport, CT, 1982), p. 193.

22. *Debates and Proceedings,* pp. 736–53, 778–80; *Constitution of New York, 1846,* Art. 8, s. 8.

23. *Constitution of New York, 1846,* Art. 8, s. 4: "The legislature shall have no power to pass any act granting any special charter for banking purposes, but corporations or associations may be formed under general laws." New York had enacted its "free banking law" in 1843 with the same provisions, but the convention delegates went through the process of establishing its banking committee and debating the issue before elevating that law to constitutional status. The new constitution called for individual liability of shareholders to the extent of their holdings in all for-profit corporations. *Constitution of New York, 1846,* Art. 8, s. 9.

24. Ibid.

25. Conventions Reports, #42.

26. *Debates and Proceedings,* pp. 66–67, 120.

27. Ibid.

28. *Constitution of New York, 1846,* Art. 8, s. 9: "It shall be the duty of the Legislature to provide for the organization of cities and incorporated villages, and to restrict their power of taxation, assessment, borrowing money, contracting debts and loaning their credit, so as to prevent abuses in assessments, and in contracting debt by such municipal corporations." See *Laws of New York, 1847,* p. 532: "An Act to provide for the incorporation of villages" (12–7–47).

29. Seavoy, *Origins of the American Business Corporation,* p. 184.

30. *Constitution of New York, 1846,* Art. 8, s. 9.

31. The Brooklyn spokesman was Henry C. Murphy. See Hendrik Hartog, *Public Property and Private Power. The Corporation of the City of New York in American Law, 1730–1870* (Chapel Hill: University of North Carolina Press, 1983), pp. 216–17. See *Debates and Proceedings,* passim, and minority reports of the Committee on Cities.

32. *Debates and Proceedings,* passim.

33. Hartog, *Public Property and Private Power,* pp. 220–39. Hartog argues that a general distrust of the legislature furthered judicial attempts to curb the legislature and the city after 1846; he places the creation of the municipal corporation in the hands of the judiciary.

34. *Laws of New York, 1844,* 4–1–44; *Ordinances of New York City,* 5–2.3–45; James F. Richardson, *The New York Police: Colonial Times to 1901* (New York: Oxford University Press, 1970), pp. 36–50; Edward K. Spann, *The New Metropolis: New York City, 1840–1857* (New York: Columbia University Press, 1981), pp. 39, 54–55, 62.

35. *Ohio Convention Debates,* J. V. Smith, reporter, (Columbus, 1851), 2 vols., I:47.

36. Ibid., I:345; the speaker was Charles Reemelin, who was from the Hamilton County delegation although he resided outside of Cincinnati's corporate limits. Reemelin played an important role in the convention, but his papers at the Cincinnati Historical Society provide little information about the proceedings.

37. Ibid., pp. 369ff.

38. Henry D. Shapiro, "City, State, and Nation: Divided Sovereignty and the Rule of Law in the United States," *Societies in Transition* (1982): 28.

39. John F. Dillon, *Treatise on the Law of Municipal Corporations* (Chicago: J. Cockroft and Co., 1872), p. 17, addresses this issue.

40. *Ohio Convention Debates*, I:350, 376; II:645–51.

41. As early as 1817, the Ohio legislature, following a year of numerous requests for town charters, had passed a law allowing for town incorporations under general terms. Several towns took advantage of the act, but town representatives and members of the general assembly found the act inappropriate in an age that considered its entities individually rather than collectively. The act was repealed in 1824. While some of the towns incorporated under the provisions of the 1817 act moved to reaffirm their grants of corporate status by seeking legislative approval for them in special acts, others moved to cancel theirs.

42. J. V. Smith, reporter, *Ohio Convention Debates* (Columbus, 1851) II:648ff.

43. *Ohio Constitution of 1851*, Art. XIII.

44. *Laws of Ohio, 1852*, 5–1–52. In 1869, when the Ohio legislature reviewed this act, it presented it as the Ohio Municipal Code, reflecting the common usage of the term "municipal corporation" applied specifically to incorporated cities and villages.

45. *Laws of Ohio, 1852*, sections 30, 40.

46. The state economic studies of the New Deal era argue that the laissez-faire attitude did not arise until after 1870. See Oscar Handlin and Mary Flug Handlin, *Commonwealth: A Study of the Role of Government in the American Economy: Massachusetts, 1774–1861* (Cambridge: Harvard University Press, rev. ed. 1969); Louis Hartz, *Economic Policy and Democrat Thought: Pennsylvania, 1776–1860* (Cambridge: Harvard University Press, 1948); James Neal Primm, *Economic Policy in the Development of a Western State, Missouri, 1820–1860* (Cambridge: Harvard University Press, 1954); John W. Cadman Jr., *The Corporation in New Jersey: Business and Politics, 1791–1875* (Cambridge, MA: Harvard University Press, 1949); and Milton Sydney Heath, *Constructive Liberalism: The Role of the State in Economic Development in Georgia to 1860* (Cambridge, MA: Harvard University Press, 1954). Hartog, *Public Property*, and Morton J. Horwitz, *The Transformation of American Law, 1780–1860* (Cambridge, MA: Harvard University Press, 1977), argue against them.

47. John C. Teaford, "Special Legislation and the Cities, 1865–1900," *American Journal of Legal History* 23 (July 1979): 189ff.

48. Joel Tarr makes this same point in "Building the Urban Infrastructure in the Nineteenth-Century City: An Introduction," in *Infrastructure and Urban Growth in the Nineteenth Century*, Essays in Public Works History, no. 14 (Chicago: Public Works Historical Society, 1985), pp. 61–85.

49. Charles Adair and Ernest S. Griffith, *A History of American City Government 1775–1870* (New York: Praeger, 1976), p. 39.

50. Dillon, *Treatise on the Law of Municipal Corporations*, p. vi. Dillon's work went through five editions in his lifetime. The first edition was one volume, as

was the second, issued one year later in 1873 with, in Dillon's phrase, "the structure unaltered." Dillon completely revised the work in 1881, explaining that "it has been necessary to *sectionize* the work anew"; a fourth edition appeared in 1890, because "the law has not only been still further extended on previous lines, but it has in material respects been modified, altered, and enlarged." Dillon's fifth and final edition appeared in five volumes in 1911. Scholars commenting on Dillon often cite the fifth edition, which, by Dillon's own account, collates a different municipal law from that in effect in the 1870s and 1880s, leading to a different reading of his work from that offered here. See, for example, Edwin A. Gere Jr., "Dillon's Rule and the Cooley Doctrine: Reflections of the Political Culture," *Journal of Urban History* 8 (May 1982): 271–98.

51. Judith Spraul-Schmidt, "Governing the American City: New York, New Orleans, and Cincinnati, 1820–1870," paper presented at the annual meeting of the Organization of American Historians, April 19, 1983, Cincinnati. Hartog, *Public Property and Private Power,* p. 220, sees it slightly differently: "In the two crucial conceptual chapters of the book . . . almost every assertion in the text found support in reference to state court decisions of the preceding forty years." There are indeed citations in Dillon to decisions before the midcentury, but many of these date to the mid-1840s, and they are greatly outnumbered by those in the 1850s and 1860s.

52. *Laws of Ohio, 1869,* 145–286: "Municipal Code," titled also "An Act to Provide for the Organization and Government of Municipal Corporations" (5–7–69). A "Code of Criminal Procedure" followed on the next page of the 1869 *Laws,* indicating the larger movement toward classification and codification of which the classification of municipal corporations was a part.

53. Dillon, *Treatise,* vii, spoke of the shortage of complete law libraries available to lawyers.

54. Dillon defined as his concern the law of cities. Although the separation of public and private corporations placed incorporated counties and other incorporated administrative subunits of state government in the public or municipal sphere, Dillon explained that those bodies were properly quasicorporations. Full-scale municipal corporations bore rights and duties identified in their charters of incorporation, their organic law, whether defined in separate or general legislative acts. They had distinct identities and discretionary powers as expressed in those charters, unlike the quasicorporations.

55. Dillon framed his list in this way:

1. Wharves
2. Ferries
3. Borrowing Money
4. Limitations on Powers to become indebted
5. Rewards for offenders
6. Public buildings
7. Police Powers and regulations

8. Prevention of Fires
9. Quarantines, and Health
10. Indemnifying of Officers
11. Furnishing entertainments
12. Impounding animals
13. Party walls
14. Public defense
15. Aid to Railway Companies, and herein of the constitutional power of the legislature, cases cited. Powers must be expressed. Construction of special grants of powers; cases cited.

56. Gere, "Dillon's Rule and the Cooley Doctrine," pp. 271–99.

57. Hendrik Hartog, whose reading of Dillon differs from mine, notes as well that most of Dillon's citations are to the period after 1830. Hartog argues that the municipal corporation was a judicial creation of the years after the adoption of New York's 1846 constitution. His argument understates the importance of the public demand for the social services of the new municipal corporation and of the cities' response to those demands and overstates the importance of the courts. As a lawyer, Hartog was trained in the case law method that perseveres to this day. Hartog, *Public Property and Private Power,* chap. 14, "The Judicial Creation of a Municipal Corporation," pp. 220–39. "Between 1835 and 1860, appellate judges created a new American law of municipal corporations. In his treatise, John Dillon gave formal—one might almost say final—expression to this new legal subject," p. 220. For alternative views, see Joan C. Williams, "The Invention of the Municipal Corporation: A Case Study in Legal Change," *American University Law Review* (Winter 1985): 370–438, and "Review—The Development of the Public/Private Distinction in American Law," *Texas Law Review* (August 1985): 230. Williams argues that by locating the invention of the municipal corporation in New York at the mid-century, Hartog's work misses the importance of earlier Massachusetts law, in which townships were deemed corporate entities during the first part of the nineteenth century and so preceded New York in formulating a law of municipal corporations. See also Jon Teaford's review of Hartog's book, "The Birth of a Public Corporation," *Michigan Law Review* 83 (February 1985): 690–701; and his "Finis for Tweed and Steffens: Reinventing the History of Urban Rule," *Reviews in American History* 10 (December 1982): 135–49; and *The Unheralded Triumph: City Government in America, 1870–1900* (Baltimore: Johns Hopkins University Press, 1984); Kenneth M. Fox, *Better City Government: Innovation in American Urban Politics, 1850–1937* (Philadelphia: Temple University Press, 1977); and Eric H. Monkkonen, *America Becomes Urban: The Development of U.S. Cities and Towns, 1789–1980.* (Berkeley: University of California Press, 1988).

Chapter Two

The Medieval Image in the Modern Mind: History, Democracy, and Turn-of-the-Century American Municipal Governance

ALAN I MARCUS

Turn-of-the-century Americans fretted about their cities. They deplored governmental corruption and greed, worried about overcrowding, expressed dismay at the heritages of those congregating in the worst neighborhoods, and generally lamented the outcome of municipal elections. Urban historians have long been fascinated by these screeds as well as by the outpouring of concern. Practical sorts, these scholars have focused on government per se. Interested in the science of political reform or the sociological forces, dynamics, or circumstances that engendered it, historians have sought to determine through what political instrumentalities contemporaries resolved their grievances. These investigations have borne considerable fruit. Historians have attributed turn-of-the-century American municipal reform to the rise of a new middle class or professional classes, an awakening to the pervasive corruption of the boss system, or an attempt to establish municipal government according to rational means and practices. In many ways, they have identified municipal reform as a triumph of modernity, as the beginning of the present American municipal system.[1]

All of the aforementioned arguments may be more or less true. But rather than focus on the mechanisms through which turn-of-the-century Americans mobilized to restructure their municipal governments, it can be useful to examine the issues through which rationales for municipal reform were expressed. Turn-of-the-century Americans labored to find meaning for the political system practiced in the United States, democracy.

But they did so in a way unlike their predecessors. Rather than praise democracy's promise or potential, common early- and mid-nineteenth-century notions,[2] they often questioned its existence and relevance for contemporary American municipalities. They debated and argued over whether democracy had outlived its municipal utility and, if not, what it now entailed and what effective means were needed to guarantee it.

These introspective citizens understood the world in which they lived as connected in fundamental ways with the historical past. And they tried to come to grips with that legacy by meeting it head on, by turning to the past and examining it. Surprisingly, they did not seek to determine from where democracy originated. They presumed that it was established in ancient Greece and Rome and gave those places only a passing nod. They concentrated their gaze on the past to see where and how things went wrong. Almost unanimously they found the culprit to be what they termed the medieval age. In this past, the tenets of municipal democracy were abandoned for other political forms. How that came about and what havoc it wreaked became an important facet of the analysis.

But reformers also recognized that American cities occupied a national and international present. That simple postulate yielded a sophisticated analytic thread that proceeded not temporally but geographically and focused on turn-of-the-century municipalities outside the United States. It recognized cities throughout the Western world as a particularistic type of unit, a complex concentration of diverse people pursuing even more diverse projects. Since these cities had sociological and demographic attributes similar to those in the municipalities of then contemporary America, turn-of-the-century Americans devoted considerable attention to how foreign cities detected their need for reformation and how they accomplished it. Americans recognized that these cities had faced and conquered many of the problems then facing American municipalities. But they also understood that democracy in a turn-of-the-century American context created its own dilemmas and required uniquely American resolutions. Foreign cities could provide assistance through potential insights, not solutions.

The geographical and temporal forms of analysis were not nearly as disparate as might be supposed. Turn-of-the-century American municipal reformers choosing to explore the intricacies of foreign cities examined them historically. Put bluntly, they assumed that municipalities outside the United States had passed through the medieval age. The successes of these places showed them to have become modern. Surely their individual histories, their trials and tribulations, could provide Americans with insights. But the collective municipal history was even more telling. Each municipality differed by place, nation, local custom, and national law, yet each had overcome its particular circumstances and history to emerge as modern. By creating in effect a multinational municipal prosopography, the essential issues of municipal modernity and the means to achieve them could be exposed. A science of municipal modernization could be revealed and applied to American cities.

The temporal and geographical approaches were nearly flip sides of the same coin. The former focused on where and how democracy was lost, while the latter accentuated where and how modernity was found and implemented. And while modernity was not exactly municipal democracy, the situation it created seemed to promise the promotion of successful municipal functioning in the United States. Yet turn-of-the-century Americans encountered difficulty almost immediately. They found that the lessons of the past could hardly be reduced to a simple, straightforward list of scientific axioms. Researchers identified any number of fractures in the past that created the less than ideal present and a like plurality of ways to achieve municipal modernity.

Recognition that the past was far more complicated than hoped led to the last and most critical facet of this two-decade-long examination of municipal governance. Turn-of-the-century Americans redrew the relationship between past and present to overcome the obstacle of a past that did not naturally conform to their needs. Two different understandings emerged. Both depended on perceptions of the present and therefore made the past hostage to the contemporary scene. One approach selected from the past those factors that could be applied to the present and future. The past now became important only so long as it was usable and contributed to the present. Another approach to the past was to forge its relevance—to use it as sociology—configuring its facts in a manner so as to serve as a call for political action in the present. Those adept at reading back into the historical record identified elements missing in the present, located them in the past, and employed that "discovery" as justification to erect these elements in turn-of-the-century America. In both cases, history as an understanding of the past on its own terms was a casualty of this modern age. What remained were traditional terms given radically different meanings by men and women lacking any historical sense and obsessed with the present. Democracy became one of those terms given new and very different meaning. New forms of municipal governance stood as testimony to the redefinition.

The quest for the medieval origins of American city government immediately encountered a potentially huge stumbling block. There was no United States during the medieval period. The earliest permanent European colonies in what would become the United States dated only from the early seventeenth century, hardly a period that the acclaimed historian of the Renaissance, Jakob Burkhardt, would call medieval. When tracing American municipalities, most investigators noted their European, particularly British, origin. And it was in this origin that they discovered a flourishing municipal democratic tradition and the interruption of that tradition in the medieval age. American municipalities were the product of that heritage and continued to cope with the manifestations in the then present.

John Fiske, the noted popular historian, proved typical as he took great pains to expose the long, convoluted history of English boroughs and towns. The high point of that history began in the twelfth century when municipalities began to free themselves from the barons and knights who had owned them. During the subsequent two centuries, guilds of "grocers, fishmongers, butchers, weavers, tailors, ironmongers, carpenters, saddlers, armourers, needle-makers," and other trades coalesced to regulate their members' activities. Soon, these guilds formed a "united brotherhood" or "town guild." This "organization at length acquired full control of city government," and "the guild hall became city hall."

Tudor and Stuart England killed this democratic arrangement. Fiske attributed the "degradation" of English municipal democracy to the "foul political intrigues and corruption which characterized the Stuart period," a consequence of "the encroachment of national politics upon municipal politics." Fiske claimed that Tudor and Stuart town officers allied themselves with the king and powerful nobles and "contrived to dispense with popular election, and thus to become closed corporations or self-perpetuating oligarchical bodies."

The timing was unfortunate for colonial America. Cities copied this system "from England at a time when city government in England was sadly demoralized." The "oligarchical abuses" persisted through the American Revolution. States sometimes took notice of this problem, but Fiske found the remedy worse than the disease. The 1857 decision by the New York state legislature to seize the administrative authority for New York City because it had grown alarmed by municipal corruption produced what Fiske viewed as a catastrophic situation. It substituted state (and national) interests for municipal concerns. Political party and party labels now defined municipal governance, a calamitous occurrence. Fiske put it simply: voting for a municipal official "because he is a Republican or a Democrat is about as sensible as to elect him because he believes in homeopathy or has a taste for chrysanthemums."

Fiske recommended severing national party concerns from municipal contests, which could be accomplished by scheduling municipal elections at times other than state and national elections and by having candidates run without party affiliation. In addition, Fiske asserted that a powerful mayor must lead city government. Rather than restore the oligarchy of old, Fiske maintained that American cities had grown much larger, more populous, and their government necessarily more complex. "The modern city," said Fiske, "has come to be a huge corporation for carrying on a huge business with many branches, most of which call for special aptitude and training." Only a strong mayor could take control of this dynamo. To Fiske, a powerful mayor, rather than a political party or machine, ensured populace-controlled municipal accountability. "To vote for candidates whom one has never heard of is not to insure popular control, but to endanger it," he argued. "It is much better to vote for one man whose reputation we know, and then to hold him strictly responsible for the appointments he makes."[3]

Albert Shaw argued from the opposite perspective. Eventually to gain fame as the American editor of the influential *Review of Reviews*, Shaw had left his position as a Minneapolis newspaperman in 1888 for a first-person survey of European municipalities. Such a survey was critical, he argued, because "studying the experience of Old World centers" prepares our American cities "for the greatness that inevitably awaits them." But Shaw's assessment of the English medieval heritage conflicted directly with Fiske's. To Shaw, the seizure of city governments by commercial and mercantile guilds proved a benison that "revived the local liberties that had languished under feudal tyranny." This approach to governance continued satisfactorily until almost the present day. Now "the new forces of modern life" have rendered "government by the self-perpetuating guilds . . . totally obsolete and inadequate." These "closed corporations with their old names and old privileges" no longer bore "any relation to industrial life, nor were they in any sense representative of the community at large." They had quickly become nothing more than wealthy "societies of gentlemen," an oligarchy seeking to maintain its traditional privileges, authority, and powers in a period quite unlike the time when they had seized authority.

Shaw took great care to report just which forces made long-established municipal government defunct, a "fossilized relic of medievalism." "Modern transportation and industrial systems" destroyed the fabric of medieval society as many major European municipalities quadrupled in size in less than a century. Rapid urban growth placed unprecedented pressure on governments, which now found themselves required to represent people and interests quite different than those initially permitted in the closed commercial municipal corporations of medieval England. "It is only lately," Shaw claimed, "that the people of advanced industrial nations have learned to accept the fact that life in cities under artificial conditions must be the permanent lot of the great majority, and that it is the business of society to adapt the urban environment to the needs of the population." A new social reality, "the new forces of urban life," had doomed old institutions and demanded the erection of new ones. "Life in the modern city should not be an evil or a misfortune for any class" became a Shaw postulate as well as a tenet of the revamped municipal democracy, and he argued that the English had answered the challenge through "central management." Beginning in the mid-1850s, England enacted a series of laws, a "general municipal system," that permitted each municipality to centralize municipal authority in a single body. Shaw argued that granting each municipality "absolute control through a directly elected authority of all administration and of all expenditure" was the sine qua non of "a fully organized municipal life." Two complementary tasks became municipal government's new agenda: municipal government now designated numerous activities as government activities—responsibilities of municipal government—and it pledged to pursue these activities systematically. In London, for example, a single board created "a system of main sewers," improved "systematically the main thoroughfares," worked "to centralize and municipalize" water and lighting, "systematized local transportation" to a considerable degree, and established minimally acceptable housing standards.

Shaw made a special point to compare contemporary British and American municipal governance. In America, mayor and council administration institutionalized checks and balances. This medieval relic proved unsuitable for contemporary life. It set the mayor up as "a sort of rival principality," which produced redundancy and waste. But the American predilection for resolving the waste problem "by choosing an absolute dictator from time to time under the title mayor" struck Shaw as "highly unrepublican, . . . incompatible with a wise continuity of policy." He recommended the British model: "one central, elective body, representing the masses of the citizens" for each municipality. This council controlled all administrative and appointment power. It formed for every municipal function—transit, sewerage, sanitation—a standing committee, "at the head of which will be a skilled executive officer appointed upon his merits."[4]

Shaw's analysis of the situation in Paris reflected similar sentiments but with more passion. Shaw maintained that Paris had been subjected to the forces of modernity for close to two centuries, but as late as the 1780s government "had not affected materially the medieval conditions." Parisian government remained "a chaos of competing authorities, a tangle of obsolete privileges, and a nest of scandalous abuses." "Ancient guilds and corporations blocked every reform; atrocious injustice and inveterate corruption reigned high-handed in the name of king, noble, or church." That situation had devolved from the ancient communities, which "had won a high degree of local autonomy" and played an important role in France's medieval past.

The French Revolution changed all that. Its "transforming energy" replaced "the iniquities of the old regime" with "the creative vigor of the new era." Municipal government began "anew upon simple principles." A "system of local representative administration" based upon "the modern electoral principle" was the keystone. Citizens elected a "corps municipal"—several men—to run Paris. This "absolutely independent and autonomous" government over the subsequent century developed functions similar to those of English municipalities and headed each functional unit with a relevant expert. Shaw noted that Paris now had become "the best lighted city in the world" and praised its system of sewers, but reserved his highest accolades for the resurrection of its physical environs. As "the most conspicuous . . . thoroughly modernized city," Paris served as a wondrous model, "teaching the world a lesson of order, system, and logic, of emancipation and iconoclasm." Paris was "the unrivaled leader" in the "brilliant nineteenth-century task of reconstructing cities in their physical characters, dealing with them as organic entities, and endeavoring to give such form to the visible body as will best accommodate the expanding life within."

By congratulating Parisians for their urban redesign, Shaw tacitly acknowledged that not all modern (and modernizing) municipalities promoted the same lesson. National circumstance, national traditions, and national history all mattered. In both the French and English cases, moreover, national life provided the events that spurned the modernization of municipal governance. In England, Parliament's passage of the Metropolis Management Act of 1855, followed by the Municipal Government Consolidation Act of 1882, provided the means, while the French Revolution of 1789 provided the opportunity. But Shaw's survey of German municipalities exposed another sort of emphasis: the response to modernizing forces by a people, which provided yet further caveats to the central lessons of modernity.[5]

To Shaw, the Germans could provide valuable lessons primarily because they seemed so unlike their European counterparts. Their history showed the universal forces of modernity. Certainly there was no expectation that Germans would successfully erect a modern municipal system. Their racial stock and national heritage were particularly unsuitable to municipal life. According to Shaw, Germans historically "have been in their habits of life a rather primitive, simple people, less fastidious" than other Europeans. These habits apparently were "unsuited to the demands of a complex, artificial civilization," such as that of the modern city. Yet Shaw noted that Germans, due to a "quickening of national pride," were in the "midst of a quick transition from an agricultural into a manufacturing people."

A key provision in the transition was passage of the Prussian municipal law of 1808, which did away with the remnants of medieval oligarchy and recognized municipalities as "ancient units of government, organic entities, with their own properties and functions, and with the right of entire self-government within the sphere of their strictly local and neighborhood concerns." When it came to "modern conveniences and improvements," Shaw found much to his surprise that Germans completely appreciated "the full force and significance of the immense modern impetus that is transforming European cities" and incorporated modern municipal principles "in a more systematic, thorough, and businesslike way than any other cities whether in Europe, America, or Australia." This, too, stemmed from German uniqueness. Shaw argued that Germans had "more of the scientific spirit and method than any other people. Their habits of thoroughness in research, and of patient, exhaustive treatment of any subject in hand, have fully characterized their new progress in the arts of civilized life." He argued that the German "system of public administration" proved "more economical and more infallibly effective than could have been found elsewhere," and that the Germans were so adept at organizing municipal governments that "they dared to assign to the municipalities spheres of action which elsewhere have been left to private effort and control." In Germany, the municipality is "an organization for business and social ends," and "it is the business of the municipality to promote in every feasible way its own welfare and the welfare of its citizens."

The Germanic embrace of municipal modernity began with the willingness of its best citizens to serve on city councils. Selection to these august bodies was a singular honor. These men only set policy. They hired an entire administrative team to implement it and to make recommendations for other initiatives. Heading this administrative team was the burgermeister, "an expert in the general art of municipal administration." His associates, who together formed a magisterial council, included "experts in law, experts in finance, experts in education to administer the schools, experts in engineering to oversee public works of every character, experts in public charity, experts in forestry and park management, experts in the technical and business management of water-and gas-supplies, and so on."

The differences between the German and American municipal systems were dramatic. Unlike the American mayor, generally a prominent citizen called temporarily to office, the burgermeister of a German city was "a civil servant—the permanent head of a permanent body of trained officials." "Given complete charge of administrative work," each member of the burgermeister-headed magisterial council had special training at universities or other appropriate schools and was paid well to reflect his specialized knowledge and talents.

These highly honed special skills paid off in other ways. Experts were unafraid to innovate. They devised new approaches to the new problems of the modern city even at the risk of public censure. Shaw argued that this freedom borne of experience and training led Germans to create a new arrangement of urban streets, "a combination of the radial and concentric with the rectangular and parallel." The German "combination system is by far the most convenient" in the modern world, a factor that encouraged commercial activities. After all, Shaw noted, "good streets are to a modern town what the circulatory system is to a living organism."[6]

Surveys of German, English, and French municipalities, coupled with similar studies of Swiss and Italian cities, compelled Shaw to conclude that a form of municipal democracy had become the guiding facet of the administration of cities "in all foreign countries." "City government controlled throughout by a central elective council" had emerged as the "simple, republican, stably balanced system" of Europe. So, too, had "municipal socialism," a term that Shaw and others employed to describe the assumption by modern municipal governments of responsibility to protect and promote the health and welfare of the entire city population. Direct application of city services equitably and regularly throughout the municipality became an important feature of municipal socialism, as did provision of the necessities of modern life—electricity, gas, and water. Rather than permit oligarchies to monopolize these crucial elements, perpetuating in effect "the selfishness of the fossilized [medieval] City corporation" into the modern world, municipal socialists demanded that governments control and regulate these facets of modernity. As important, Shaw maintained that such sentiments reflected not just his opinion but rather that of modern municipal man. Municipal socialism "originated in the population," he contended, as citizens of each city began "waking up with a sense of unity and with an appreciation of great things to be done through united municipal action for the common welfare."[7]

Shaw's and Fiske's examinations of the medieval municipal past and the entrance of European cities into the modern world outlined or exposed virtually all the issues that formed the basis of municipal agitation in turn-of-the-century America. Freedom from outside jurisdictions—home rule—strong mayor, nonpartisan elections, expert administration, commission form of governance, and city manager were imbedded in and evident from these analyses. All found their genesis in the same desire: to overcome the heritage of the medieval past, which in each instance was deemed oligarchy, government in the hands of a few. Yet most of the turn-of-the-century American proposals for modifying municipal governance also relied on the establishment of an oligarchy. City manager, commission, or strong mayor systems all were oligarchies. Each of these proposed turn-of-the-century American oligarchies would have to have received the consent of the governed, as had their oligarchical antecedents in colonial America or often European municipalities. But none of those earlier or European cities had to placate a populace that championed universal manhood suffrage. Democracy wrought large appeared antithetical to "good" turn-of-the-century American governance.

L. S. Rowe, professor of political science at the University of Pennsylvania, made the same point and based his conclusions upon the highest tenets of science. He examined the contemporary world and pronounced traditional notions of democracy as expressed in America doomed. Rowe came to his assessment by applying "the doctrine of evolution." "Its leading principle of the adaptation of form to function" spelled democracy's demise. American democratic principles were crafted in the eighteenth century and polished in the first half of the nineteenth. These principles championed local governments, especially cities, as protectors of "individual rights." Local governments were "the bulwark against the possible tyranny of the state and federal governments" and served to check them so as to not damage "personal responsibility and initiative."

Local government, then, simply kept the state and federal governments from encroaching on the individual. Rowe argued that the success of that philosophy ironically led to its downfall by "contribut[ing] so much toward our industrial development." But that development, coupled with "the concentration of population and the growth of great industrial centers[, has] brought to the foreground a mass of new problems which the community is compelled to face." Democracy, those "ideas of governmental organization which we have borrowed from an earlier period [the medieval] and which have worked great good . . . are no longer applicable to the conditions that prevail in cities." This was especially unfortunate to Rowe because turn-of-the-century Americans "continue to reason as if the political principles of the eighteenth century had lost none of their force." "The political ideas which have dominated our political thinking for more than a century are no longer adequate to meet the complex conditions of modern city life."

Specifically, Rowe targeted the bifurcated nature of municipal governance. Traditional democracy placed city council, the local representative assembly, in juxtaposition with and in opposition to the popularly elected "higher administrative officials of the city," which blunted any hope of dramatic initiatives while protecting individual options. But the forces of modernity operating throughout society both in Europe and America "proved" that form of organization obsolete. The effect of those forces was inevitable. "We cannot hope permanently to preserve the illusion that by some occult force political organization can be kept free from the influences which are dominant in every other department of our national life," Rowe reasoned. He claimed that business, educational, charitable, and even church organizations had vested management control "in one individual." In all cases, concentration of and increase in executive power "have been accompanied by a marked increase in efficiency."

Increased efficiency was pitted against democracy. Rowe found that Americans in the modern age were "worshippers of efficiency." Therefore, the quaint eighteenth-century idea of democracy now seemed a pernicious atavism, a symbol of the medieval age. The doctrine of the survival of the fittest required democracy's demise. Turn-of-the-century Americans would necessarily institutionalize expert administration, ceding their decision-making authority to others who could operate the municipality and its new functions at peak efficiency.

Rowe also contended that the "political superstitions" of the eighteenth century—that is, the principles of democracy—were a modern-age sham because they in fact removed the people from the political equation. By placing the mayor in opposition to council, giving municipal officeholders overlapping jurisdictions, and making terms of office as short as possible, Rowe believed, "we have beguiled ourselves." We have fashioned "the illusion that we can construct a mechanism of government which requires the attention of the citizen body only at stated election periods." The result of "belief in a self-acting governmental mechanism" was to lower civic participation, to remove the most prominent, well-respected urbanites from municipal affairs except during elections. At all other times, the mechanism of legislated checks and balances between the administrative and executive was depended on "to secure honesty." This approach, which Rowe claimed attempted to ensure integrity "through statutes rather than through men," was the single greatest "influence to retard municipal progress."

The road was clear. City governments needed to scrap their long-standing system of municipal checks and balances and put aside fears of "absolutism," a relic of the medieval age. Efficiency now commanded the day. For any sort of legislative prerogative to persist in modern times, efficiency needed to be served; governmental organization required complete separation of administrative and legislative functions and autonomy for each. Local representation in municipal governance would be a necessary casualty; it had already become untenable. To Rowe, local representation—a ward-based council system—"clogs positive action and prevents the systematic planning and economical execution of great public improvements." Only through a small council, elected citywide, could a discrete legislative unit play a role in municipal affairs, and then only in a neatly circumscribed way, by superintending financial considerations. Composed of the city's best men, the small council would restore virtue and responsibility to municipal government. By maintaining financial balance and responsibility, the council could help the municipal system run like a well-oiled machine. To not accept Rowe's design meant that city government would inevitably be entirely consumed by the executive and his administrative team. American democracy, formulated in the eighteenth century to preserve individual initiative from government, needed to yield to efficiency for the management of complex modern sociopolitical systems.[8]

Rowe's paean to municipal efficiency echoed the municipal socialism of Shaw and others as well as the municipal democracy of Fiske. Each explained why an oligarchy was required in the new modern city, and each championed rhetoric to mark the differences of his notions from what had transpired in the past. What each proposed was not the restoration of previous successes but rather a new program, one in consonance with the modern forces reconstructing contemporary society. All recognized cleavages, radical disjunctions. Yet the turn-of-the-century American leitmotif did not permit abrupt discontinuity. What was necessary, then, was acceptance that the present developed out of the past.

The practical aspects of having to deal with such an apparently restrictive formulation led to a subtle yet momentous reconceptualization. The key was to focus not on an ongoing relationship between past and present but on the fact that the present developed out of the past. By this cognitive redefinition, the present was radically different from the past and therefore ought not to be constrained by outmoded ideas and traditions. The present needed ideas and conventions suited to its peculiar requirements.

What of history in this turn-of-the-century American formulation? What could history add, how could history be made usable, at a time when the present seemed so fundamentally dissimilar to what preceded it and the form of governance erected as recently as the late eighteenth century already seemed to lack utility? History's lessons were not germane, except for demonstrating that the past was very unlike the present. That in itself was useful and usable. It would provide justification for adapting municipal government to the city's "present" requirements as well as solace to individuals experiencing the trauma of dislocation. Creation of a pathway to the present—the new municipal history—must place emphasis not on examining the details of the past but on a kind of municipal sociology. Forces buffeting cities now and in the most recent past were examined, classified, and explained as a prelude to action; they had rendered what had been the old city government inadequate, irrelevant, or inappropriate. In this new milieu, representative government entailed representing "the best interests" of the populace—what the good government types deemed best for the urban population—not the wishes of individual citizens according to some sort of numerical or proportional basis. Histories of municipalities and municipal governments of the past had become correspondingly peripheral.

One other major avenue remained for using the past. As municipal reformers throughout the country engaged in this sociological/quasihistorical recreation, they generally identified in the past two closely linked factors associated with successful municipalities. Citizens of primitive, independent, flourishing municipalities had character and exhibited civic virtue. Both characteristics were viewed as qualities of past successful civic administrations, as if the laws of sociology required that sort of outlook and those traits to prevail in all positive social groupings. Reformers contended that character and civic virtue were necessary for favorable collective living no matter the time and place. Indeed, they could be found in the progressive modern cities of Europe.[9]

That sociological conception made both character and civic virtue appear essential to the proper functioning of turn-of-the-century American cities. Character's definition was straightforward. It supposed morality, progressiveness, honesty, and humanity. Civic virtue was somewhat less well defined. In a municipal context, it suggested a sort of virtue within an individual that led him or her to conceive of the municipality as a whole, as a hierarchically ordered social system of discrete yet related parts. The individual imbued with civic virtue used it for the municipality in toto, for the good of the municipality. The civically virtuous individual had a duty or responsibility for support of good city government—which in the modern age meant application of an oligarchy of experts to rationalize municipal government systematically and the city generally—and for active participation in municipal affairs. Together in modern America, civic virtue and character added up to a fundamental appreciation of efficiency and advocacy of that program as a requirement for city living.

Contemporaries explored two possibilities. Either individuals of good character and civic virtue failed to step forward, or they did not exist in numbers sufficient to ensure municipal efficiency in modern America. Both were matters of concern. Washington Gladden, a member of the clergy and a city councilman in Columbus, Ohio, argued that cities were severely hampered when "the natural leaders of society," "the men to whom the political leadership of the community belongs," failed "to come to the front and take hold of" government. The lessons of history, asserted Gladden, teach that when these men refuse to exert their governmental responsibilities they handicap the body politic, a catastrophe analogous to a "human body with its eyes put out and its hands cut off." Rather than demonstrate the time-honored trait of what Gladden called "municipal patriotism" or "civic religion," they exhibited the modern disease of acting "too selfish, . . . unwilling to sacrifice their financial and professional interests" for the "thorough and faithful performance of the duties of citizenship." Their craven neglect ruined not only the municipality but America. "The nation can no more prosper" when its cities are misgoverned, Gladden claimed, "than a tree can prosper while its several branches are covered with nests of worms and blight."

Gladden's solution and the solution of numerous others was to create in each city an institution to gather reticent professionals and businessmen together in the spirit of civic virtue to accept their social responsibility. Such a reform club would not only mobilize its members' sentiment but also provide a single focus from which to pursue municipal reform; it would centralize effort. But Gladden's thoughts about civic virtue went further. He wanted these organizations to express their members' virtue by imitating "scientific organizations" such as the American Association for the Advancement of Science, which were organized in sections with "each section [in charge of] some specific branch of inquiry and investigation." Gladden, then, wanted these organizations to bring their members' expertise as well as virtue systematically to bear on modern municipal problems.[10]

Gladden's and other turn-of-the-century Americans' reliance on organization and combination reflected the more general assumption that organization and combination—specialized, hierarchically administered systematization—marked the best practice in the modern age and therefore was the best way to accomplish all tasks. John S. Billings, deputy surgeon-general of the United States, put it simply: "From the viewpoint of the physician, the best city government is that which preserves the health of the people, best cares for the sick and injured who require municipal aid, and gives most opportunities for the increase and diffusion of medical knowledge in connection with such care." That sentiment broached the second of the two possibilities: that civic virtue and good character were in short supply in modern America. Again, modern forces were culpable, at least in part. "Physical contiguity"—dense population—was the "starting point of all distinctly urban influences" and was in turn "caused by commerce and manufactures." Population density, "the frequent contact of man with man," had created a new personality type—"nervous, impatient, irritable, at times almost ecstatic or hysterical, one who depends for stimulus habitually upon his surroundings." Neurasthenia—or "the modern disease," as it was called by its foremost proponent, the psychologist George Beard—complicated the character and civic virtue issue. Character and civic virtue would have to be created within these urban Americans if municipalities were to establish positive, harmonious government.[11]

In a good turn-of-the-century manner, reformers assumed that their arguments were so logical and rational and their case so persuasive that its pronouncement would educate and thus transform most listeners. Put simply, they figured that a clear examination and dispassionate exposition of past and present would inevitably lead others to the same conclusions that the analysts had reached; they believed that the evidence was self-evident, not open to conflicting interpretations. It was in this spirit that big city–based college and university men published various studies that addressed a wide spectrum of questions of municipal well-being. Johns Hopkins University sponsored a series of monographs on municipal affairs. Columbia University scholars wrote numerous essays, choosing to publish them in the *Political Science Quarterly*. Harvard was also active, but its researchers gravitated to the *Quarterly Journal of Economics*.[12]

Others, not affiliated with major universities, characteristically called for collective action, demanded more formal mechanisms, and quickly located educational efforts within their new civic clubs. For example, Boston's Edwin Mead's "scientific patriotism" sought to capitalize on the "new devotion to the study of our national history" to improve municipal government. It is our job, Mead maintained, "to educate ourselves and to educate the people," "to awaken the reverence and emulation of the present generation." This could be accomplished by exposing Bostonians and other urbanites to the municipal past. The Society for the Promotion of Good Citizenship was leading the way in Boston. According to Mead, its members recognized that "history is a great power to bring to bear upon the present and the future," and he urged citizens in all major cities to exercise "the high privilege" of recounting the stories of civic virtue and character in the past to the uninitiated in the here and now.[13]

No single group pursued this aim more systematically than the National Municipal League. Created in 1894 by men and women "who realize that it is only by united action and organization that good citizens" can reform municipal government, the league restricted membership to civic associations "having the object the improvement of Municipal government." By "multiply[ing] the numbers, harmoniz[ing] the methods, and combin[ing] the forces" of civic associations nationwide, the league could establish a standardized American municipal system. More than 450 associations had

joined the league by 1900. It attracted civic organizations in cities as different and far apart as New York City; Beloit, Wisconsin; and Portland, Oregon.
These organizations were represented at league meetings by an equally
impressive and diverse selection of good government types—college professors, women, professionals, and businessmen. The league's municipal
program, which it announced in 1898, included an amendment to be added
to each state constitution to guarantee within each state (and therefore
nationwide) a particular relationship between state government and municipalities. It also drafted a municipal corporations act that if adopted in state
after state would have become a single national municipal charter. This charter provided for uniform municipal accounting, uniform gathering of
municipal statistics, and uniform municipal services. Experts in the requi-
site areas would provide all municipal services.[14]

The league undertook this grand plan of standardization because,
according to Baltimore resident Charles Bonaparte, a member of the U.S.
Civil Service Commission and chairman of the National Municipal
League's executive committee, "the evils of municipal government in the
United States were substantially the same in all our American cities." These
evils "were traceable in the last analysis" not "to local and political causes"
but rather "to moral and permanent" ones. And it was at Bonaparte's insti-
gation that the league began a campaign to standardize character and civic
virtue nationwide.

Bonaparte made the character/civic virtue case neatly. He reminded
league representatives that "the object of the National Municipal League"
was "promoting a better municipal government by promoting a desire or
demand thereof." And then Bonaparte flatly stated that "we are endeavoring, I say, to raise the moral tone of the community in regard to a most
important branch of its government." "You cannot have good government
until you have a sentiment for good city government, and you cannot have
a sentiment for good city government unless the men and women of a city
want good city government," he continued. Education in civic virtue and
character was the only effective means to straighten out municipal affairs.
"Now, create your public sentiment," Bonaparte concluded, "and your
public sentiment will very soon find a way of working itself out and
putting itself into force and effect."[15]

Bonaparte's initiative led the league to appoint a committee to learn
how the promotion effort had been faring. Composed mainly of college
and university men, the committee evinced its scientific spirit by making
its first official act the gathering of data. Arguing in essence that the study
of municipal governance was a cutting-edge discipline, the committee sur-
veyed American colleges and universities to see what municipal governance courses they were teaching and to bring "to the attention of college
authorities the necessity of offering more extended instruction."[16]

That the Bonaparte-inspired committee began by looking at higher education should not surprise. There the future was formed. Potential leaders of municipal government, both administratively and philosophically, gained the special training and skills necessary to battle and control modern forces. It was in colleges and universities that the demand for good government had to be created and codified if the municipal future was to be better than the municipal past. Character and civic virtue needed to be the products of a college education as much as engineering skills or accounting.

The committee sent its circular to more than 300 institutions and received 222 replies. Most reported work in civics or American government, but only 19 percent claimed to offer "distinct undergraduate courses more or less extended in Municipal Government." Among the 19 percent, all sections of America, except the South, received roughly equal representation. Only a handful of courses were not taught in a department that included history; few departments with political science and even fewer with sociology in their designations provided municipal government courses. Municipal government courses used two kinds of texts: general civics or American government texts or volumes written to spur municipal reform. None of either kind of text had been drafted specifically to teach municipal government at colleges. Many were written by league members or others, such as Fiske and Shaw, passionately interested in the present and future of the city. The league's municipal program functioned as a text in more than one school.[17]

The committee was gratified by the results of its survey but recognized that much more needed to be accomplished. To that end, it set itself up as a central clearinghouse for the study of municipal governance. The committee offered "its assistance to all colleges" in supplying schools "with a bibliography of books and articles" useful for municipal governance courses and furnishing free of charge the league's annual proceedings. The committee also established a speakers bureau to send speakers to college campuses to address municipal affairs. Finally, it determined that its responsibilities included "suggesting subjects" for teaching about municipal government; the committee had an obligation to create a standard municipal government course for American colleges and universities. Furnishing syllabuses of courses that the committee deemed appropriate to all American colleges and universities remained the mechanism to accomplish this. Each of these committee-approved syllabuses showed how the contemporary municipal situation evolved out of the medieval urban past. All devoted a unit to the character and passionate embrace of the entire city by early medieval guilds as they struggled to free themselves from the nobility. Beyond that, however, history as expressed in these syllabuses was irrelevant; its only relevance was to show the irrelevancy of the lessons of the past to resolving the problems of the present, with the sole exception of demonstrating the critical nature of virtuous citizens and civic virtue.[18]

The league formed another education committee a year or so later. This

new committee concentrated on popular education, the teaching of municipal governance at American elementary and secondary schools. Composed of principals and superintendents of large city public schools, it sur-
veyed municipal school systems to find out what they offered about
municipal government. History's hold on the public school market was
found to be even more tenuous than it had been in higher education. To be
sure, the past persisted to be viewed as a period very different from and foreign to the present and useful primarily to demarcate the grand divide. And
a few used the idea of biography—great men in America's, Rome's, and
Greece's past—to teach the universality of the merits of character and civic
virtue. But increasingly interest in public elementary and secondary schools
turned to what educators called "citizenship," the training of boys and girls
to assume the full-time duties of living in a cooperative community.[19]

Schoolchildren, a distinct cohort, had a special role to play in the modern city. Unlike college men and women, who were expected to emerge as
the modern municipality's leaders, schoolchildren were not to lead but to
become the means to power. As interpreted by American educators
responding to the committee's inquiries, citizenship was the very embodi-
ment of modernity. "The first essential of good citizenship" is "to foster a
sense of social obligation." "The child needs to be taught that, even as a
child, he cannot live for himself alone; that his own well-being is inextri-
cably connected with the well-being of others; that he is affected by their
acts, and they by his; and that there is a mutual obligation to self-restraint
and to active service."[20]

Acquisition of citizenship by the young had to be regularized. Citizenship was not something learned by reading, rote, or recitation. It was a contemporary, not a medieval, notion. It could not incorporate or use the past;
citizenship demanded hands-on experience. The locus of practical training
occurred in either of two places. Students worked with and through city
government—reading and analyzing reports and memorizing bureaucratic tables of organization and city charters—or at their school. This latter practicum was often called the School City and it was marked by governance of the school as if it were city government. Proponents of the
School City argued that citizenship was the goal of popular education and
that only through the mechanism of a living interactive demonstration—
in this case, treating the school as if it were a little municipality—would
these future citizens gain an awareness of their responsibility to work
together for mutual efficiencies and embrace their duties to each other and
the community.

School City theorists reasoned that the boss-infested municipality had
much in common with the traditional school. Each was a monarchy, an
aristocratic oligarchy. Only by installing this new communitarian ethos
could citizens exert their citizenship and make their mutual voices heard.
Through active participation in the School City young men and women of

the future could learn of their mutual dependence; accept the differences among people, professions, races, religions, and classes that marked modern municipal life; and support the institutionalization of those differences in their daily affairs.

In this movement, systematization ruled the day. Operating under the Golden Rule, the first principle of the School City's charter, children ran "the school as a miniature municipality." They "elect their own officers and exercise legislative, judicial and executive functions." But the most important factor was not what these indoctrinated students learned in school but what they would do when they finished school. "Fully conscious of their civic responsibilities," recent graduates "will so regenerate the cities that their government will become the pride rather than the shame of the Republic."[21]

Articulation of the School City symbolized the end of the turn-of-the-century municipal debate. It marked a point so far from the debate's initial moment that there could be no return. Nor could there be much of a meaningful connection. By the time the School City generation took its adult place in the modern city, the idea of the medieval origins of modern cities and the problems caused by these roots were hardly a memory outside of some antiquated college courses. Medievalness had lost its power to explain, just as the past was rendered obsolete by the present. The question that fueled Fiske and the other early analysts—how did we come to the present—yielded to considerations of how we ensure the future. Democracy, formerly the protection of the minority from the tyranny of the majority, gave way to the modern, more nebulous idea of the good of the community, now recognized as distinctly hierarchical, composed of discrete and specialized groups and peoples. Full participation in this new democracy meant oxymoronically participating in the appropriate place, in the appropriate manner, at the appropriate time, in the appropriate way. Even political agitation had by and large ceased. In a few short years, Americans had redrawn their understanding of the past and the present with critical implications for the municipal and American future. The various municipal governments they erected were testimony to those new ideas.

Notes

1. The historical literature on municipal reform is considerable. See, for example, Samuel P. Hays, "The Politics of Reform in Municipal Government in the Progressive Era," *Pacific Northwest Quarterly* 55 (October 1964): 157–69; Robert H. Wiebe, *The Search for Order, 1977–1920* (New York: Hill and Wang, 1967), particularly pp. 111–32; Zane L. Miller, *Boss Cox's Cincinnati: Urban Politics in the Progressive Era* (New York: Oxford University Press, 1968); Martin J. Schiesl, *The Politics of Efficiency: Municipal Administration and Reform in America,*

1880–1920 (Berkeley: University of California Press, 1977); Michael H. Ebner and Eugene M. Tobin, eds., *The Age of Urban Reform: New Perspectives on the Progressive Era* (Port Washington, N.Y.: Kennikat Press, 1977); Alan I Marcus, "Professional Revolution and Reform in the Progressive Era: Cincinnati Physicians and the City Elections of 1897 and 1900," *Journal of Urban History* 5/2 (February 1979): 183–207; Jon C. Teaford, *The Unheralded Triumph, City Government in America, 1870–1900* (Baltimore: Johns Hopkins University Press, 1984); Bruce M. Stave and Sondra Astor Stave, eds., *Urban Bosses, Machines, and Progressive Reformers,* 2d rev. ed. (Malabar, Fla.: R. E. Krieger, 1984); and Kenneth Finegold, *Experts and Politicians: Reform Challenges to Machine Politics in New York* (Princeton, N.J.: Princeton University Press, 1995).

2. On early- and mid-nineteenth-century democracy in America, see R. W. B. Lewis, *The American Adam: Innocence, Tragedy, and Tradition in the Nineteenth Century* (Chicago: University of Chicago Press, 1955); Fred Somkin, *Unquiet Eagle: Memory and Desire in the Idea of American Freedom, 1815–1860* (Ithaca: Cornell University Press, 1967); John William Ward, *Andrew Jackson: Symbol for an Age* (New York: Oxford University Press, 1955); and Bernard Wishy, *The Child and the Republic: The Dawn of Modern American Child Nurture* (Philadelphia: University of Pennsylvania Press, 1967).

3. John Fiske, *Civil Government in the United States Considered With Some Reference to Its Origins* (Boston: Houghton, Mifflin, 1890), pp. 99–139. Fiske has been the subject of several biographies. See Milton Berman, *John Fiske: The Evolution of a Popularizer* (Cambridge: Harvard University Press, 1961), and George P. Winston, *John Fiske* (New York: Twayne, 1972). The American connection with England and the classical past was often cited. The third edition of James Bryce's *The American Commonwealth* (New York: Macmillan, 1895) was easily the most important volume in this genre. Also see Bryce's "The Essential Unity of Britain and America," *Atlantic* 82 (1898): 22–39. Of interest are Adolph Moses, "Popular Government: Its Development and Failure in Antiquity," *American Journal of Politics* 5 (July–December 1894): 381–91; A. V. Dicey, "England and America," *Atlantic* 82 (1898): 441–45; and Edwin Burritt Smith, "Municipal Self-Government: Council and Mayor," *Atlantic* 89 (1902): 391–97.

4. Albert Shaw, "Municipal Government in Great Britain," *Political Science Quarterly* 4 (June 1889): 197–229; "Glasgow: A Municipal Study," *Century* 39 (1889–90): 721–36; and "How London Is Governed," *Century* 41 (1890–91): 132–47. Also see Shaw's *Municipal Government in Great Britain* (New York: Century Co., 1895). Shaw has also been the subject of a biography. See Lloyd J. Graybar, *Albert Shaw of the* Review of Reviews, *an Intellectual Biography* (Lexington: University Press of Kentucky, 1974). Also of note is "The City in Modern Life," *Atlantic* 75 (1895): 552–56; "The Government of English Cities," *Century* 50 (1895): 314–15; Washington Gladden, "The Government of Cities," *Century* 49 (1894–95): 155–57; and J. W. Martin, "A Cure for City Corruption," *Harper's* 99 (June–November 1899): 641–46.

5. Albert Shaw, "Paris. The Typical Modern City," *Century* 42 (1891): 449–66.

6. Albert Shaw, "The Government of German Cities: The Municipal Framework," *Century* 48 (1894): 296–305, and "What German Cities Do For Their Citizens. A Study of Municipal House-Keeping," *Century* 48 (1894): 380–88.

7. Albert Shaw, "The Municipal Problem and Greater New York," *Atlantic* 79 (1897): 733–47, and "How London Is Governed." Shaw summed up his European analyses in *Municipal Government in Continental Europe* (New York: Century Co., 1895). Also see his "Municipal Administration at Home and Abroad," *Independent* 46 (1894): 1183–84. Of use for municipal socialism is Milo Roy Maltbie, "Municipal Functions: A Study of the Development, Scope and Tendency of Municipal Socialism," *Municipal Affairs* 2/4 (1898): 579–787; Richard T. Ely, "Municipal Ownership of Natural Monopolies," *North American Review* 172 (1900): 445–55; Josiah Quincy, "The Development of American Cities," *Arena* 17 (1897): 529–37; John C. Chase, "Municipal Socialism in America," *Independent* 52 (1900): 249–51; and "How Municipal Ownership Succeeds. Testimony From a Score of Cities," *Independent* 49 (1897): 577–79. Americans continued to look to Europe for ideas and inspiration. See, for example, William Bennett Munro, *The Government of European Cities* (New York: Macmillan, 1909).

8. L. S. Rowe, "The Relation of Municipal Government to American Democratic Ideals," *Proceedings of the New York Conference for Good City Government and the Eleventh Annual Meeting of the National Municipal League*, 1905, pp. 170–79. Rowe expressed similar points elsewhere. See, for example, his "American Political Ideas and Institutions in Their Relation to the Problem of City Government," *Proceedings of the Louisville Conference for Good City Government and the Third Annual Meeting of the National Municipal League*, 1897, pp. 75–88. Rowe had great admiration for German municipalities. See his "City Government As It Should Be and May Become," *Proceedings of the National Conference for Good City Government*, 1894, pp. 111–21. Rowe was involved with the administration of Puerto Rico after the Spanish-American War and so had helped construct local government in an imperial context. Also of interest is "Address of Hon. William Dudley Foulke," *Proceedings of the Indianapolis Conference for Good City Government and the Fourth Annual Meeting of the National Municipal League*, 1898, pp. 135–42; T. St. Pierre, "Responsibility in Municipal Government," *Arena* 27 (January–June 1902): 39–46; Thomas G. Hayes, "A City Controlled on a Business Basis," *Independent* 53 (1901): 479–80; and W. J. Ghent, "The Next Step: A Benevolent Feudalism," *Independent* 54 (1902): 781–88.

9. In addition to the material already cited, see, for instance, George F. Parker, "An Object-Lesson in Municipal Government," *Century* 53 (1896–97): 71–89; George R. Parkin, "Australian Cities. The Anglo-Saxon in the Southern Hemisphere," *Century* 41 (1890–91): 690–96; Delos F. Wilcox, "The City Government of Athens," *Independent* 49 (1897): 1200–1201; E. L. Godkin, "Peculiarities of American Municipal Government," *Atlantic* 80 (1897): 620–34; Robert P. Porter, "The Municipal Spirit in England," *North American Review* 161 (1895): 590–601; C. E. Pickard, "Great Cities and Democratic Institutions," *American Journal of Politics* 4 (January–June 1894): 378–91; J. Eugene Whitney, "Proportional Representation:

A Remedy for Municipal Misrule," *American Magazine of Civics* 8 (January–June 1896): 127–33; and Herbert Welsh, "The Movement for Good Government," *American Journal of Politics* 5 (July–December 1894): 67–75.

10. Washington Gladden, "The Cosmopolis City Club. Why and How the Club Was Organized," *Century* 45 (1893): 395–406. Also see Gladden, "Civic Religion," *Proceedings of the Second National Conference for Good City Government and the First Annual Meeting of the National Municipal League and the Third National Conference for Good City Government, 1895*, pp. 508–16. Gladden was a prolific correspondent and writer. For a catalog of his microfilmed material, see Gary J. Arnold, *The Washington Gladden Collection: An Inventory to the Microfilm Edition* (Columbus: Archives-Library, Ohio Historical Society, 1972). For similar sentiments, see, for instance, "Misgovernment of Cities," *Century* 40 (1890): 798–99, and "Responsibility for Political Corruption," *Century* 44 (1892): 473–75; James Hoffman Batten, "The Problem of Municipal Government," *Arena* 24 (July–December 1900): 589–93; and "Responsibility for Misrule," *Independent* 53 (1901): 2481–82.

11. John S. Billings, "Good City Government From the Standpoint of the Physician and Sanitarian," *Proceedings of the Second National Conference,* pp. 492–99; and James T. Young, "University Instruction in Municipal Government," *Proceedings of the Rochester Conference for Good City Government and the Seventh Annual Meeting of the National Municipal League, 1901,* pp. 226–31. On neurasthenia and Beard, see, for example, his *A Practical Treatise on Nervous Exhaustion (Neurasthenia). Its Symptoms, Nature, Sequences, Treatment* (New York: William Wood, 1880). This classic work was in its fifth edition in 1905. Also see "The Problem of City Life," *Independent* 53 (1901): 1087–89, and "The New City," *Independent* 53 (1901), pp. 1932–33. Adna Ferrin Weber's *The Growth of Cities in the Nineteenth Century* (New York: Macmillan, 1899) proved a particular favorite source of inspiration and documentation for those pointing to the pressure of populations as a central modern force. Also see Walter Wellman, "Rise of the American City," *McClures* 17 (1901): 470–75.

12. The *Quarterly Journal of Economics* was edited at Harvard, and William Bennett Munro, the college's municipal political scientist, was a frequent contributor. Columbia's Frank J. Goodnow published considerable research in his university-edited *Political Science Quarterly*. Herbert Baxter Adams, Edward P. Allinson, and Boies Penrose, all Johns Hopkins faculty, contributed several pieces to *Johns Hopkins University Studies.*

13. Edwin D. Mead, "The Promotion of Municipal Reform By Education," *Proceedings of the National Conference,* pp. 167–76. Of value is Adolph Roeder, "The Civic Oversoul," *Arena* 28 (1902): 346–53.

14. *Proceedings of the National Conference,* pp. 1–48 and 303–40, and *Proceedings of the Indianapolis Conference,* pp. 1–52. Also see Clinton Rogers Woodruff, "The Progress of Municipal Reform, 1894–95," *American Magazine of Civics* 7 (July–December 1895): 66–73, and "Conference for Good City Government," *Independent* 49 (1897): 638–39; and Frank J. Goodnow, "The National Municipal League's Municipal 'Program,'" *Independent* 51 (1899): 3228–30. Support for

the league's municipal program often found its way into texts. See, for instance, J. A. James and A. H. Sanford, *Government in State and Nation* (New York: Charles Scribner's Sons, 1904), pp. 31–47.

15. Charles J. Bonaparte, "Remarks," *Proceedings of the Milwaukee Conference for Good City Government and Sixth Annual Meeting of the National Municipal League,* 1900, pp. 5–7, 21–27, and "The Essential Element in Good City Government," *Proceedings of the Milwaukee Conference,* pp. 88–93. Also see Bonaparte, "The Movement for Honest Government," *Proceedings of the Boston Conference for Good City Government and Eighth Annual Meeting of the National Municipal League,* 1902, pp. 246–59.

16. *Proceedings of the Milwaukee Conference,* pp. 41–42. The centrality of the university in modern times was noted in Nathaniel S. Shaler, "The Transmission of Learning through the University," *Atlantic* 73 (1894): 115–24.

17. Thomas M. Drown, "Report of the Committee on Instruction in Municipal Government in American Colleges," *Proceedings of the Rochester Conference,* pp. 218–25, and "Bibliography," *Proceedings of the Rochester Conference,* pp. 232–34. Also of interest is Harry A. Garfield, "The College Man in Public Affairs," *Proceedings of the New York Conference,* pp. 184–92.

18. Drown, "Report," pp. 224–25; L. S. Rowe, "Outline of Course on Municipal Government and Institutions Offered at the University of Pennsylvania," *Proceedings of the Rochester Conference,* pp. 235–41; Robert C. Brooks, "Outline of Course on Municipal Government in Europe and the United States Offered at Cornell University," *Proceedings of the Rochester Conference,* pp. 242–44; Clinton Rogers Woodruff, "Municipal Government in the United States," *Proceedings of the Rochester Conference,* pp. 245–47; Thomas M. Drown, "Instruction in Municipal Government in American Educational Institutions," *Proceedings of the Boston Conference,* pp. 268–71; Samuel E. Sparling, "Syllabus of Course on Municipal Government," *Proceedings of the Boston Conference,* pp. 272–80; Charles Zueblin, "American Municipal Progress Syllabus," *Proceedings of the Boston Conference,* pp. 281–88; "List of Lecturers," *Proceedings of the Boston Conference,* pp. 289–91; L. S. Rowe, "University and Collegiate Research in Municipal Government," *Proceedings of the Chicago Conference for Good City Government and the Tenth Annual Meeting of the National Municipal League,* 1904, pp. 242–48; L. S. Rowe, "Report of the Committee on 'Co-ordination of University and Collegiate Instruction in Municipal Government,'" *Proceedings of the New York Conference,* pp. 180–83; and *Proceedings of the Atlantic City Conference for Good City Government and the Twelfth Annual Meeting of the National Municipal League,* 1906, pp. 416–18.

19. William H. Maxwell and J. J. Sheppard, "Instruction in Municipal Government in Secondary and Elementary Schools," *Proceedings of the New York Conference,* pp. 256–80. Also see Josiah Strong, "The Problem of the Twentieth Century City," *North American Review* 165 (1897): 343–49.

20. Maxwell and Sheppard, *Proceedings of the New York Conference,* p. 259. For explorations of late-nineteenth- and early-twentieth-century public education, see Lawrence A. Cremin, *The Transformation of the School: Progressivism in American Education, 1876–1957* (New York: Knopf, 1961); Raymond E. Callahan,

Education and the Cult of Efficiency (Chicago: University of Chicago, 1962); and David B. Tyack, *The One Best System. A History of American Urban Education* (Cambridge: Harvard University Press, 1974).

21. On the School City and other efforts, see John A. Fairlie, "Instruction in Municipal Government," *Proceedings of the Detroit Conference for Good City Government and the Ninth Annual Meeting of the National Municipal League,* 1903, pp. 222–30; J. B. Davis, "The Teaching of Municipal Government in the High Schools of Our Large Cities," *Proceedings of the Detroit Conference,* pp. 231–35; "Friday Afternoon Session," *Proceedings of the Chicago Conference,* pp. 58–68; Thomas R. Slicer, "The School City as a Form of Student Government," *Proceedings of the Chicago Conference,* pp. 283–93; Frederic L. Luqueer, "A Tentative Program for the Teaching of Municipal Government and of Civics in the Elementary School," *Proceedings of the Chicago Conference* , pp. 249–77; Oliver B. Cornman, "The School City. An Inquiry Concerning Its Success and Value," *Proceedings of the New York Conference,* pp. 280–89; John F. Finley, "Report of the Literature of Instruction in Municipal Government," *Proceedings of the New York Conference,* pp. 289–92; William Chauncy Langdon, "A Fundamental Principle of Civic Education," *Proceedings of the Atlantic City Conference,* pp. 409–15; and Wilson L. Gill, "The School City," *Proceedings of the Detroit Conference,* pp. 236–46. Gill directed the Cuban schooling effort under the American occupation. The School City was used there to accomplish one of the stated goals of American imperialism: to raise up the masses through the promotion of democracy.

Chapter Three

Advocating City Planning in the Public Schools: The Chicago and Dallas Experiences, 1911–1928

ROBERT B. FAIRBANKS

The two great issues in American municipalities today are citizen making and city planning. They are two parts of one whole. Both are inseparable.[1]

—JOHN NOLEN

In *Our Cities To-Day and To-Morrow* (1929), their well-known survey of planning and zoning progress in the United States, Theodora Kimball Hubbard and Henry Vincent Hubbard included in their chapter "Educating the Public to Support City Planning" a section on "Teaching of City Planning in Public Schools."[2] In it the authors not only discussed the nation's first elementary school textbook on city planning, *Wacker's Manual of the Plan of Chicago*, published in 1911, but also referred to several other texts for schools in Dallas, Buffalo, Boston, and New York City. Those four books appeared in the 1920s and could be called community civics texts instead of planning texts. All four differed significantly in focus from the Chicago text but were cited by the Hubbards because they included references to city planning and because their overall message was essential to the promoters of planning in the 1920s—the inextricable linkage of each city's parts to the others and to its whole. A comparison of one of these 1920s texts, *Our City—Dallas: A Community Civics*, with *Wacker's Manual* can help us better understand subtle but significant shifts in the advocacy of planning in public schools at this time and the way changing conceptions of the city shaped the focus and emphasis of planning.

Wacker's Manual of the Plan of Chicago appeared as an outgrowth of Walter Dwight Moody's ambitious efforts to promote the Chicago Plan of 1909.

That plan, undoubtedly the most important and influential one of the decade, was established due to the efforts of the Merchant's Club, an organization that merged with the more prestigious Commercial Club as the project got under way. In 1907 the Merchant's Club organized a committee with Charles D. Norton as chair and Charles H. Wacker as vice chair and initiated efforts to secure a plan. Only after it had merged with the Commercial Club were Daniel Burnham and Edward H. Bennett hired to develop the project.[3] The completed plan focused on six areas: (1) the development of the lakefront; (2) the improvement and consolidation of railroad terminals; (3) the creation of a system of highways outside of the city to connect the suburbs and the center; (4) the development of an extensive park system linked by tree-lined boulevards; (5) a systematic arrangement of streets and avenues to facilitate movement to and from the business district; and (6) the development of "centers of intellectual life and administration, so related as to give coherence and unity to the city."[4]

Such an approach to the more coordinated planning of public works was not the first in this country, nor did it address new issues in Chicago development needs. Indeed, the plan's introduction noted that "If many elements of the proposed plan shall seem familiar, it should be remembered that the purpose of the plan has not been to invent novel problems for solution, but to take up pressing needs of today, and to find the best methods of meeting those requirements, carrying each particular problem to its ultimate conclusion as a component part of a great entity—a well-ordered, convenient, and unified city."[5] The plan's significance was its ability to bring the various strategies and calls for improvement into one document providing more centralized and coordinated solutions to the city's needs.

Although the plan was impressive in its own right, it was also noteworthy because of the massive promotional campaign employed to secure voter approval of many of its public works proposals. Shortly after the plan was announced, Chicago mayor Fred A. Busse appointed a Chicago Plan Commission (CPC) on November 1, 1909, to direct government in carrying out the plan and publicize it to the city as a whole. The commission, comprised of "328 leading men of Chicago," according to the plan's promoters, was "made as representative as possible of every section and element in our population."[6] Its first chairman, Charles H. Wacker, asked Walter D. Moody, managing director of the new body, to orchestrate a massive publicity blitz for the plan. Moody had been the general manager of the Chicago Association of Commerce with a background in sales and promotion, experience that made him an ideal candidate for this task. He was, according to Thomas J. Schlereth, "one of the new breed of public executives who made careers out of managing civic organizations."[7] His first important public relations effort for the CPC was the publication and distribution of *Chicago's Greatest Issue: An Official Plan*. Unlike the hardcover complete plan that sold for twenty-five dollars, the *Greatest Issue*, a ninety-page reference book on the Plan of Chicago, was distributed free to more than 165,000 Chicago residents.[8]

Wacker's most original contribution to the CPC would be the strangely titled *Wacker's Manual of the Plan of Chicago,* a text adopted by the Chicago public schools for use in their eighth-grade civics classes. While such action seems odd to us today, it made sense at a time when notions about planning, education, and the city were very different from our contemporary ones.

Moody undertook this project after Daniel Burnham, unhappy with the failed implementation of his plan for San Francisco, suggested he promote the Chicago plan in the city's schools. Moody decided to go beyond Burnham's idea to provide lectures and distribute literature on the Chicago plan to the city's schoolchildren and developed a text for use in the classroom. It was named for the Chicago Plan Commission's chairman, Charles H. Wacker, because Moody thought that the post was so important that its occupant needed to be well known. The completed text was adopted by the Chicago public school board for use in its newly created eighth-grade civics class, which gave special attention to the civic life of Chicago.[9] The school board approved the book not only because of the prestige of the Commercial Club, which helped organize the CPC, but because it seemed to meet the curriculum needs of the school system.

The Chicago schools were at the forefront of a significant transformation of curriculum at this time. Unhappy with the old emphasis of public education, John Dewey and his generation wanted a more relative course of study that helped students cope with the realities of urban industrial society. As a result, educational innovators pushed schools to take on broader social and economic functions. At a time when cities seemed to be disintegrating before the eyes of Americans, and the newness and largeness of American cities appeared to be destroying any sense of civic responsibility among their residents, an emphasis on teaching good citizenship surfaced at the turn of the century. Although the nineteenth-century curriculum had taught appropriate behavior by including classes in morals and manners, at the turn of the century a new interest in promoting civic loyalty resulted in courses on citizenship supplanting the older emphasis.

While most civics classes at this time emphasized national loyalty and focused on the federal government, Chicago took an alternative approach after a committee investigating the Chicago school district in 1898 issued the Harper Report, which called for a more detailed, systematic, and specific focus on developing good citizenship.[10] Such a movement eventually led to the eighth-grade civics class, the home for *Wacker's Manual.* Unlike other civic classes that used texts that taught what it meant to be a citizen of the United States, the Chicago program used Wacker's text, which emphasized loyalty to Chicago. Although this could be dismissed as another example of Chicago boosterism, it suggests that educators realized the city was a distinctive unit in twentieth-century American society and that urban students needed civics lessons arranged to address the needs and problems found in such a setting.

Moody, who was not an educator, might seem a strange choice to author such a book, but as chief propagandist for the plan he understood the significance of instructing the school population on its importance. Because he thought completion of the plan might take well more than fifty-eight years, the amount of time it took to finish Baron Eugene Haussmann's nineteenth-century Paris plan, he knew that the students of 1912 would be asked to support bonds for projects called for in the plan during their adult years. As a result, he believed that they needed to be thoroughly indoctrinated in the benefits of the plan. But the book would be more than propaganda. It would be a perfect fit into a civics class because it emphasized the needs of the larger city as opposed to the needs of particular neighborhoods, and it encouraged students to better understand how promoting the larger public good benefited each individual. In the prefatory note to his book, Moody warned students that "Neglect of the citizen to give some of his time, some of his thought, and some of his money for the public good, if widely distributed, would mean disaster to the community."[11] Moody wanted to introduce schoolchildren to the responsibilities of good citizenship by using planning as the focus and the Chicago Plan of 1909 as the specific localized example.

The text roughly followed the pattern of the actual plan, with twelve of its sixteen chapters specifically about planning. Also, two of the three purposes of the text related to planning. The author not only hoped the book would promote "the ultimate accomplishment of the plan in future years through an enlightened citizenry," but also thought it might draw "the attention and sympathy of the parents through their children as a medium." Moody also expected that the book would train "a future citizenry to become responsible in matters of governmental control." Indeed, the author thought planning was an excellent tool with which to teach the meaning of good citizenship. Both planning and citizenship focused on the welfare of the larger community, and both looked to the future. Not only would planning promote "impulses for good order, cleanliness, honesty and economy in the physical growth and political conduct of our cities," it would instruct students in "their obligations to their fellows and to cities which shelter and develop them."[12]

Moody consulted with University of Chicago faculty as well as the Chicago Historical Society and the Art Institute. He was aware that German educators had been teaching children about urban planning since the 1880s. His final product, however, reflected how American planning advocates thought best to publicize and promote planning at this time.[13] Moody believed that "nothing can be accomplished in the move toward city betterment without public understanding and appreciation of city planning needs, problems, and advantages."[14]

Published in 1911, the 139-page textbook included more illustrations than found in the plan and incorporated drawings from the original along with other charts and pictures. In 1912, the Chicago Board of Education adopted and purchased nearly fifteen thousand copies of the book at thirty-four cents apiece for the second half of a civics course offered to eighth-graders. Eighth grade seemed a particularly suitable time to introduce students to Chicago civics and planning because it was the last year of the required grammar school and many students dropped out of school after that. Eighth grade also was when children were most impressionable, according to contemporary thought.[15]

Moody furnished a teachers' handbook for *Wacker's Manual* as well. The introduction to the handbook emphasized many themes associated with planning and also with the broader Progressive movement. It promised that the Chicago Plan of 1909 would promote the future growth of the city in a systematic and orderly fashion. It also criticized personal self-interest and selfish sectionalism within the city and emphasized that the focus needed to be on the "city's needs as a whole" since "a benefit to one part is a benefit to the whole city." Indeed, a major goal of not only the text but all publicity for the plan was to develop "a cohesion of all interest . . . by persuading the people to see and realize nothing can be accomplished except by blending all interests into a grand harmonious whole." The manual also stressed the need for efficiency and the elimination of waste. To make sure students understood and remembered what they read, the textbook contained 667 questions appearing at the end of its sixteen chapters.[16] Such an interrogative method reflected a nineteenth-century pedagogical emphasis, but the subject matter clearly reflected the concerns of the twentieth.

The textbook was roughly divided between a broad discussion of the benefits of planning and a more focused examination of the Chicago Plan of 1909. A prefatory note made it clear what the book was about. Although the text included "brief notice . . . of Chicago's past, thoughtful consideration of Chicago's present, and deep effort made to foresee Chicago's future," these sections were to "prepare the student's mind for the reception of that portion of *Wacker's Manual* which is devoted to the study of the Plan of Chicago."[17] (Page references to the manual here and in the following paragraphs are given in parentheses.) Such a textbook, then, would introduce students to "the science of city planning, as related to the future glory of Chicago and the prosperity and happiness of all her people" (10).

Several themes dominated the first half of the book, but none was more apparent than the idea that planning brought efficiency to the city. Not only would planning bring more order, cleanliness, and beauty to the city, it would promote what the author called "municipal economy." The first three chapters traced the factors behind Chicago's growth and explored some of the consequences of inadequate planning. The book also predicted that Chicago could achieve true greatness only by planning for its future

(17). Chapters 4 and 5 developed those themes by looking at European city building, starting with ancient Rome and proceeding to compare modern Paris as a successfully planned city with London as one of missed opportunities. German cities also won praise from the text, as did the country's strong planning tradition that produced cities built for "the comfort and convenience of its people" (46). In chapter 6 the text examined the planning tradition in America and looked at the planning successes associated with Washington, D.C., and Cleveland, as well as the influence of Chicago's own "White City" during the Columbian Exposition. Using the experience of European cities as evidence, this chapter emphasized how proper planning would promote a convenient and healthy Chicago for its people (57). The next two chapters explained why Chicago needed a plan. Chapter 7 stressed the material and moral reasons for planning and reminded readers that it promised an ordered and humane city. At one point in that chapter Moody warned, "We must work to a plan that stops waste of time, effort, money and labor in carrying on the work of our city and its industries" (62). But the park system called for in the plan was also necessary, according to Moody; without it "the people will become inferior in morals, mind and even in physical size and strength" (63). Chapter 8 emphasized the value of permanency and stressed how city planning would promote it. As a result, the textbook suggested that the Chicago Plan of 1909 would gradually develop "good order and attractiveness" for the city (71).

The rest of the book focused on the Chicago plan. Chapters 9 and 10 probed the background and commercial possibilities of the plan, with the former emphasizing how its chief goal was to "create order out of chaos" (80). Chapter 9 also detailed the movement for the plan and provided the text of a speech the mayor made about the plan on July 6, 1909, as well as the speech made by the chair of the Chicago Plan Commission at its first meeting (78). Chapter 10, largely made up of talks given at a dinner hosted by the Chicago Plan Commission by the Commercial Club, anticipated the many benefits that would come from a planned city. One speaker concluded that "Aside from the aesthetic and hygienic value an orderly, systematic and beautiful development of our city will produce, the commercial asset is of incalculable value" (87).

The final six chapters focused more specifically on replicating the themes from the plan's text. Chapter 11 set the groundwork by exploring the purpose and meaning of the plan. Efficiency and order, as well as a concern with congestion, traffic, and public health, seemed to attract the most attention. But so did another issue. According to the manual, the plan's purpose was to "make Chicago a real, centralized city instead of a group of overcrowded and overgrown villages." Such a new centralized city would make it easier and cheaper to carry on business, and the larger parks and playgrounds and wider streets would "make the whole people more healthy and better able to carry on the work of commerce and civilization in our great city" (95).

These chapters, then, paraphrased the plan and approached the city's problems in the same fashion as did the actual plan. Discrete chapters focused on Chicago's transportation problems, its street system, the development of Michigan Avenue, the park system, and the need for a civic center. According to Moody, "the most essential thing in a great city" is the "convenience and orderliness in its street arrangements" (125). In this context, the textbook called for the carrying out of the plan's proposed street system, since delay would not only increase the financial burden but prolong "discomfort, continued danger to health, and continued and increasing loss to the city's business, trade and commerce" (105). Streets would be widened and additional arteries created to provide "more direct routes throughout the city, and so stopping the crowding of traffic into the city's business district." The plan's complete system of diagonal streets would also do away with "crowding and congestion in various parts of the city" and add beauty to each neighborhood. Finally, the text explained to students the need for "a system of outer roadways and highways encircling the city to connect the various parts of Chicago with each other, with the center of the city and with the outlying sections" (111). A separate chapter was given to the development of Michigan Avenue, a project that would increase property values in the nearby area, provide for the city's most attractive thoroughfare, and be a major link connecting the north and south sides of Chicago (116, 121). Such an emphasis underscored the planner's concern with making Chicago an efficient working whole, a real entity where the parts were tied together through a well-planned street system.

The same theme of coordination came through in chapter 12, "Solving Chicago's Transportation Problems." This chapter provided guidance on how to make railroads "more effective in commerce [, t]o bring them all together as one great machine in the service of the city" (99). Again the emphasis was on coordinating railroads in such a way to facilitate transportation in the city for railroad freight as well as passengers.

Chapter 15 underscored the importance of parks in creating a better Chicago. According to the text, parks made for "the beautification of the city" and were necessary for "the preservation of public health" (125). Moody suggested that parks could be "compared with the lungs of a person, as the means by which the city and its people get the stimulus of fresh air so necessary to normal well-being" (125). Only the street system deserved a higher priority in the list of city needs, according to the text.

The chapter on the plan's proposal for a civic center explained that it would give "life to the spirit of unity in one city." By erecting imposing buildings that housed government agencies, the city would be allowed to "express there the pride and spirit of the people" (136). Indeed, according to the manual, a center so "stately and magnificent" would "indelibly impress Chicago's greatness upon the mind of every beholder." Planning the physical city, then, promised to make Chicago "both unified and beautiful"(137). *Wacker's Manual* used planning to instruct students on the virtues of the plan and also promoted "citizen building" and the development of "community patriotism."[18]

This pioneering textbook focused on the disorder of the physical city and why it threatened all citizens, and trumpeted the Chicago Plan of 1909 as the solution. Although it briefly discussed the city's history as well as factors in urban development, it was clearly a textbook on the good of planning in general and the Chicago plan specifically. It reflected the turn-of-the-century progressive mode of focusing on specific problems—congestion, bad housing, inadequate play space—rather than on the city as a starting point. The text began with the premise that the best way to get support for planning efforts was to educate children about planning and how it benefited the public interest. Indeed, planning would be useful not only in promoting the proper development of the physical city but in teaching students good citizenship, since citizenship meant supporting the needs of the larger city.

Although there appeared to be some controversy over the appropriateness of the text for eighth-graders—some thought the book too difficult for that level—*Wacker's Manual* remained a part of the Chicago schools' curriculum into the 1920s and went through four editions.[19] The last edition included an addendum that examined what had been done toward carrying out the Chicago plan during the fifteen years since the plan was presented.[20] The book's long life suggested it proved satisfactory for the civics class, and the constant requests for copies of the text from school districts around the country indicates it elicited great interest outside of Chicago.[21] Such demand makes sense because the book broke new ground: it taught civics by focusing on the city rather than on the nation state, a model that seemed relative to other large urban school districts.

Despite the significant publicity that the text generated, and despite Moody's belief that *Wacker's Manual* had launched "one of the most important and far reaching movements in the annals of the history of common school education in this country,"[22] it is interesting to note that when another planning advocacy group in Dallas developed a school text to promote planning in that city in the 1920s, its book had a very different form and emphasis. So did the other texts that were mentioned by the Hubbards in their 1929 survey of planning and zoning. Although several explanations might be possible for the change, the new texts appear to reflect differing ideas about planning and the city in the 1920s.

The text with the closest ties to the planning movement in the 1920s was *Our City—Dallas: A Community Civics*, published by the Kessler Plan Association (KPA) in 1927. The organization had been created in 1924 thanks to the efforts of the Dallas Property Owners Association (DPOA), a group of downtown businessmen committed to improving the decaying western part of the central business district. Shortly after its creation in 1919, the DPOA invited George Kessler, a nationally respected planner from St. Louis, to return to the city and revise a plan he had created for the city in 1911. Frustrated by their inability to rally city-wide support for the revisions, as well as for portions of the original plan, leaders of the DPOA disbanded and created a new planning advocacy group called the Kessler Plan Association, committed to the "the entire Kessler Plan and scientific development of every part of Dallas."[23]

The Kessler Plan of 1911 mirrored the emphasis of the Chicago Plan of 1909 by focusing on efforts to alleviate congestion, promote better circulation of traffic, and improve citizens' health and safety through parks and other public works projects. The forty-page plan contained a list of nine improvements: a levee system for the Trinity River and reclamation of the bottoms, a belt railroad system, a union terminal passenger station, a freight terminal, a civic center, the elimination of grade crossings in the downtown area, the opening of downtown streets, a comprehensive system of parks and boulevards, and additional playgrounds.[24] However, the revisions that Kessler made when he returned to Dallas after World War I expanded the plan's purpose by trying to better accommodate the automobile and by calling for comprehensive zoning. Unlike the earlier plan, as well as the Chicago Plan of 1909, which focused on centralizing and coordinating public works in the city, the postwar planning emphasis in Dallas (and elsewhere) expanded to include a truly comprehensive approach covering all the city's land, emphasizing the regulation of both private and public land through zoning, as well as the other planning elements present earlier.

The Kessler Plan Association, a planning booster group, shared the same goal as the Chicago Plan Commission, to persuade the city and its citizens to support the completion of the plan. Toward this end, the KPA employed John E. Surratt, who in many ways paralleled Walter Moody as a public executive who made a career out of managing civic organizations. Surratt had started with the Dallas Chamber of Commerce, went on to run chambers of commerce in Sherman, Texas, and Little Rock, Arkansas, and then returned to Dallas to head the Dallas Property Owners Association. As a result, he seemed the logical choice to lead the KPA as executive secretary and help "rejuvenate city planning" in Dallas.[25] Surratt, as had Moody, believed that educating the public about planning was the key to guarantee that rejuvenation. Toward this end he brought in national speakers such as J. C. Nichols of Kansas City and E. M. Bassett of New York, and helped secure the prestigious National Conference on City Planning for Dallas in 1928. He also lectured and showed lantern slides at a variety of church and civic groups of black and white citizens.[26] The chief aim in those lectures, according to the president of the KPA, Dr. E. H. Cary, was to show "leaders of each group and district that things they needed would benefit other districts and that by joining and putting over the entire Kessler program all would be served."[27] Surratt saw that the chief goal of the KPA was "simply that of selling the plans already prepared."[28] He did this, however, not only by explaining the plan but by emphasizing how the entire city benefited from it.

Such a commitment to sell the plan explains the KPA's decision to sponsor the development of a community civics text for the seventh grade, the last year of required education in the city. This text would be substantially different from *Wacker's Manual*, not only because of its size—384 pages compared to 139—but because of its emphasis. Moody had built his book around the history and benefits of planning in general and the Chicago Plan of 1909 specifically. The Dallas book discussed planning in about one-third of the text and focused on a variety of other civic issues, including government, education, and public utilities, as well as giving forty-six pages to the city's history—a history that continually emphasized the role of cooperative, civic-minded citizens in Dallas's development and the close interconnectedness of the parts to each other and to the whole.

According to the author, Justin F. Kimball, Dallas succeeded because "her early citizens pushed and worked and strove to make it grow and develop." Early on, Kimball continued, citizens developed the "Dallas Spirit," characterized by loyalty to the city, enthusiasm, enterprise, industry, teamwork, "and above all the willingness to make sacrifices for the good of the city and her people."[29] While Moody had hoped to create support for the Chicago Plan of 1909 by emphasizing the promise of that plan, the Dallas text started with an appeal to civic patriotism to rally support for comprehensive planning for the good of the city. It began with the city as opposed to planning, and viewed good citizenship as a key to carrying out the plan, rather than as an end result of planning. The Dallas text, then, focused primarily on the role of good citizenship rather than merely on the role of planning in the city.

One possible reason for this different emphasis might be the book's author. Justin F. Kimball had been superintendent of Dallas public schools for ten years before being forced out of office in 1924 by a combination of ill health and pressure from the Ku Klux Klan. The fifty-two-year-old Kimball had degrees from Mount Lebanon College in Louisiana and Baylor University in Texas, and had done postgraduate work at the University of Chicago and the University of Michigan. After stepping down from the superintendency and while taking a year off to recover his health, he agreed to write a community civics text for Dallas that included extensive discussions of planning.[30] Because of his background, he must have been aware of the growing emphasis on community civics by 1915, an emphasis that accelerated greatly after World War I.

Under the guidance of the Department of Civic Education, established within the U.S. Bureau of Education in 1914, civics moved from an emphasis on simply educating students about their governments and their need to vote to a course whose goal was to promote "harmonious and efficient team work in society."[31] Although early civics classes had focused primarily on the national government and emphasized the organization and legal powers of that government, a new preoccupation with what was called community civics gained momentum after 1915. According to Civic Education Circular No. 1, issued by the U.S. Bureau of Education, the aim of community civics was to "help the child know his community" and cultivate in him or her "the essential qualities and habits of good citizenship." The focus on the city or town made it easier for students "to realize [their] membership in the local community, to feel a sense of personal responsibility for it, and to enter into actual cooperation with it, than in the case of the national community."[32] Kimball wrote a community civics text that was both organized and focused differently than Moody's Chicago text. The book's enthusiastic reception by KPA leadership suggested they wholeheartedly embraced this approach to promoting planning.

Unlike Moody, who emphasized the importance of planning to the city's proper growth, Kimball stressed the role of civic-minded citizens in the city's development and focused on the history of the city rather than merely on planning. And unlike Moody's focus on the history of planning and how other cities had been shaped by great and ambitious plans, Kimball accentuated the role of citizens and the larger city-building experience. Early chapters titled "How Dallas Began" and "How Dallas Grew and Why" never mentioned city planning. It was not until chapter 4, "How Other Cities Have Been Planned," that students were introduced to planning. And only with chapter 5, "The Coming of George Kessler," did seventh-graders read anything about planning in Dallas. Even in this chapter, the author focused on the failure of Dallas's citizens to fully carry out the 1911 plan or the revisions of 1919. Indeed, the chapter lamented that there had been "no concerted plan or organization" for the effort.[33] Kimball repeated the theme in another chapter when he observed that "the city of Dallas had never undertaken the plan as a whole" and bemoaned the fact that it had only been "worked out in disconnected parts." The point that the plan was for the entire city and not just some parts was repeated in a parenthetical note to teachers in chapter 6. It reminded them that "the essential feature in teaching this chapter is to impress upon the child the fact that Mr. Kessler made a plan for the *city as a whole*" and that it provided one plan "for the city as a unit, and at the same time gave us a plan that touches every part of the city." Only then did the book proceed to identify and discuss features that inhibited the city's proper growth and development, including badly placed railroad tracks, lack of thoroughfares, inadequate housing, and the meandering Trinity River with its smelly and unusable flood plain.[34] After listing the problems, the book explored how the Kessler plan proposed to remedy them, while paying special attention to the city's need to secure comprehensive zoning since "there can be no adequate city planning without some kind of zoning."[35]

The book did not end with this promotion of planning, however. Chapters 14 through 29 examined a variety of topics from "Our Threefold Citizenship" to "How Cities are Governed." Although many of these pages documented the work of specific parts of city government, they also explained the complexity of that government and implicitly emphasized the interdependence of the parts with each other and with the whole. Indeed, the book even concluded that the city and county were so interdependent now that Dallas and its suburbs needed a single, unified government. Besides this emphasis, the book returned to the theme that had guided its early chapters—the critical role of good citizenship in proper community building. "Fifteen years ago," Kimball observed, "our leaders in thought and action were thinking somewhat more seriously than now about the general betterment of Dallas, the development of her personality, the stimulation of her livableness. We ought to get back to that point of view."[36] The book's last page returned to the larger issue of civic loyalty by asking students to serve their city "devotedly, unselfishly, and without thought of gain."[37]

Wacker's Manual had treated planning as an answer to a discrete problem—bad land use—and focused on the importance of planning in general and the Chicago plan specifically to solve that problem and make Chicago a more orderly and efficient city. It also suggested how such physical improvement through good planning could encourage good citizenship. Even though themes of the city's interconnectedness and implicit appeal to citizenship appeared in the book, it was not the central emphasis. That was not the case for the Dallas text, which had a very different premise. It argued that Dallas's greatest need was for a dedicated and educated citizenry who understood that every city problem affected the city as a whole and every other part of the city and each citizen in some way. By educating seventh-graders on the inextricable linkage of the parts to the whole, the Dallas text hoped to make them good citizens—citizens who clearly understand the significance of the Kessler Plan's importance and who would promote its completion. Although the different authorship of the two texts might explain the varied emphasis of the two books, the growing popularity of texts such as *Our City—Dallas* in civics classes and the absence of any new text on planning history suggests a change in the way people approached planning in the 1920s. *Wacker's Manual* reflected the turn-of-the-century emphasis on focusing on separate parts or problems of the city, while the Dallas text emphasized the city over its parts or problems.[38]

Despite the apparent success of *Wacker's Manual*, it is interesting that all the other texts cited by the Hubbards followed the community civics format, focusing on the city rather than its parts and on making better citizens instead of simply promoting better plans. Indeed, the 1920s texts emphasized the civic spirit behind making a plan, rather than detailing the specifics of the plan, just as the emphasis in citizenship went from learning about government to developing traits necessary to become a supportive and cooperative citizen so as to promote "harmonious and efficient team work in society."[39]

For instance, John F. Barry and Robert W. Elmes's *Buffalo's Textbook*, adopted by the Buffalo Department of Education for use in its public schools in 1924, mentioned planning only in chapter 8 and closely followed the form of a community civics text. Nevertheless, it appeared in the Hubbards' chapter "Educating the Public to Support City Planning." The book outlined "the commercial industrial advantages of Buffalo, its educational and recreational facilities, and indeed all those assets which contribute to make it a city in which citizenship should be prized." The book's purpose was to "stimulate and engender local pride, strong belief in the city's possibilities and loyalty to high ideals of citizenship."[40] Leadership played much less of a role in this history of Buffalo than in the Dallas book. Indeed, a theme of the text appeared to be the inevitability of Buffalo's greatness. But the point remains that this book emphasized Buffalo, rather than focusing on some part or a single problem.

Another school text mentioned by the Hubbards, a 423-page book entitled *Citizenship in Boston: Plan and Text*, written by Joseph Burke Egan and published in 1925, also followed the community civics format, emphasizing the important role of citizenship in promoting Boston's growth in addition to providing the standard introduction to the various functions of government. Indeed, the preface to the book reminded students they were not about to read a complete history of Boston; rather, the book was meant to "stimulate teacher and pupils to study the various factors that make for efficient citizenship."[41] Although organized chronologically, the book was divided into sections that were defined by the eleven laws of the Hutchins *Children's Code of Morals*, published by the National Institute for Moral Instruction in 1919.[42] For instance, the book showed how self-reliance, one of the laws of the code, helped early Bostonians conquer the wilderness and develop a great city. The discussion of planning played an important role in the book's section on teamwork. Boston, the book observed, was a result of teamwork, something that is "the most vital factor in modern living and working together. " Chapter 18, "Boston's Planning Board a Potent Influence," discussed early planning efforts in Boston but concluded that it was the citizens rather than the physical plans that were the key to Boston's prosperity. Planning for the whole city, the chapter continued, was "the one common meeting ground of community interests, where differences of race and riches, color, creed, and party should all be lost sight of in the effort of a public spirited people for the welfare of their own

municipality." Only then can "any community . . . prosper and endure."[43]
This book followed the pattern of the Dallas and Buffalo texts, emphasizing the importance of developing good citizenship to achieve planning
goals. And like the other two texts, the city and its citizens were emphasized rather than planning.

The New York City school text that the Hubbards cited followed a
slightly different format, although this book, *Our City—New York: A Text-
Book in City Government,* also clearly belongs in the category of the community civics text rather than the planning text associated with *Wacker's
Manual.* High school students from nineteen schools helped prepare the
book for use in the city's ninth grade. Unlike the Buffalo and Dallas books,
this one did not provide chapters detailing the history of New York City
but incorporated historical chapters into the broader text. Early chapters
focused on the city's water supply, the protection of the city's food supply,
regulation of buildings and the workplace, sewerage, recreation, health,
welfare, planning, and public safety. Other chapters looked at the city's
public utilities, as well as the actual process of making and carrying out
laws, financing the city, and the court system. Chapters on the role of the
citizen and education completed the 406-page text. Chapter 10, "City Planning and Civic Beauty," emphasized how good planning promoted efficiency and how improved circulation of people and goods permitted the
wise use of city monies. Special attention was also given to the power of
planning to better unify the various parts of New York, to address the city's
serious congestion problems, and to beautify the city.[44]

The failure of other cities to follow Chicago's example and produce a
planning text may seem curious, considering the wide-scale interest
Wacker's Manual elicited in the educational and planning communities
when it appeared. However, the Hubbards' comprehensive survey of the
teaching of city planning in public schools could find no similar book published in the 1920s. Rather, what appeared was community civics texts on
specific cities that included chapters on planning as part of the larger picture of the city and its problems and solutions. Just as important, these texts
emphasized not just the mechanics of government but the obligations and
responsibilities of the citizens to understand and support the city. Even the
Dallas text, one sponsored by a planning organization, followed this format. Such a commitment to community civics texts might be explained by
a new postwar emphasis on patriotism and citizenship building or even by
educational reforms stressing the need to teach "useful" knowledge.[45] But
even these causes do not necessarily explain the changes, since the turn of
the century was a period when many were concerned about the future of
the city and the need to promote better civic loyalty.

Rather, the shift in emphasis from planning text to community civics text
may well reflect changing notions about planning as it relates to the city. If
the city was viewed as a system of functionally different parts and needs

that are interdependent in the sense that the malfunction of one disrupts the whole but not necessarily the other parts, then a textbook on planning made sense because it addressed a specific need of the city. However, if, as it turns out, a new notion of the city as system emerged after 1915—a notion that emphasized that the city's parts and needs are so interdependent that one defective part affected all the other parts as well as the city, or that one specific need could not be isolated without understanding its connection to the whole—then a community civics text made more sense even for the advocates of planning because it emphasized the interconnectedness of the parts to the whole and to each other.[46] And that is what appeared in the 1920s: texts introduced students not only to planning but to the city's economic, social, demographic, and political needs and their relationship to each other. And only then, once students were taught the interdependence of the whole city, did comprehensive planning make sense as a solution to the city's physical needs. Understanding the nature of the city, then, would encourage students to be advocates of comprehensive planning.

The new focus on the city found in *Our City—Dallas*, as opposed to the emphasis on planning in *Wacker's Manual*, might be more than a mere quirk in the history of textbooks sponsored by planning associations. Indeed, if the changing nature of school texts is linked to a significant shift in thought about the nature of the city, such a discovery might well inform future writing on the history of planning and urban reform.[47]

Notes

1. The epigraph is from Chicago Plan Commission, *Chicago's World-wide Influence in City Planning* (Chicago: Chicago Plan Commission, 1914), p. 17.

2. Theodora Kimball Hubbard and Henry Vincent Hubbard, *Our Cities To-Day and To-Morrow: A Survey of Planning and Zoning in the United States* (Cambridge: Harvard University Press, 1929), pp. 95–96.

3. Kristen Schaffer, "Fabric of City Life: The Social Agenda in Burnham's Draft of the Chicago Plan," in Daniel H. Burnham and Edward H. Bennett, *Plan of Chicago*, ed. Charles Moore (New York: Princeton Architectural Press, 1993 [1908]), p. vi.

4 Burnham and Bennett, *Plan of Chicago*, p. 121; Sally Chapell, "Chicago Issues: The Enduring Power of a Plan," in *The Plan of Chicago: 1909–1979: An Exhibition of the Burnham Library of Architecture* (Chicago: Art Institute, 1979), pp. 7–8.

5. Burnham and Bennett, *Plan of Chicago*, p. 4.

6. Walter D. Moody, *Wacker's Manual of the Plan of Chicago*, 4th ed. (Chicago: Chicago Plan Commission, 1924), pp. 77–78. Even though the CPC was composed of "citizens from every section of the city," including at least one from each ward, it was in no way representative of the various classes of the city. Its

72 ROBERT B. FAIRBANKS

primary membership came from industrial, commercial, financial, educational, religious, and political leaders, as well as "prominent men of all nationalities" and the "leaders of thought and action." The smaller executive committee that would actually run the organization was much less representative of the entire city. One-third of its twenty-four-member executive committee would be from the Commercial Club. Walter D. Moody, *What of the City? America's Greatest Issue—City Planning, What It Is and How to Go about It to Achieve Success* (Chicago: A. C. McClurg, 1919), p. 420; Neil Harris, *The Planning of the Plan: An address given . . . to the 695th Regular Meeting of The Commercial Club of Chicago at the Art Institute of Chicago, November 27, 1979, in observance of the opening of the exhibition, The Plan of Chicago: 1909–1979, John Zukowsky, Architectural Archivist* (Chicago: The Club, 1979), p. 11.

7. Thomas J. Schlereth, "Burnham's Plan and Moody's Manual: City Planning as Progressive Reform," in *The American Planner: Biographies and Recollections*, 2d ed., ed. Donald A. Krueckeberg (New Brunswick, N.J.: Center for Urban Policy Research, 1994), pp. 135–36.

8. Roger P. Akeley, "Implementing the 1909 Plan of Chicago: An Historical Account of Planning Salesmanship" (M.S. thesis, University of Tennessee, 1975), pp. 95–96.

9. Arthur R. Dunn, "Civic Education in Elementary Schools as Illustrated in Indianapolis," *United States Bureau of Education, Bulletin No. 17* (Washington, D.C.: Government Printing Office, 1915), p. 7; Moody, *What of the City*, p. 96.

10. Joel Spring, *The American School, 1642–1985: Varieties of Historical Interpretation of the Foundations and Development of American Education* (New York: Longmans, 1986), pp. 149–52, 173; Mary J. Herick, *The Chicago Schools: A Social and Political History* (Beverly Hills: Sage Publications, 1971), p. 85.

11. Walter D. Moody, *Wacker's Manual of the Plan of Chicago: Municipal Economy* (Chicago: Chicago Plan Commission, 1913), p. 9

12. Moody, *What of the City?* pp. 96–97, 34.

13. Thomas J. Schlereth, "Planning and Progressivism: Wacker's Manual of the Plan of Chicago," in *Ideas in America's Cultures: From Republic to Mass Society*, ed. Hamilton Cravens (Ames: Iowa State University Press, 1982), p. 129; Moody, *What of the City?*, p. 97.

14. Moody, *What of the City?* p. xi.

15. Schlereth, "Planning and Progressivism," p. 129.

16. Walter D. Moody, *Teachers' Handbook: Wacker's Manual of the Plan of Chicago* (n.p.: n.p., 1912), pp. 3, 6–8.

17. Moody, *Wacker's Manual*, p. 8.

18. Walter D. Moody, Prefatory Note, *Wacker's Manual of the Plan of Chicago*, 4th ed. (Chicago: Chicago Plan Commission, 1924).

19. Moody, *What of the City?* pp. 99–100.

20. Moody, *Wacker's Manual*, p. 141.

21. By 1914, requests for copies of *Wacker's Manual* had been received from

110 cities in the United States. Thirty-six cities from abroad also asked for copies. Chicago Plan Commission, *Chicago's World-wide Influence*, pp. 4–5.

22. Quote from Akeley, "Implementing the 1909 Plan," p. 107. For more on the national publicity see pp. 132–33.

23. Quoted in Robert B. Fairbanks, *For the City as a Whole: Planning, Politics, and the Public Interest in Dallas, Texas, 1900–1965* (Columbus: Ohio State University Press, 1998), p. 48.

24. George Kessler, *A City Plan for Dallas* (Dallas: Dallas Park Board, 1912); Louis Head, "The Kessler Plan for Dallas: A Review of the Plan and Its Accomplishments" (Dallas: *Dallas Morning News*, 1925).

25. George Dealey to Eda A. Stuteimeister, March 8, 1923, George Dealey Papers, box 3, Dallas Historical Society; Marshall Surratt to the author, July 23, 1999. For more on the Kessler Plan Association see Robert B. Fairbanks, "Making Better Citizens in Dallas: The Kessler Plan Association and Consensus Building in the 1920s," *Legacies: A History Journal for Dallas and North Central Texas* 10 (Fall 1999): 26–36.

26. John Surratt to Fred F. Florence, Jan. 16, 1933, John Surratt Papers, University of Texas at Arlington Special Collections.

27. *Dallas Morning News*, Jan. 2, 1925.

28. Secretary's Report to the Directors of the Kessler Plan Association (1924?), George Dealey Papers, folder 28, Dallas Historical Society.

29. Justin F. Kimball, *Our City—Dallas: A Community Civics* (Dallas: Kessler Plan Association, 1927), p. 69.

30. Kimball became a professor of education at Southern Methodist University in 1925. Ron Tyler, ed., *New Handbook of Texas*, vol. 4 (Austin: Texas State Historical Association, 1996), p. 1097; Walter J. E. Schiebel, *Education in Dallas: 92 Years of History* (Dallas: Dallas Independent School District, 1966), pp. 173–74; Interview, Marshall Surratt, April 28, 1999; Kimball, *Our City—Dallas*, p. 5.

31. "Civic and Moral Instruction in The Public Schools," *American City* 11 (July 1914): 69; A. G. Cranes, "Psychology of Citizenship Training," *School and Society* (July 14, 1928): 34.

32. Quoted in Special Committee of the Commission on the Reorganization of Secondary Education, National Education Association, "The Teaching of Community Civics," *United States Bureau of Education Bulletin, 1915, No. 23* (Washington, D.C.: Government Printing Office, 1915), p. 11; J. Lynn Barnard, "The Teaching of Civics in Elementary and Secondary Schools," *Journal of Proceedings and Addresses of the Fifty-First Annual Meeting of the National Education Association of the United States* (Ann Arbor: The Association, 1913): 84.

33. Kimball, *Our City—Dallas*, p. 67.

34. Ibid., p. 80.

35. Ibid., p. 194.

36. Ibid. p. 360.

37. Ibid., p. 364.

38. For more on this see Fairbanks, *For the City as a Whole*, pp. 11–33.

39. Cranes, "Psychology of Citizenship Training," p. 34.

40. John F. Barry and Robert W. Elmes, *Buffalo's Textbook: Authorized by the Council of the City of Buffalo and adopted by the Department of Education for use in the Public Schools in the Study of Buffalo* (Buffalo: Robert W. Elmes, 1924), p. 8.

41. Joseph Burke Egan, *Citizenship in Boston: Plan and Text* (Philadelphia: John C. Winston, 1925), p. vii.

42. The code, written by Oberlin Theological Seminary professor William J. Hutchins, was the winning submission in a contest that awarded five thousand dollars for the best children's code of morals submitted. Hutchins's son, Robert, went on to become the controversial president of the University of Chicago. The eleven laws of the Hutchins Moral Code were self-reliance, teamwork, self-control, good workmanship, reliability, health, fair play, charity, duty, loyalty, and obedience to duly constituted authority. Mary Ann Dzuback, *Robert M. Hutchins: Portrait of an Educator* (Chicago: University of Chicago Press, 1991), pp. 23–24; William J. Hutchins, *Children's Code of Morals* (Washington, D.C.: National Institute for Moral Instruction, 1919); Egan, *Citizenship in Boston*, p. viii.

43. Egan, *Citizenship in Boston*, p. 150.

44. Frank A. Rexford, ed., *Our City—New York: A Text-Book in City Government* (Boston: Allyn and Bacon, 1924), see especially pp. 185–211.

45. For more on the new emphasis on patriotism and good citizenship after the war, see Bessie Louise Pierce's contribution to the American Historical Association's investigation of the social studies in the schools entitled *Citizens' Organizations and the Civic Training of Youth* (New York: Charles Scribner's Sons, 1933). Also see Charles E. Merriam, *Civic Education in the United States* (New York: Charles Scribner's Sons, 1934), another contribution to the AHA investigation.

46. The redefinition of the city paralleled the idea of systems in the 1920s. According to one historian of technology, systems at the turn of the century were thought to be "static entities, composed of diverse, fixed, and limited parts." By the 1920s systems were seen as "dynamic, predicated on a much more complex relationship among the parts." Alan I Marcus and Howard P. Segal, *Technology in America: A Brief History*, 2d ed. (Fort Worth: Harcourt Brace College Publishers, 1999), p. 207.

47. For more on an approach to urban history that emphasizes the role of human perception as opposed to social forces, see Alan I Marcus, "Back to the Present: Historians' Treatment of the City as a Social System During the Reign of the Idea of Community," in *American Urbanism: A Historiographical Review*, ed. Howard Gillette Jr. and Zane L. Miller (New York: Greenwood Press, 1987), pp. 9–11.

Chapter Four

The Boss Becomes a Manager: Executive Authority and City Charter Reform, 1880–1929

ROBERT A. BURNHAM

Many historians have noted that municipal reformers during the late nineteenth and early twentieth centuries sought to apply business principles to city government with the intent of achieving greater efficiency and eliminating the evils of boss rule. Some reformers even went so far as to assert that a city, as a municipal corporation, had more in common with a business enterprise than it did with state or federal government because it existed primarily for the purpose of performing administrative functions rather than making broad policies. The business analogy, moreover, lent support to the contention that the city ought to operate in a businesslike manner, which meant finding the most cost-effective way to do its work. Those who espoused such notions also tended to believe that partisan politics had no place in administrative affairs, claiming that there was no Democratic or Republican way of cleaning the streets, only the efficient or inefficient way.[1] This effort to apply business principles to city government supposedly culminated in the 1910s and 1920s with the widespread adoption of the city manager form of government, which sought to remove politics from administration by placing executive authority in the hands of an expert manager who would provide the city with businesslike government.[2] Historians also tend to view the shifting trends in charter reform during the late nineteenth and early twentieth centuries as progressive steps, each one a further refinement of the last, toward achieving one or another reform goal, whether ending corruption, promoting efficiency, establishing a bureaucratic order, tilting the balance of political power toward the middle class, or addressing new "realities" created by rapid urban growth and technological change.[3] Unfortunately, this approach often has the effect of conflating forms of city government that were very different from one another with respect to the organization of executive authority. It also fails to consider that every one of the commonly recognized reform goals pervaded the entire period, raising the question of how such seemingly static formulations can explain quite different phenomena. In addition, simply saying that reformers adopted a business ethos, as identified with their calls for efficiency and cost cutting, ignores the fact that business thought and practice also changed significantly during the period.[4]

The direction that charter reform and executive authority took during the Progressive Era suggests that the reform agenda shifted after 1910 as a result of the emergence of a new conception of the city and American society. During the late nineteenth and early twentieth centuries, contemporaries tended to see the city as composed of separate and inherently unequal groups, parts, and systems that could be ranked hierarchically according to their perceived importance. This helps account for the affinity that reformers had for the strong mayor plan of city government, which vested primary authority in a single strong man, the good boss, who would impose order upon the city's unequal and often conflicting groups, parts, and systems from the top down. By the 1910s, however, reformers had begun to view the city as a pluralistic entity composed of separate but interdependent and potentially equal groups, parts, and systems. The notion of interdependence required that each component be considered in relationship to all others, which raised questions about the advisability of hierarchical rankings and piecemeal approaches to urban problems. This shift in the way people perceived the city also led to a new understanding of the exercise of executive authority wherein the boss became a manager whose primary function was to facilitate coordination and cooperation among the various separate but interdependent elements that comprised the city.[5]

In the 1880s and 1890s, both municipal reform and American business culture tended to focus attention on the one powerful man, the boss, who exercised control from the top down. As one manifestation of this, municipal reformers devoted much of their energy to combating the evils of boss rule, which they considered the cause of waste, inefficiency, and corruption. The object of their attacks was the big city boss who functioned as the de facto head of the city government by maintaining control over a local party organization and the distribution of political patronage. Reformers referred to such a party organization as a "political machine," which they characterized as a military-like structure designed to ensure that the boss's orders were carried out in lockstep fashion.[6] While reformers never seemed to tire of railing against boss rule, their efforts to address the issue typically did not call for the elimination of the boss, but for replacing the bad boss with a good boss, which meant an honest, responsible boss who would place the welfare of the city as a whole above any desire for political spoils. And given their inclination to equate the operations of city government with those of business, securing a good boss normally took the form of recruiting some prominent businessman to run for mayor under the assumption that such an individual would naturally possess the knowledge and skills needed to manage city affairs efficiently.[7]

Reformers also sought to change the prevailing form of city government, which placed various administrative functions under the control of separately elected boards or commissions. This sort of administrative structure bothered reformers because it failed to provide for a "hierarchy of officials"—necessary to "subordinate one officer to another"—within the system itself.[8] The "complex" needs of the modern city, they argued, required a centralized form of administrative organization. As Woodrow Wilson put it, life in the modern city was "many-sided and without unity, and voters of every blood and environment and social derivation mix and stare at one another at the same voting places." Such conditions, he claimed, fostered "confused, irresponsible, unintelligent, [and] wasteful" government. For Wilson, placing a decentralized and divided form of administrative organization in the hands of popularly elected officials only served to replicate social divisions, stemming from racial, religious, and ethnic differences, within the government itself. In other words, not only was there no Republican or Democratic way of cleaning the streets, there was also no Irish, Italian, or Scandinavian way. On the basis of this analysis, Wilson concluded that forms of administrative organization "which served us admirably well while the nation was homogeneous and rural, serve us often-times ill enough now that the nation is heterogeneous and crowded into cities."[9]

Reformers also claimed that the absence of any central executive authority within the system itself had contributed to the rise of the boss, an extralegal figure who performed the necessary function of coordinating the city's various administrative boards and commissions.[10] To address this concern, they advocated the adoption of the so-called strong mayor plan, which provided for a hierarchically organized administrative structure that centralized authority and responsibility in the office of the mayor.[11] Basically, the strong mayor plan sought to put the boss into the system by empowering the mayor to appoint and remove department heads, veto ordinances and individual items in appropriation bills, prepare an annual budget estimate, and participate in the deliberations of the city council. In addition, strong mayor charters normally reorganized and streamlined governmental structure by replacing independent boards and commissions with single-headed departments that answered to the mayor and by reducing the total number of departments through the consolidation of functions.[12] Between 1880 and 1900, the strong mayor plan was adopted by Brooklyn, Philadelphia, Cleveland, Boston, and a host of smaller cities.[13] Also, the National Municipal League, the foremost municipal reform organization in the United States at the time, embraced the strong mayor plan in its model city charter of 1899. [14]

In support of the strong mayor concept, Charles Richardson, who helped draft the model charter of the National Municipal League, stressed that "in all great undertakings, concentration of power is essential for attaining the highest degree of efficiency and economy." According to Richardson, this truism applied just as strongly to city government as it did to "the armies of a nation" or a "great corporation." Each of them needed "one supreme head who can decide all questions, combine and direct all efforts, and secure the loyal service and harmonious co-operation of all subordinates."[15] This also required a centralized and hierarchically organized administrative structure in which power flowed from the top down.[16]

With its emphasis on hierarchy and subordination, the strong mayor plan provided an organizational framework that fit neatly with the late-nineteenth- and early-twentieth-century tendency to view the city as an "organic unit" composed of separate and unequal groups, parts, and systems that could be ranked hierarchically according to their perceived importance or level of advancement. The various groups, parts, and systems were also seen as interdependent, but only in the sense that they shared a common relationship to the city as a whole, not to each other. Consequently, a defect in one would not necessarily corrupt the others. It would, however, prevent the city as a whole from functioning at peak capacity or reaching its full potential.[17] Securing the welfare of the city as a whole, then, meant dealing with particular groups, parts, and systems without worrying much about their relationship to all others, an approach that yielded separate policies and plans for each perceived problem. In this context, the strong mayor plan seemed an ideal mechanism for addressing the needs of the modern city. By centralizing power in the mayor, the elected representative of the whole city and the person at the top of the governmental hierarchy, the strong mayor plan provided for a good boss who would coordinate the various separate and unequal groups, parts, and systems that comprised the city with the intent of achieving some sense of unity and order.[18]

For good or ill, the overall course of charter reform during the 1880s and 1890s pointed toward the expansion of executive authority, or what one observer called "the Czar or good father theory of city government."[19] This emphasis on the executive was also reflected by the considerable national attention given to various reform mayors of the period. Men such as Hazen Pingree of Detroit, Samuel "Golden Rule" Jones and Brand Whitlock of Toledo, Tom Johnson of Cleveland, and Seth Low of New York received numerous accolades for advancing the cause of municipal reform and improving the quality of city government.[20]

While these and other lesser known reform mayors were all depicted as good bosses, not all of them gave highest priority to the advancement of businesslike government, which after all represented only one thrust of municipal reform. Those who did adopt the business ethos tended to devote considerable attention to eliminating governmental waste, inefficiency, and corruption. Others, however, placed less emphasis on improving the way the machinery of government worked than on using government to secure social justice for the less wealthy segments of urban society.[21]

Those who took the latter approach, most notably Jones, Johnson, and Pingree, functioned as champions of "the people," a term that Progressive Era reformers used to distinguish between average working Americans and the wealthy businessmen who oppressed them.[22] Reformers also made it clear that "the people" did not include only wage laborers. As Mayor Pingree boasted, the "anti-monopoly measures of my administration have been supported by all classes"; the "small property-owners have supported them as zealously as the wage-earners." The only dissenting voices, he said, came from "what are called the best citizens," who sought to dominate the economic life of the community for their own gain.[23] Though "the people" did not mean everyone, it meant almost everyone; consequently its use had the effect of lumping together all of the various racial, religious, and ethnic groups that comprised the city, thus eliminating, at least rhetorically, all lines of division except those that separated powerful business elites from everyone else. And as the champion of the people, the reform mayor represented, in Brand Whitlock's words, "the father of all."[24]

The threat to the people posed by entrenched wealth seemed quite real to many reformers. In an article that glorified the mayoralty of "Golden Rule" Jones, Washington Gladden, the Social Gospel movement leader, claimed that "the organization of corporate wealth . . . is ready to spend money by the millions in the bribery of legislatures and city councils and judges and newspapers in order that it may fasten its grip on the people and suck their blood by slow tribute."[25] In the face of such a powerful and pervasive force, the people appeared to be helpless victims who needed a champion, a powerful individual capable of standing up to "the interests." Expressing this point of view, Henry Demarest Lloyd, writing to Hazen Pingree, remarked that without "some such Hercules as you, the work [of reform] will never be done."[26]

The perceived helplessness of the people, along with the fact that the reform mayor rarely came from the ranks of the people—"Golden Rule" Jones, Tom Johnson, and Hazen Pingree were all wealthy businessmen—suggested an air of paternalism, the "good father theory," which apparently troubled neither the people nor their protectors. The only criticism seemed to come from frustrated political opponents who called attention to the paternalistic, top-down nature of reform administrations by accusing mayors such as Johnson and Pingree of exercising dictatorial power or, in the lexicon of the day, "bossism," a charge that the reformers did not always rush to deny.[27] Indeed, Frederic Howe, who served on the Cleveland City Council during Johnson's administration, matter-of-factly stated that "the boss appears under" any form of city government; but "under a system of centralized responsibility," as provided by the strong mayor plan, "the boss becomes responsible."[28] From the position of power that he enjoyed as Cleveland's strong mayor, Tom Johnson created his own political machine, which managed to gain control over the Democratic party in Ohio.[29]

Though the socioeconomic standing of reform mayors tended to place them far apart from the people, it actually enhanced their status as father figures, men whom the people were supposed to be "looked up to." Similarly, their business backgrounds generated little concern because such experience supposedly better equipped them to do battle with the interests. Familiar with the rough-and-tumble world of corporate capitalism, these champions of the people were thought to possess the knowledge and skills needed to fight the malefactors of great wealth on their own turf.[30]

Ironically, when one looks beyond the great contest between the people and the interests, the reform mayor becomes the political equivalent of his nemesis, the wealthy entrepreneur, the patriarch of the company, the one great man who represented the face of American business during the late nineteenth and early twentieth centuries. The fact that the names Rockefeller, Carnegie, and Vanderbilt became "household words" attests to the close connection that Americans made between the business life of the nation and a few powerful men who were thought to control things from the top down.[31] Alternately viewed as either good bosses (captains of industry) or bad bosses (robber barons), these men, much like their counterparts in city government, were depicted as rare individuals who rose to the top through personal "genius." They also exhibited determination, courage, and an independent spirit that made them willing to go it alone. Such attributes supposedly enabled the great entrepreneurs and reform mayors to accomplish things that average men could not.[32] The thin line that separated the champion-of-the-people type of reform mayor from the robber baron might best be illustrated by a single example. When the wealthy shoe manufacturer turned mayor Hazen Pingree entered into a fight over the street railway franchise for the city of Detroit during the mid-1890s, he was pitted against one of the most powerful street railway magnates in the Midwest—Tom Johnson, who had not yet become the people's champion of Cleveland.[33]

But even as reform mayors and wealthy businessmen were capturing the imagination of the American people, the apotheosis of the one great man faced a challenge from efforts to turn public administration into a "science," which represented another means of dealing with the modern city viewed as a complex entity composed of separate and unequal groups, parts, and systems. The application of science, at first glance, appeared to eliminate the need for a boss, or to replace one boss with many, in the form of well-trained technical experts who would oversee the specialized functions of the city government. But it actually sought to enshrine knowledge, acquired through scientific study, as the new boss. Through science, the "best men" would be replaced by the best methods, and personal genius would give way to technical training.[34]

The movement to create a "science of administration" began in the late 1880s when Woodrow Wilson advocated the idea of subjecting public administration to "systematic" study with the intent of finding the most efficient, "businesslike" methods for performing administrative tasks.[35] Wilson's proposal rested, in part, on his contention that modern city government was becoming increasingly complex and technical, necessitating the recruitment of well-trained experts for administrative offices. Other reformers shared such views, which were expressed with greater frequency over the course of the 1890s. When it came to administrative matters, many felt that there was simply less and less room for amateurs in city government—and that included businessmen.[36] Indeed, the idea that business acumen automatically gave a person the "typical training and ideals of a city father" began losing some its resonance.[37] Although reformers continued to make the analogy between business and city government, they recognized that the city was its own kind of business, as identified with the various specialized administrative services it provided. By the early 1900s, the importance that reformers placed on those who either directed or performed the technical work of the city even had the effect of de-emphasizing the role of the mayor. Noting that mayors come and go, some reformers began to view the election of a good boss as a less critical matter than the filling of municipal offices with permanent, professional administrators who would provide the city with continuous expert service.[38]

During the same period, the notion of the one great man in business also faced a challenge in the form of "scientific management," a theory of business management devised by Frederick Winslow Taylor, a mechanical engineer who began developing his ideas in the 1880s. Sounding much like those who advocated the creation of a science of public administration, Taylor wanted to turn business management into a "true science," which would eliminate guesswork and greatly increase productivity and efficiency.[39] As part of that effort, he called for the abandonment of the "old view" that "if you have the right man the methods can be safely left to him."[40] As Taylor saw things, "no great man" could "compete with a number of ordinary men who have been properly organized so as efficiently to cooperate."[41] Basically, Taylor sought to determine the best way to do the work of any given concern by subjecting every aspect of the manufacturing process to careful, "scientific" study.[42] This task, moreover, would be performed by a "planning department" composed of trained technical experts, each of whom would preside over a particular area of specialization. Taylor placed great importance on the planning department. In his view, the "shop (indeed the whole works) should be managed, not by the manager, superintendent, or foreman, but by the planning department."

And if the planning department did its job properly, "the works could run smoothly even if the manager, superintendent, and their assistants ... were all to be away for a month." While Taylor did not call for the elimination of the person at the top of the company hierarchy, he had little to say about the role of that individual. Hence, the boss, the one great man, seemed somewhat superfluous in Taylor's vision of management.[43]

Taylor also proposed the abandonment of what he called the "military plan" of business organization that featured a hierarchical managerial structure in which orders flowed from the top down in a single unbroken stream. In its place he wanted to substitute "functional management," which would organize managerial authority functionally rather than hier-archically. Under this scheme workers would no longer take orders from a single superior but from a number of functional managers who had sole authority over their respective areas of speciality. As a result, specialized knowledge of a particular aspect of the work determined managerial authority, not the place one held within the hierarchy.[44]

Taylor's functional management had a kind of rough municipal reform equivalent in the commission plan, which came into vogue during the early 1900s. Attesting to its popularity, the commission plan was adopted by more than three hundred American cities between 1901 and 1913.[45] Those who promoted this new form of city government stressed some of the same basic themes that had given rise to the strong mayor plan. They hoped to secure businesslike efficiency by centralizing responsibility and simplifying governmental structure. But they also proposed a very different way of organizing executive authority. The commission plan, as first introduced in Galveston, Texas, in 1901, vested both legislative and executive authority in a five-member commission elected at large. In the view of one historian, this decision to combine legislative and executive authority in a single body constituted an "extreme form of centralizing."[46] In essence, the commission plan attempted to achieve the goals of centralization and simplification by concentrating authority in as few elected officials as possible. In the process, it abandoned the principle of separating legislative and executive author-ity, forsook ward representation, and reduced the number of administrative departments by consolidating functions. It also eliminated the office of mayor—its most significant departure from the strong mayor plan. In the absence of a single boss, executive authority under the commission plan was divided among the members of the commission, each of whom served as the director of an administrative department. This created a functionally decentralized executive, which was similar to the form of business organi-zation that Frederick Taylor proposed.[47]

Those who developed and advocated the commission plan, however, never seemed to notice this similarity. Even though they self-consciously sought to create a form of city government modeled after a business cor-poration, there is little evidence that they were following (or even aware of) Taylor's ideas. When they compared the commission plan to a business, they always made the same simple analogy, which equated voters with stockholders and the members of the commission with a board of directors. Nonetheless, they embraced an organizational structure that approximated Taylor's functional management, even if not by conscious design.[48]

Though the form of executive authority that characterized the commission plan and Taylor's functional management enjoyed considerable support during the 1900s, it would become the subject of much criticism during the 1910s, when a new view of the city and American society emerged. In a significant shift from the late nineteenth and early twentieth centuries, urban experts in the 1910s began to perceive the city as a pluralistic entity composed of separate but interdependent and potentially equal groups (racial, religious, and ethnic); parts (neighborhoods, districts, townships); and systems (transportation, parks, recreation). This conceptualization tended to proscribe ranking the various groups, parts, and systems hierarchically, which created uneasiness with the old order and prompted efforts to forge a decentralized and horizontally organized society and governmental system. At the same time, the assumption of interdependence meant that no single element could be addressed without considering its relationship to all others. This helps explain why urban experts during the period began insisting upon the need for comprehensiveness, which required consideration of all of the various groups, parts, and systems of the city when making any policies or plans.[49] The most obvious manifestation of this was the comprehensive city planning movement, which held that every aspect of the city's development needed to be considered "with reference to each other on a comprehensive basis, so that not only will each be a perfected unit of itself, but that each will support the other as far as desirable."[50] Or, in the words of Frederick Law Olmsted, comprehensive city planning sought to provide an "aggregation of accepted ideas or projects for physical changes in the city, all consistent with each other, and each surviving, by virtue of its own inherent merit and by virtue of its harmonizing with the rest."[51]

Others during the period expressed similar ideas about American society generally, as seen in the work of political scientist Mary P. Follett. In her most well-known book, *The New State* (1918), Follett posited a theory of politics and social relations that rested on the notion that society was "neither a collection of units nor an organism but a network of human relations." In making this case, Follett criticized "pluralist" political theory for stressing the separateness of social and political groups, claiming that this merely replaced the "individualistic" particularlism of the nineteenth century with a new group-based particularlism. As a preferable alternative, she thought that primacy ought to be placed on the relationships between groups with the intent of helping to "unify our differences." But unity did not mean uniformity. Indeed, Follett showed just as much disdain for the idea of assimilation as she did for separatism, asserting that "[w]e do not want Swedes and Poles to be lost in an undifferentiated whole." Rather, she called for an "articulated whole," which would enable "different peoples to be part of a true community—giving all they have to give and receiving equally."[52]

Follett also attempted to apply her theory of social relations to business organization. A business, she argued, ought to strive for what she called "integrative unity." This meant a business with "all of its parts so co-ordinated, so moving together in their closely knit and adjusting activities, so linking, interlocking, interrelating that they make a working *unit*." But, based on her observation of American business practices, she determined that "integrative unity" had not been fully realized because of a lack of coordination between departments.[53]

This assessment was in tune with that of American business scholars, who during the 1910s began criticizing Frederick Taylor's functional management scheme. Functional management, they argued, failed to make adequate provisions for coordinating the efforts of separate departments and for directing the work of the business as a whole. This job of coordination, of course, had been traditionally performed by the boss, the person at the top of the company hierarchy, who took a back seat to the planning department under Taylor's system of management. But the critics did not advocate the return of the boss, for they too rejected the idea of creating a centralized and hierarchically organized managerial structure. Moreover, they disliked the connotation of the term "boss," which suggested coercion, dominance, and inflexibility. Their solution called for replacing the boss with a manager. Their conception of a manager, however, was quite different than that envisioned by Taylor. From their point of view, Taylor's functional manager was not much of a manager at all, but rather a mere technical expert who oversaw a particular aspect of doing the work. Their manager was a top-level executive who would coordinate the work of the various specialized departments and devise a comprehensive plan for the business as a whole.[54]

A strikingly similar set of criticisms was leveled against the commission plan by urban experts during the 1910s and 1920s. Expressing concern over the decentralization of executive authority along functional lines, William Bennett Munro, professor of municipal government at Harvard University, observed that the commission plan had created a "five-headed" executive in which no commissioner was answerable to any other commissioner. As a result, no single authority had the power to make the administrative departments of the city government work together or to plan the city's administrative work as a whole. This lack of "co-ordinating supervision," as Munro put it, was considered the single most significant defect of the commission plan.[55] But critics raised other concerns as well. In their view, the consolidation of legislative and executive authority in a single body represented another serious mistake because it encouraged commissioners, in their capacity as legislators, to make policy decisions on the basis of their particular departmental interests rather than the interests of the city as a whole.[56] Also, by putting popularly elected officials in charge of specialized administrative departments, the commission plan did little to ensure government by experts. The thought that anyone capable of winning an election might become the head of a public utilities department or a public safety department troubled those reformers who believed that administrative affairs should be directed by well-trained professionals.[57]

Such concerns led reformers to embrace the city manager plan, which after 1912 supplanted the commission plan as the latest advance in municipal reform. More than two hundred American cities adopted the city manager plan during the 1910s and 1920s. Also, the National Municipal League was so convinced of the merits of this new form of city government that it abandoned the strong mayor plan for the city manager plan in the model city charter that it adopted in 1915.[58]

Reformers expected the city manager plan to correct the defects of the commission plan by separating legislative authority from executive authority and by providing for a coordinator, the city manager, who would oversee all of the administrative departments of the city government. Although the city manager plan gave a single individual authority over administrative affairs, it did not mean the return of a boss, not even a good one. Rather the boss became a manager, a term that denoted an entirely different concept of executive authority. Under the strong mayor plan, executive authority rested with the mayor, the highest elected official in the city government, who not only had jurisdiction over all administrative matters but also served as the representative of the whole city, a good boss who embodied the will of the people. In contrast, the city manager did not represent anyone. The only elected officials under the city manager plan were the members of the city council, who had the power to appoint and remove the manager. In a sense, the city manager functioned as an agent of the council, but charter provisions normally tried to ensure a true separation of powers by prohibiting council members from interfering in administrative affairs and by giving the manager sole authority to appoint department heads and other administrative officials. Also, the city manager, unlike the strong mayor, had no veto power, thus limiting the ability of the executive to influence legislation.[59]

Those who devised this arrangement claimed that they modeled it after a business corporation: city council, in the role of a board of directors, made broad policy decisions but hired a chief executive to carry out the day-to-day operations of the enterprise. Under such a system, the city manager was supposed to be a trained professional who would provide the city with continuous expert service. By stressing the need for government by experts, the proponents of the city manager plan merely seemed to be reiterating a theme that had captivated reformers since the 1880s. During the late nineteenth and early twentieth centuries, however, reformers tended to call for technical experts to manage specific departments, not an expert manager to coordinate the work of the city as a whole.[60]

The new view of executive authority ushered in by the city manager plan also rejected the kind of centralized and hierarchically organized administrative structure that had emphasized subordination and control from above. By the 1920s, urban experts who advocated the city manager plan began criticizing the centralization movement of the late nineteenth and early twentieth centuries, which had led the supporters of the strong mayor plan, and later the commission plan, to press for departmental streamlining through the consolidation or elimination of functions—the administrative equivalent of assimilation. The critics believed that these efforts had gone too far, resulting in the placement of too many "unrelated" functions under the jurisdiction of a single department. The penchant for streamlining, noted one observer, had led to "such incongruities as a department of public safety entrusted with police and fire protection, elevator inspection, and operation of the municipal market and employment bureau."[61] Those who raised this issue felt that grouping unrelated functions together virtually ensured that those that fell outside the department head's area of expertise or interest would not receive the attention they deserved. Put another way, the consolidation and subordination movement failed to recognize the importance of each function to the working of the city government as a whole. In voicing this concern, urban experts noted that they were not opposed to centralization per se, but to centralization achieved through the consolidation of unrelated functions. What bothered them was the heterogeneous nature of individual departments and the possibility that certain functions would not receive equal treatment. In the belief that "dissimilar" functions "should be kept in separate departments," they called for the grouping of "related" functions so as to create separate but equal departments.[62]

While they insisted on the need for separation, urban experts also assumed that the various departments of the city government were interdependent, not simply by virtue of the relationship they shared as units within a larger whole, but also by their relationship to each other. This understanding of interdependence meant that a defect in any one department had the potential to undermine the efficiency of the others and the administration as a whole. Yet the inherent separateness of the departments, which inclined each one to focus on its own area of specialization, discouraged concerted action. Hence, it was necessary to provide for a coordinator, who would ensure that the various departments worked together in the best interest of the city as a whole. But under such an administrative framework, the coordinator did not play the role of the boss, who controlled things from the top down. Again, the boss became a manager, who facilitated interaction between what were otherwise separate and autonomous departments. As explained in the 1926 issue of *Municipal Activities*, an annual publication of the city of Cincinnati, which had adopted the city manager plan in 1924, the city manager was expected to "co-ordinate and harmonize the activities of the Departments through the Department Heads, while allowing free range to initiative within each Department on its special problems."[63] Performing the function of coordination, moreover, required that the city manager take a comprehensive approach toward administrative affairs. Speaking to this issue, R. W. Rigsby, the city manager of Durham, North Carolina, stressed that the "successful city manager acquires perspective by freeing himself as much as possible from the routine details of operation and is thereby enabled to co-ordinate more effectively the work as a whole."[64] This managerial approach not only emphasized coordination over control, but also eschewed the authoritarian imagery associated with the term "boss." For example, Harry H. Freeman, the city manager of Kalamazoo, Michigan, asserted in 1919 that the manager must "substitute boss rule, dominance and power, for a quality of leadership,—a willingness to treat men as human beings . . . and to co-operate and expect their co-operation in order to get things done."[65]

By stressing cooperation, coordination, and comprehensiveness, the form of executive authority envisioned by the city manager plan sought to meet the needs of the city perceived in a new way. During the 1910s and 1920s, the tendency to view the city as a pluralistic entity composed of separate but interdependent and potentially equal groups, parts, and systems called into question the forms of executive authority and administrative organization that had been introduced during the late nineteenth and early twentieth centuries. This suggests that the city manager plan did not merely represent the culmination of a long-standing effort to apply business principles to city government in the name of efficiency. Though its advocates sounded many of the same "good government" themes (efficiency, expert service, businesslike administration, fixed responsibility, and so on) that had fueled municipal reform since the 1880s, the city manager plan introduced a new concept of executive authority and a new view of the organization of municipal government. As a consequence, the boss, who was supposed to impose order from the top down within a centralized and hierarchical system, gave way to the manager, who facilitated interaction within a functionally decentralized and pluralistic system.[66]

Notes

1. Charles W. Eliot, "City Government by Fewer Men," *World's Work* 14 (October 1907): 9420; "One Remedy for Municipal Misgovernment," *Forum* 12 (October 1891): 166, 168; "Mayor vs. Council," *Municipal Affairs* 1 (September 1897): 567–68; Frank J. Goodnow, "The Place of the Council and of the Mayor

in the Organization of Municipal Government—The Necessity of Distinguishing Legislation From Administration," *Proceedings of the Indianapolis Conference for Good City Government and the Fourth Annual Meeting of the National Municipal League* (Philadelphia: National Municipal League, 1898), pp. 72–73; Horace Deming, "The Municipal Problem in the United States," *Proceedings of the Indianapolis Conference for Good City Government and the Fourth Annual Meeting of the National Municipal League* (Philadelphia: National Municipal League, 1898), pp. 54–55, 61.

2. James Weinstein, "Organized Business and the City Commission and Manager Movements," *Journal of Southern History* 28 (May 1962): 175; Samuel P. Hays, "The Politics of Reform in Municipal Government in the Progressive Era," *Pacific Northwest Quarterly* 55 (October 1964): 157–69; Melvin G. Holli, *Reform in Detroit: Hazen S. Pingree and Urban Politics* (New York: Oxford University Press, 1969), pp. 163, 175, 178–79; Richard J. Stillman, *The Rise of the City Manager: A Public Professional in Local Government* (Albuquerque: University of New Mexico Press, 1974), pp. 8, 20–21.

3. Holli, *Reform in Detroit*, pp. 163, 178; Samuel Haber, *Efficiency and Uplift: Scientific Management in the Progressive Era, 1890–1920* (Chicago: University of Chicago Press, 1964), p. 104 n. 12; Robert H. Wiebe, *The Search for Order, 1877–1920* (New York: Hill and Wang, 1967), p. 149; Martin J. Schiesl, *The Politics of Efficiency: Municipal Administration and Reform in America* (Berkeley: University of California Press, 1977), pp. 139, 145–46, 176, 222 n. 21.

4. Alfred D. Chandler Jr., *The Visible Hand: The Managerial Revolution in American Business* (Cambridge: Harvard University Press, 1977), pp. 8–9, 381, 415, 450–51, 460, and "Management Decentralization: An Historical Analysis," in James P. Baughman, ed., *The History of American Management* (Englewood Cliffs, N.J.: Prentice-Hall, 1969), pp. 189, 191, 238–39.

5. For changing conceptions of the city during the late nineteenth and early twentieth centuries, see Zane L. Miller and Bruce Tucker, *Changing Plans for America's Inner Cities: Cincinnati's Over-the-Rhine and Twentieth-Century Urbanism* (Columbus: Ohio State University Press, 1998), pp. 4–13; Alan I Marcus, "Back to the Present: Historians' Treatment of the City as a Social System during the Reign of the Idea of Community," in Howard Gillette Jr. and Zane L. Miller, *American Urbanism: A Historiographical Review* (New York: Greenwood Press, 1987), pp. 13–16; Robert B. Fairbanks, *For the City as a Whole: Planning, Politics, and the Public Interest in Dallas, Texas, 1900–1965* (Columbus: Ohio State University Press, 1998), pp. 2–3.

6. Alexander B. Callow Jr., *The Tweed Ring* (New York: Oxford University Press, 1966; New York: Galaxy Books, 1969; rep., 1972), pp. 116–17; Zane L. Miller, *Boss Cox's Cincinnati: Urban Politics in the Progressive Era* (New York: Oxford University Press, 1968; Phoenix Edition, 1980), pp. 86–93.

7. E. L. Godkin, "What A Mayor Should Be," *Nation* 59 (October 11, 1894): 262–63; Miller, *Boss Cox's Cincinnati*, pp. 173–74.

8. Woodrow Wilson, "Democracy and Efficiency," *Atlantic Monthly* 87 (March 1901): 295.

9. Ibid., p. 296.

10. Milo R. Maltbie, "Municipal Political Parties," *Proceedings of the Milwaukee Conference for Good City Government and Sixth Annual Meeting of the National Municipal League* (Philadelphia: National Municipal League, 1900), p. 237; Frank J. Goodnow, *Politics and Administration* (1900; reissued, New York: Russell and Russell, 1967), pp. 173–75.

11. Clinton Rogers Woodruff, "The Progress of Municipal Reform," *Municipal Affairs* 1 (June 1897): 311–12; E. J. Blandin, "Municipal Government of Cleveland," *Proceedings of the Second National Conference for Good City Government* (Philadelphia: National Municipal League, 1895), pp. 112–15; John A. Butler, "Some Essential Features of the New Municipal Program," *Proceedings of the Milwaukee Conference for Good City Government and Sixth Annual Meeting of the National Municipal League* (Philadelphia: National Municipal League, 1900), pp. 95, 100–101; Maltbie, "Municipal Political Parties," p. 237; Frederic C. Howe, *The City: The Hope of Democracy* (New York: Charles Scribner's Sons, 1905; University of Washington Press, 1967), p. 185.

12. New York, *Laws of the State of New York Passed at the One Hundred and Third Session of the Legislature*, vol. 1 (1880), pp. 557–60; *New York Times*, May 25, 1880, p. 1; Edward M. Shepard, "The Brooklyn Idea in City Government," *Forum* 16 (September 1893): 40–47; James Allen Scott, "The Businessman, Capitalism and the City: Businessmen and Municipal Reform in Philadelphia From the Act of Consolidation (1854) to the Bullitt Bill (1885)" (Ph.D. dissertation, University of Delaware, 1974), p. 106; Pennsylvania, *Laws of the General Assembly of the Commonwealth of Pennsylvania* (1885), pp. 38–40, 42–45, 47–49, 50–52; Ohio, *General and Local Acts Passed and Joint Resolutions Adopted by the Sixty-Ninth General Assembly* (1891), vol. 88, pp. 106, 108–10, 112, 117, 120.

13. Ernest S. Griffith, *A History of American City Government: The Conspicuous Failure, 1890–1900* (New York: Praeger, 1974), p. 108.

14. "Municipal Corporations Act," *Proceedings of the Indianapolis Conference for Good City Government and Fourth Annual Meeting of the National Municipal League* (Philadelphia: National Municipal League, 1898), pp. 3–38.

15. Charles Richardson, "Does the New Municipal Program Confer Dangerous Powers on the Mayor," *Proceedings of the Milwaukee Conference for Good City Government and the Sixth Annual Meeting of the National Municipal League* (Philadelphia: National Municipal League, 1900), pp. 120–21.

16. Goodnow, " Place of the Council and of the Mayor," p. 80.

17. L. S. Rowe, "American Political Ideas and Institutions in Their Relation to the Problem of City Government," *Proceedings of the Louisville Conference for Good City Government and the Third Annual Meeting of the National Municipal League* (Philadelphia: National Municipal League, 1897), pp. 80–81; Ada Ferrin Weber, *The Growth of Cities in the Nineteenth Century: A Study in Statistics* (New York: Macmillan, 1899), p. 183; Richard M. Hurd, *Principles of Land Values* (New York: Record and Guide, 1903), pp. 17–18.

18. Zane L. Miller, "Thinking, Politics, City Government: Charter Reform in Cincinnati, 1890s-1990s," *Queen City Heritage* 55 (Winter 1997): 24–26.

19. Horace E. Deming, "Public Opinion and City Government Under the Proposed Municipal Program," *Proceedings of the Columbus Conference for Good City Government and the Fifth Annual Meeting of the National Municipal League* (Philadelphia: National Municipal League, 1899), pp. 80–81. Also see Russell McCulloch Story, *The American Municipal Executive* (Urbana: University of Illinois Press, 1918; rep. New York: Johnson Reprint, 1970), p. 33; Clinton Rogers Woodruff, "The Progress of Municipal Reform," *Municipal Affairs* 1 (June 1897): 312.

20. Washington Gladden, "Mayor Jones, of Toledo," *Outlook* 62 (May 6, 1899), p. 17; Joseph Dana Miller, "President Roosevelt and Mayor Johnson As Typical Representatives of Opposing Political Ideals, *Arena* 30 (1903): 145, 148–51; Holli, *Reform in Detroit*, pp. 54–55, 72; Gerald Kurland, *Seth Low: The Reformer in an Urban and Industrial Age* (New York: Twayne, 1971), p. 49.

21. It is important not to draw too sharp a distinction between these two types of reform mayors, as some historians have done. Some of the reform mayors who have been viewed as pushing efficiency and honesty above all else also adopted policies designed to promote social reform. Similarly, some of the reform mayors who have been identified primarily with social reform sought to apply business principles to city government. It is also worth noting that during the Progressive Era there emerged an influential group of urban "experts," most notably Henry Bruere and Frederick Cleveland, who championed efficiency as a means of serving social welfare needs. See Kurland, *Seth Low* , pp. 73, 101, 103; Holli, *Reform in Detroit*, p. 153; Augustus Cerillo Jr. "The Impact of Reform Ideology: Early Twentieth-Century Municipal Government in New York City," in Michael H. Ebner and Eugene M. Tobin, eds., *The Age of Urban Reform: New Perspectives on the Progressive Era* (Port Washington, N.Y.: Kennikat Press, 1977), pp. 69–70, 80–81, 83–85; Kenneth Finegold, *Experts and Politicians: Reform Challenges to Machine Politics in New York, Cleveland, and Chicago* (Princeton: Princeton University Press, 1995), pp. 21–22; Haber, *Efficiency and Uplift*, p. 111.

22. B. O. Flowers, "A New Champion of the People's Cause," *Arena* 28 (November 1902): 537–40; Frank Parsons, *The City for the People* (Philadelphia: C. F. Taylor, 1901), p. 9; Charles H. Hession and Hyman Sardy, *Ascent to Affluence: A History of American Economic Development* (Boston: Allyn and Bacon, 1969), p. 582.

23. Hazen S. Pingree, "Detroit: A Municipal Study," *Outlook* 55 (February 6, 1897): 437.

24. Quoted in Story, *American Municipal Executive*, p. 33.

25. Gladden, "Mayor Jones," p. 17.

26. Quoted in Holli, *Reform in Detroit*, p. 55. While some reformers attributed the need for a champion to the helplessness of the people, others attributed it to the apathy of the people, who seemed willing to allow themselves to be bossed for good or ill. See Lincoln Steffens, *The Shame of the Cities* (New York: S. S. McClure, 1902; New York: Hill and Wang, 1957), pp. 1 -2, 7, 42.

27. Eugene C. Murdock, *Tom Johnson of Cleveland* (Dayton: Wright State Uni-

versity Press, 1994), pp. 10, 13, 17–19, 123, 180–81; Holli, *Reform in Detroit*, pp. 7, 55, 139, 141, 154–55.

28. Howe, *The City*, p. 185.

29. Murdock, *Tom Johnson*, pp. 73, 122–23; Schiesl, *Politics of Efficiency*, pp. 81–82.

30. Henry George Jr., "Captains of Industry: Tom Lofton Johnson," *Cosmopolitan* 34 (November 1902): 95; Thomas F. Campbell, "Mounting Crisis and Reform: Cleveland's Political Development," in Thomas F. Campbell and Edward M. Miggins, eds., *The Birth of Modern Cleveland, 1865–1930* (Cleveland: Western Reserve Historical Society, 1988), p. 305; Wiebe, *Search for Order*, p. 172.

31. Edward D. Jones, *The Administration of Industrial Enterprise* (New York: Longmans, Green, 1916), p. 127; Louis M. Hacker, *The World of Andrew Carnegie: 1865–1901* (Philadelphia: J. B. Lippincott, 1968), pp. xviii–xx, xxxiv–xxxvi; Edward C. Kirkland, *Industry Comes of Age: Business, Labor, and Public Policy, 1860–1897* (New York: Holt, Rinehart, and Winston, 1961), p. 213; Chandler, "Management Decentralization," pp. 189, 191, 238–39.

32. Burton J. Hendrick, *The Age of Big Business* (New Haven: Yale University Press, 1919), pp. 21, 33, 35, 40, 67, 187; Jones, *Administration of Industrial Enterprise*, p. 126; Hacker, *World of Andrew Carnegie*, pp. 405–7; George, "Captains of Industry," p. 95; Flowers, "New Champion of the People's Cause," p. 534; Gladden, "Mayor Jones," p. 17.

33. Holli, *Reform in Detroit*, p. 108.

34. Frank Barkley Copley, *Frederick W. Taylor, Father of Scientific Management*, vol. 1 (New York: Harper and Row, 1923): 290–91. Also see Haber, *Efficiency and Uplift*, p. 29.

35. Woodrow Wilson, "The Study of Administration," *Political Science Quarterly* 2 (June 1887), pp. 197–98, 202–3, 206. Wilson's article is usually credited with launching the field of public administration in the United States. See Richard J. Stillman II, *Public Administration: Concepts and Cases*, 5th ed. (Boston: Houghton Mifflin, 1992), p. 4.

36. Wilson, "Study of Administration," pp. 197–99, 201, 209–10; Eliot, "One Remedy for Municipal Misgovernment," p. 155; Edmund J. James, "The Elements of a Model Charter for American Cities," *Proceedings of the Second National Conference for Good City Government* (Philadelphia: National Municipal League, 1895), pp. 170–71; Richardson, "Does the New Municipal Program," pp. 119–20.

37. Franklin MacVeagh, "The Business Man in Municipal Politics," *Proceedings of the Louisville Conference for Good City Government and the Third Annual Meeting of the National Municipal League* (Philadelphia: National Municipal League, 1897), p. 133.

38. Eliot, "City Government by Fewer Men," pp. 9420–21.

39. Frederick Winslow Taylor, *The Principles of Scientific Management* (New York: Harper and Brothers, 1911), p. 7.

40. Frederick W. Taylor, "Shop Management," *Transactions of the American Society of Mechanical Engineers* 24 (1903): 1341.

41. Taylor, *Principles of Scientific Management*, pp. 6–7.

42. Taylor, "Shop Management," pp. 1369, 1400, 1443–46; *Principles of Scientific Management*, pp. 38–39, 104, and "A Piece-Rate System," *Transactions of the American Society of Mechanical Engineers* 16 (1895): 869–72.

43. Taylor, "Shop Management," pp. 1369, 1398, 1409. Also see *Principles of Scientific Management*, pp. 124–23.

44. Taylor, "Shop Management," pp. 1386–87, 1390.

45. Thereafter, however, its popularity began to wane, as indicated by the steady decline in the number of cities that adopted it during the late 1910s and early 1920s. See Bradley Robert Rice, *Progressive Cities: The Commission Government Movement in America, 1901–1920* (Austin: University of Texas Press, 1977), p. 53.

46. Stillman, *Rise of the City Manager*, p. 13.

47. Carl Dehoney, "Commission Government and Democracy," *American City* 2 (February 1910): 76–78, and "Breaking Down Ward Lines in American Cities," *World To-day* 18 (May 1910), pp. 487–90; Rice, *Progressive Cities*, p. xiii.

48. In doing the research for this study, I found only one self-conscious effort to apply scientific management to city government, and it had nothing to do with the commission plan. See Morris L. Cooke, "Scientific Management of the Public Business," *American Political Science Review* 9 (August 1915): 488–95.

49. Frederick Law Olmsted Jr., "Introduction," in John Nolen, ed., *City Planning* (New York, 1916), p. 1: Frank Backus Williams, *The Law of City Planning and Zoning* (New York: Macmillan, 1922), pp. 4, 27; Austin F. MacDonald, *American City Government and Administration* (New York: Thomas Y. Crowell, 1929), p. 457. Also see Zane L. Miller and Bruce Tucker, "The New Urban Politics: Planning and Development in Cincinnati, 1954–1988," in Richard M. Bernard, ed., *Snowbelt Cities* (Bloomington: Indiana University Press, 1990), pp. 91–92; Henry D. Shapiro, "The Place of Culture and the Problem of Identity," in Allen Batteau, ed., *Appalachia and America: Autonomy and Regional Dependence* (Lexington: University of Kentucky Press, 1983), pp. 131–33; Robert A. Burnham, "Planning versus Administration: The Independent Planning Commission in Cincinnati, 1918–1940," *Urban History* 19 (October 1992): 231–32.

50. William A. Magee, "The Organization and Functions of A City Planning Commission," *Proceedings of the Fifth National Conference on City Planning* (1913), p. 81.

51. Frederick Law Olmsted, "A City Planning Program," *Proceedings of the Fifth National Conference on City Planning* (1913), p. 5.

52. Mary P. Follett, *The New State* (Gloucester, Mass.: Peter Smith, 1965; Longmans, Green, 1918), pp. 7, 10, 36, 106.

53. Henry C. Metcalf and L. Urwick, eds., *Dynamic Administration: The Collected Papers of Mary Parker Follett* (New York: Harper and Brothers, 1940), p. 71.

54. Robert G. Valentine, "The Progressive Relation Between Efficiency and Consent," *Bulletin of the Society to Promote the Science of Management* 1 (November 1915): 26; Jones, *Administration of Industrial Enterprise*, pp. 22, 123, 126, 144–45, 292–93; Alexander Hamilton Church, *The Science and Practice of Man-*

agement (New York: Engineering Magazine, 1918), pp. 36, 56, 74, 77; Lee Galloway, *Office Management: Its Principles and Practices* (New York: Ronald Press, 1918), pp. v, viii, 3–4; Richard H. Lansburgh, *Industrial Management* (New York: John Wiley and Sons, 1923), pp. 35, 38; Edward Eyre Hunt, ed., *Scientific Management Since Taylor* (New York: McGraw Hill, 1924), pp. 32, 59, 71, 78, 239.

55. William Bennett Munro, *Municipal Government and Administration,* 2 vols. (New York: Macmillan, 1923), vol. 1, pp. 410–11. Also see H. S. Gilbertson, "Some Serious Weaknesses of the Commission Plan," *American City* 9 (September 1913): 237; Clinton Rogers Woodruff, ed., *A New Municipal Program* (New York: D. Appleton, 1919), p. 152; William Anderson, *American City Government* (New York: Henry Holt, 1925), p. 324.

56. Rice, *Progressive Cities,* p. 91.

57. Dunbar F. Carpenter, "Some Serious Defects of Commission Government," *Annals of the American Academy of Political and Social Science* 38 (November 1911): 199; Gilbertson, "Some Serious Weaknesses," p. 237.

58. Rice, *Progressive Cities,* p. 108; National Municipal League, *A Model City Charter and Municipal Home Rule: As Prepared by the Committee on Municipal Program of the National Municipal League* (Philadelphia: National Municipal League, 1916).

59. Harry Aubry Toulmin Jr., *The City Manager: A New Profession* (New York: D. Appleton, 1915), pp. 99, 158–59; Richard S. Childs, "How the Commission-Manager Plan Is Getting Along," *National Municipal Review* 4 (July 1915): 372; Munro, *Municipal Government and Administration,* vol. 1, pp. 416, 423; National Municipal League, *Model City Charter,* pp. 12, 29.

60. Eliot, "One Remedy for Municipal Misgovernment," p. 165; Delos F. Wilcox, "The Inadequacy of Present City Government," in Edward A. Fitzpatrick, ed., *Experts in City Government* (New York: D. Appleton, 1919), p. 40.

61. MacDonald, *American City Government and Administration,* p. 368. Also see Luther Gulick, "Notes on the Theory of Organization," in Luther Gulick and L. Urwick, eds., *Papers on the Science of Administration* (New York: Institute of Public Administration, 1937), p. 10.

62. Munro, *Municipal Government and Administration,* vol. 2, pp. 14–16; and MacDonald, *American City Government and Administration,* pp. 368–71. As Robert Fairbanks has shown, housing reformers in the 1920s sought to create separate but equally important homogeneous neighborhoods, which was analogous to creating separate and distinct homogeneous administrative departments within the city government. See Fairbanks, *Making Better Citizens: Housing Reform and the Community Development Strategy in Cincinnati, 1890–1960* (Urbana: University of Illinois Press, 1988), pp. 52–53.

63. City of Cincinnati, *Municipal Activities* (1926), p. 56.

64. R. W. Rigsby, "The Technique of City Management," *Public Management* 10 (March 1928): 174.

65. "Administrative Duties and Problems," *City Managers' Association, Yearbook* 5 (1919), p. 129.

66. Even cities that chose not to adopt the city manager plan embraced the new managerial ethos. For example, numerous mayor-council governed cities hired a "chief administrative officer" who functioned much like a city manger. See Stillman, *Rise of the City Manager,* pp. 24–25. Also, there emerged in the 1910s a new breed of reform mayors who had the qualifications expected of city managers. Typified by Newton D. Baker of Cleveland, John Purroy Mitchel of New York, and Henry Hunt of Cincinnati, these reform mayors did not come from the ranks of business but were highly regarded public administrators. Referring to Baker and Mitchel, one contemporary noted that the "mayor system has evolved two administrations headed by men who can satisfy the demand for skilled and trained executives just at the moment when the city manager plan appears to lay special emphasis upon the necessity for public servants of that type." See Story, *American Municipal Executive,* p. 177.

Chapter Five

Before the Neighborhood Organization Revolution: Cincinnati's Neighborhood Improvement Associations, 1890–1940

PATRICIA MOONEY-MELVIN

As the United States entered the 1970s, a chorus of noisy neighborhood organizations advocating a variety of programs for local betterment emerged. Slogans such as "Power to the Neighborhoods" and both popular and scholarly articles focusing on "resurgent neighborhoods" captured the spirit of this strident localism. An article in the *Christian Science Monitor* reported that "a groundswell movement of citizens" existed across the country, ready, so it seemed, to rise to the defense of the nation's neighborhoods.[1] The country was in the midst of a neighborhood organization revolution.

Amid all the enthusiasm for neighborhood development, the founder of the National Association of Neighborhoods, Milton Kotler, suggested that the neighborhood movement's ability to appeal to widely divergent groups helped account for its popularity. The movement lacked, however, a clearly articulated set of strategies to orchestrate neighborhood demands and exercise substantive power. Kotler urged those interested in neighborhoods to look to the roots of the movement for guidance. "We must remember where the neighborhood movement came from and what happened to create the present situation," he wrote. "The neighborhood movement did not fall from heaven yesterday. It began in the 1960s." During that decade, according to Kotler, neighborhood residents, community organizers, activist clergy, and government workers joined together to involve those living in poor neighborhoods in efforts to shape their own future. The movement worked then, Kotler argued, because it included an ethical vision that promoted social responsibility and justice to achieve real power. If the various strands of the 1970s neighborhood movement reincorporated the ethical vision of its early years, Kotler contended, it would stand a better chance of success.[2]

More recent analysts have pushed the movement's origin back to the late 1940s,[3] although they accept Kotler's vision of what constituted appropriate organizing initiatives at the neighborhood level. According to these scholars, the modern neighborhood movement or revolution grew out of the efforts of concerned citizens, organizers, local clergy, and government activists to empower the nation's urban poor after the end of World War II. Once organized, these neighborhood residents were able to begin the process of "converting interests into politically relevant issues,"[4] work for the betterment of local conditions, and have a voice in the planning process. The creation of federated coalitions, often portrayed as a new addition to the tactical arsenal of local activists, allowed neighborhood residents to break free of the potentially parochial dynamic in campaigns for local betterment and share responsibility for the larger urban community.[5]

Still other scholars interested in the neighborhood movement acknowledge that it was not completely new in either the 1940s or 1960s. They situate its origins between 1890 and 1920 when "progressives and liberals" created local organizations to confront the challenges associated with turn-of-the-century cities. According to this argument, neighborhood activists focused their efforts on the needs of newly arrived ethnic groups or other members of the urban poor and emphasized poverty-related issues as well as building community and citizenship through the establishment of settlement houses and community centers. After 1920, these analysts contend, those involved in neighborhood-based work abandoned their residential orientation for a more individualized casework and small-group focus, and organizing on the local level disappeared. Neighborhood-based organizing would not resume as an identifiable force until the late 1940s.[6]

This shift in emphasis on the part of those active in neighborhood work coincided with changing beliefs about neighborhoods and their role in the city that lessened the importance of the neighborhood as an arena for either social or political action between 1920 and 1950. Chicago sociologists argued that the dynamics of modern metropolitan life destroyed the homogeneity they believed necessary to sustain a vibrant community life at the neighborhood level, and the resulting social disorganization negated localized efforts to organize residents. The adoption of comprehensive city plans, which shifted power from the neighborhood to city hall, attempted to recapture residential homogeneity, stressed city needs over local issues, and downplayed neighborhood activism in favor of a greater civic identity and for an efficiently regulated urban system. According to those scholars influenced by the Chicago sociologists' vision of urban life or those who focus on planners, it was not until the late 1940s, when a different understanding of the city and its constituent parts emerged, that neighborhood organizing resurfaced as a significant element of urban life.[7]

None of the above scenarios suggests that neighborhood-based organizations served as important vehicles through which to identify and meet local needs between the 1920s and the late 1940s. However, if the definition of neighborhood organization between 1890 and 1920 is broadened to include other than social service–oriented groups such as settlement houses or community centers and to focus on infrastructure in addition to poverty and social service delivery, the situation looks somewhat different. Because people continued to "share a common relation to [their] place of residence" since it was where they lived and raised their families,[8] *place* remained important. As a result, other types of neighborhood organizations continued to operate after 1920. They possessed arsenals of strategies and tactics strikingly similar to those in use during all phases of the neighborhood organization revolution. Their existence counters the discontinuity suggested by those who date the origins of the movement between 1890 and 1920 and see it as virtually nonexistent between 1920 and 1940, those who locate its emergence at the end of the 1940s, or those who emphasize its relative newness. In addition, the examination of these other organizations highlights the relationship between urban definition and action that guides the ways in which city dwellers understand their community and prescribe activities to solve urban problems.

Among the most ubiquitous of late-nineteenth- and early-twentieth-century local organizations were neighborhood improvement associations.[9] While not necessarily always viewed as reformist or progressive, as were settlements and community centers, they were nonetheless important neighborhood organizations. Strictly residential in nature, these associations focused their activities on local betterment. Despite a myriad of ties that drew residents out of the neighborhood, these organizations provided the arena in which residents "demonstrated a commitment to their home district by debating, petitioning, rallying, and lobbying the government about issues affecting the welfare of their neighborhood."[10] They promoted community building and civic loyalty. More active during some years than others, they often survived when other locally based organizations seemed to have disappeared. If we explore the activities of these groups, it becomes clear that the neighborhood movement did not rise and fall between 1890 and 1920, emerge after 1940, or "fall from heaven" in the 1960s[11] but persisted from its emergence during the late nineteenth century.

An examination of three neighborhood improvement associations in Cincinnati, Ohio, between 1890 and 1940—the Westwood Civic Association, the Bond Hill Civic Association, and the Price Hill Civic and Businessmen's Club—illustrates that the neighborhood organization movement developed as the modern city took shape during the late nineteenth century and endured during the years between 1920 and 1940. Despite the implementation of a city plan and different beliefs about the nature of the city and its constituent parts, place—the particular locale where people lived and invested a significant portion of their time—remained important to urban dwellers. As a result, it is not surprising that neighborhood organizing continued, albeit different in range and intensity, during the interwar years.

During the nineteenth century rapid social and economic changes negated the prevailing definition of the city as an undifferentiated whole. When confronted with this disparity between the old urban definition and the "new city" of the late nineteenth century, with its specialized land-use pattern and system of socioeconomic segregation, Americans searched for a new definition of the city that corresponded more closely to the segmented urban community around them. Borrowing an analogy popular in descriptions of society, Americans portrayed the city as an organism composed of interdependent units or neighborhoods. It is at this point that the neighborhood as a discrete unit formally enters the urban landscape.[12]

Between 1850 and 1910 Cincinnati underwent the transition from the walking city of the nineteenth century to the metropolitan community of the twentieth century. A combination of technological innovations in intracity transportation, population growth, industrial expansion, and successful annexations enlarged city boundaries from 6 square miles in 1850 to 50.26 square miles by 1910.[13] Central in this process of physical growth was the emergence of a differentiated urban structure in which the expanded central business district of the new city appeared to be surrounded by zones that exhibited distinct residential and industrial functions.[14] In Cincinnati, three discernible zones emerged: the Slums, the Zone of Emergence, and the Hilltops.[15]

It was in the Hilltop neighborhoods that local improvement associations first appeared. While not isolated from the rest of the city (many Hilltop dwellers either worked or had ties in the city), the Hilltop represented residential havens for Cincinnati's economically successful citizens. In order to protect their living spaces and interests, Hilltop residents formed a host of organizations during the late nineteenth century, among which were improvement associations. Some of these organizations existed before an area's annexation to Cincinnati, such as the Bond Hill Improvement Association (1892) and the Hyde Park Improvement Association (1893). Other associations grew out of the fight against annexation, while still others emerged after annexation, such as the Westwood Improvement Association (1896). Whenever their formation, these organizations were designed to promote and improve conditions in the Hilltop communities.[16] Once they were operating in the Hilltop suburbs, other Cincinnati neighborhoods and unincorporated areas surrounding the city formed similar organizations to advance their interests.

However, as the author of *The Suburbs of Cincinnati* remarked as early as 1870, "one bad tendency in individual suburbs [was] to make streets and other improvements without regard to similar enterprises in adjacent territory."[17] By the 1890s, inner-city neighborhoods as well as the Hilltop communities began to learn that major improvements affected more than just a single area and that by joining together it was possible to exert greater influence upon city officials responsible for the desired improvements. As a result, after a period of more locally oriented activities, the various improvement associations entered into a citywide federation to coordinate efforts that touched common problems. Following the recognition of common problems came an understanding that a connection between local improvements and the entire metropolitan community existed.

The experience of the Westwood Civic Association illustrates the move from local concerns to an appreciation of cooperative action on the part of many local organizations during the period 1890 to 1920, and it captures the flavor of this type of neighborhood organization. The Westwood Civic Association was an outgrowth of the pre-annexation Westwood, Cheviot, and Dent Improvement Association and the post-annexation Westwood Improvement Association and Westwood Businessmen's Club. Its roots reach back to the 1890s, and it continues in operation today.

The area that became known as Westwood lay on one of the hilltops that rose to the west of Cincinnati's central business district. A primarily farming settlement at first, Westwood soon attracted wealthy residents with ties to Cincinnati. As these residents increased in number they organized a local government and incorporated the village of Westwood in 1868. Throughout the remainder of the nineteenth century the area prospered, and further growth was secured with the establishment of a railroad line that provided regular service between Westwood and Cincinnati.[18]

Westwood's growth and prosperity attracted the attention of Cincinnati's politicians. Like most late-nineteenth-century cities, Cincinnati sought to increase its boundaries through the annexation of surrounding territory. In 1889 Cincinnati's mayor stressed the importance of annexing the rapidly growing suburban population. During the 1894 election Cincinnati voters formally endorsed this position and launched the city on a drive to annex the wealthy, populous suburbs that encircled the city. Five suburban villages were of concern in 1894: Avondale, Clifton, Linwood, Riverside, and Westwood. Despite the outraged protests of these suburbs, Cincinnati capitalized on the recently passed Lillard Law that allowed the votes of the city annexing to be counted together with the votes of the target suburbs, a procedure that effectively wiped out any suburban opposition.[19] On January 1, 1896, these suburbs became part of the city of Cincinnati.[20]

Following annexation, residents of the former village of Westwood believed it important to continue the improvement of their new neighborhood and maintain a sense of community identity. Prior to annexation Westwood had worked for local improvements through the Westwood, Cheviot, and Dent Improvement Association,[21] which focused its efforts primarily on securing appropriate railroad ties with Cincinnati and on developing a system of roads in those communities.[22] After annexation, leading Westwood residents decided to form their own improvement organization. The Westwood Improvement Association (WIA) came into existence in 1896. As one of the association's founding members later remarked, "[I]t was very important that the interests of this part of the city should be looked after closely."[23] The intent of the WIA was to do just that, and following its organization the association pushed for a variety of improvements that were believed necessary for the development and further enhancement of Westwood.

The WIA soon found that in order to secure certain improvements cooperative action with other groups often helped facilitate its efforts. This was particularly true in the drive to eliminate four dangerous grade crossings, known as "Dead Man's Crossing," that separated the western part of Cincinnati from the central portion of the city. Westwood had fought for this improvement to no avail since 1888. After years of frustration, the Westwood association joined forces with the North Fairmount Improvement Association and the Central Fairmount Improvement Association in 1897.[24] Together these organizations pressured the city to implement the provisions of a bill passed by the state legislature in 1890 that permitted cities of the first class to construct viaducts "for the purpose of providing against overflow from high water and the dangers of grade crossings of steam railways."[25] This pressure forced the city to acknowledge the problem; it took a bit longer to get the city to act upon it.

Finally, on May 10, 1899, a particularly serious accident at the "crossing" sparked a general public outcry, and the three organizations captured the moment and issued a resolution charging the Board of City Affairs with the "murders" of all persons killed at the "crossing." In response, the board approved the construction of a viaduct to span the area. By 1901 the board had authorized the issue of a bond to raise the money for the project and a condemnation order so that the construction could proceed once the money had been secured.[26]

Following the resolution of a series of lawsuits contesting the validity of such bond issues and condemnation procedures as well as the vigilant oversight provided by the concerned associations, the construction of the viaduct began. In late 1906 work commenced on the abutments and piers, and the steel superstructure was completed in August 1908. At the opening on September 19, 1908, of the Harrison Avenue Viaduct, members of the three improvement associations recognized that the viaduct stood "as a monument of the untiring and unselfish devotion" of the three organizations.[27] Singly each organization had failed in its efforts to move the city to action between 1888 and 1898. Working together, despite the delays, the three associations were able to secure the completion of the project.

Based on the viaduct experience, the Westwood Improvement Association voted to become a member of the Federated Improvement Association (FIA) in 1908.[28] Members of the WIA believed this would facilitate West-

wood's future development by systematizing the collective efforts of organizations interested in projects important to Westwood yet impinging
upon other Cincinnati communities. In short, the WIA felt that unification
would strengthen rather than impede local community development.

The FIA was the brainchild of William C. Culkins, a member of the Hyde
Park Businessmen's Club, and Joseph J. Castellini, a member of the
Evanston Welfare Association. In early 1907 Culkins and Castellini, frustrated by the lack of progress their organizations experienced in a variety
of areas, decided to organize a citywide civic association.[29] In June 1907
seven organizations came together to form the Federated Improvement
Association. According to the FIA's newspaper, the *Civic News*, while
Cincinnati's associations had "developed a local sentiment keenly alive to
the needs of their neighborhoods," they "often found that improvements
suggested or needed" demanded the attention of more than just their own
particular group. The formation of the FIA was based on the belief that the
local groups could "be of mutual assistance" to one another. Through
"concerted action," local associations could "extend the scope of their
activities."[30]

Once in existence, the FIA operated on two levels. Local organizations
focused on identifying and securing improvements for their own localities.
The FIA handled larger issues of more general concern to the entire city
and coordinated efforts that touched on more than one community. All in
all, as far as its organizers were concerned, the FIA represented the "awakened interest and understanding" on the part of the people of the "responsibility" they possessed in public affairs.[31] Its reliance upon citizen
activism and emphasis on civic loyalty indicated that it was part of a larger
outburst of civic involvement that appeared in all sorts of communities
during the late nineteenth and early twentieth centuries.[32]

By 1912 the FIA had grown to include thirty-two organizations, each of
whom sent three representatives to meetings.[33] Of the organizations
involved, most came from the Zone and Hilltops communities, and their
delegates to the FIA represented a cross section of Cincinnati businesses,
professions, ethnic groups, and religious denominations. With few excep-
tions, however, the leadership of the organization rested in the hands of
the delegates representing improvement associations in the Hilltops.[34]
Delegates from the WIA could be counted among some of the more active
leaders of the FIA.

As a result of action orchestrated by the FIA, the Westwood Improvement Association, known as the Westwood Civic Association (WCA) after
1911,[35] was able to secure lateral sewers to eliminate a sewage problem in
Boudinot Creek, the adoption of a plan to create a comprehensive sewer system that would benefit Westwood as well as the rest of the city, proper-
capacity water pumps, streetcar route changes, contracts for street lighting,
and general street improvements.[36] For all these projects the Westwood

organization presented its needs before a citywide forum, joined with other local groups interested in the same issues, and then, under the umbrella of the FIA, offered a unified front toward and exerted increased pressure on Cincinnati's city council.

Throughout this period the Westwood association was able to maintain its own identity and work for its own needs. Yet during its first twenty-five years of existence it came to recognize the interdependence of urban needs and the utility of organized action. An editorial in 1915 by then FIA president John Markworth, an early member of the Westwood association, captured the essence of the improvement association experience during this period. According to Markworth, "certain needs of the particular locality possessed a relationship of an importance more vital to the city at large than to the locality." Accordingly, it "became necessary to view the matter from a larger and more cosmopolitan standpoint and thus arose the dual relationship of every improvement association, a relationship now universally recognized." There was, Markworth emphasized, "no service that benefits all that doesn't benefit each."[37] Neighborhood improvement associations served as a vehicle to forge a closer relationship between local activism and the larger urban community.[38] Working together, the neighborhood organizations were able to convert local concerns into "politically relevant issues."[39]

In a city without a plan, local neighborhood organizations, both alone and through cooperative action in city federations,[40] possessed the opportunity to exercise influence over the direct placement or improvement of the city's infrastructure, activities deemed important in virtually all campaigns for local betterment. Local initiatives and interneighborhood cooperation seemed an appropriate response to both neighborhood and citywide needs in the city of interdependence as defined at the turn of the century. The city was, according to Robert A. Woods of Boston's South End House, "a cluster of interlacing communities, each having its own vital ways of expression and action, but all together creating the municipality which shall render the fullest service through the most spirited participation of its citizens."[41] Activism by neighborhood improvement associations reflected an approach to urban problem-solving consistent with beliefs about the interdependence of the city and its constituent parts as defined by Woods and his contemporaries. At the same time, this activism—with its emphasis on the interrelationship believed to exist among localized needs, social issues, the building of community and citizenship, and the improvement of the larger urban community—was in keeping with the orientation of reform activities associated with neighborhood organization during the first two decades of the twentieth century.

By 1925 Cincinnati possessed a comprehensive city plan, and while neighborhoods remained part of the urban equation, the understanding of the neighborhood and its operation within the metropolitan community was different. The plan perceived neighborhoods not as residential spaces within the city that served as arenas for local activism, but rather as "functional 'community' units" that operated in an "ecologically interdependent way in which a defect in one not only impaired it and the whole but also *each* of the other units." Neighborhoods could not be left to take care of themselves; problems or concerns manifested in one area needed to be attacked simultaneously across the city in order to preserve metropolitan stability and coherence and avoid the debilitating effect of particularism on the welfare of the whole.[42] Neighborhoods were to be managed, not self-directed.

Cincinnati's 1925 plan, reflecting the insights of the Chicago sociologists, sought to control the social and cultural disorganization that was believed to accompany the urbanization process. Such disorganization alienated citizens, fostered group conflict, and encouraged intolerance. City plans, with the potential to shape the social as well as physical environment, could construct "competent communities"[43] that, when combined with social welfare initiatives, exhibited cohesion and unity. By redistributing population and rationalizing it on the basis of race, ethnicity, and class, for example, the plan possessed the opportunity to create the homogeneous units deemed so essential by Chicago sociologists to preserve both social and moral order. Cooperation, an expectation in a city of "interlacing communities,"[44] was not anticipated in an urban community composed of "mosaics of little cultural worlds"[45] and defined by function. Instead, the development of efficient communication and transportation networks would facilitate the web of secondary relations that brought all the various functional communities—residential, commercial, industrial—into a smoothly operating whole.[46]

Under conditions that required the management of urban space and community needs for the greater good of the metropolitan unit, the neighborhood ceased to be considered as a partner in the planning process. If the analysis of the Chicago sociologists and their supporters was correct, and Cincinnati's planners operated as if it was, the only role left for neighborhood improvement associations was to foster the internal restructuring of their neighborhoods to create community centers to facilitate "local identity and social and civic intersection."[47] No expectation existed for the associations individually or in concert through the Federated Improvement Association to identify and press for the resolution of local needs.

However, the world of city planners and the 1925 plan was not necessarily the same world inhabited by neighborhood residents. Despite connections to interest groups not associated with a particular locale, residence remained important and people "forged solidarities on the basis of interests . . . inherent in that relation."[48] As a result, it is not surprising that organizational life on the neighborhood level existed beyond the 1920s. Regardless of their neighborhood's composition, residents still wanted infrastructure improvements and other local amenities. Managed care by planners did not necessarily meet local needs in a proactive way. Neighborhood improvement associations continued to operate and promote the needs of their communities. The Federated Improvement Association, renamed the Federated Civic Association (FCA) in the mid-1920s, remained as well, although it acted as much as a city booster organization that coordinated support for more general projects with a larger citywide focus as it did a dynamic advocate for local infrastructure needs. It saw itself as an advocate of the "welfare and development of [Cincinnati's] local communities" through its ability to assist in projects for which local efforts alone proved unsuccessful. At the same time, as it had earlier, the FCA pursued measures that affected the "city as a whole."[49]

On both the FCA level and the neighborhood level, the city plan and the altered notion of urban organization that accompanied it did not discourage improvement association activity, although the range and intensity of such activity may have diminished somewhat. Improvement organizations pressed for local needs believed unmet by city government and other related institutions. They cooperated with one another if the occasion appeared to warrant it. The FCA provided pressure or more integrative services whenever necessary. All in all, the associations continued to play a role in the lives of neighborhood residents. A brief examination of the activities undertaken by the Bond Hill Civic Association illuminates two aspects of neighborhood improvement association activity in the years between 1920 and 1940, the continued local campaigns for improvements and enhanced amenities and the continuance of federated activity that coordinated local activities for the larger public good and pressured city government into action.

The village of Bond Hill lay to the northeast of Cincinnati's downtown. Although primarily agricultural in the mid-nineteenth century, by the early 1860s the area included two institutions, St. Aloysius Orphanage and Longview Asylum, which had been attracted to the quiet and underpopulated countryside. The establishment of the Marietta & Cincinnati Railroad[50] during the late 1860s increased access to the area, and in 1871 the Cooperative Land and Building Association laid out a village, Bond Hill,[51] and offered lots for sale. Despite its rail connections the community, incorporated as the village of Bond Hill in 1886, initially failed to attract many inhabitants.[52]

The Bond Hill Improvement Association (BHIA) came into existence in 1892 to secure a variety of improvements for the village. Issues relating to improved rail connections and street improvements received particular attention. In the late fall of 1892 the association secured a rate reduction for the stretch of road between Bond Hill and Cincinnati from the Baltimore & Ohio Railroad. As 1892 ended, the association's legislation committee was empowered to formulate a request to the Hamilton County commissioners for the widening and improvement of Paddock Road, located at the western edge of the village. Once the appropriate legislation had been secured from the Ohio legislature, the BHIA monitored the project closely to ensure that the commissioners would complete the improvements. Other issues of interest to the BHIA during its early years were street lighting, the procurement of water from Cincinnati, and village beautification projects.[53]

Growth continued to be slow, and Bond Hill retained its predominately pastoral character. Nonetheless, as with Westwood, the community attracted the attention of an expansion-minded Cincinnati, and the city annexed Bond Hill in 1903.[54] At some point after annexation, the BHIA changed its name to the Bond Hill Welfare Association (BHWA) and, as did its predecessor, championed a variety of campaigns for local betterment. Improved rail connections continued to concern local residents, although the emphasis had shifted from the B&O Railroad to streetcars. In January of 1911, the Bond Hill Welfare Association renewed its push for streetcar service. The association was able to get coverage of its plight in one of Cincinnati's local newspapers, the *Commercial Tribune*,[55] and like many other organizations found that strength in numbers could be beneficial. As a member of the Federated Improvement Association, the BHWA turned to the FIA for help. Because the introduction of the Bond Hill streetcar line would ultimately impact other localities, the FIA joined the fight for streetcar service and put pressure on the Cincinnati Traction Company through its transportation committee. The BHWA organized community residents to sign petitions to present to the Traction Company and to attend city council meetings whenever the issue of streetcar route expansion was on the agenda.

By midsummer of that year a victory appeared imminent with an announcement from the Traction Company that it was willing to accommodate the community's streetcar needs.[56] However, soon after its apparent agreement, the company dragged its feet and suggested that the community did not possess enough people to ensure consistently high levels of ridership. At the same time, once the plans for the location of the rails were made public, property owners balked at giving up the necessary rights of way. A series of court cases followed, and the process dragged on for another four years without resolution. Finally, on December 17, 1916, the Bond Hill streetcar line began operation. Although the battle proved much longer than either organization had expected, the combined and continuous pressure of both groups finally brought positive results.[57]

Industrial development in the nearby Mill Creek Valley after World War I helped spark interest in the small community. During the 1920s an area-wide housing boom revitalized Bond Hill's real estate market, and agricultural land was transformed into housing tracts. Population surged,[58] and the Bond Hill Welfare Association was there to champion the interests of the community. The combination of population growth and an increase in membership in the BHWA led the organization to reaffirm its vision and role in the neighborhood. The association sponsored a local newspaper, the *Bond Hill News,* to inform residents about community issues and encourage participation in local affairs. It revisited its constitution and bylaws in 1932 and again in 1936, changing its name to the Bond Hill Civic Association (BHCA) and stressing that its purpose was "to function as a body only for the improvement of existing conditions, and to sponsor and encourage needed improvements, legislation and developments in the interests of Bond Hill primarily, and the City of Cincinnati in general." Committees addressed issues relating to sewers, street lighting, transportation, and the library, as well as entertainment and recreation. During these years the association counted among its important achievements the promotion of the Bloody Run sewer project to lessen area flooding and the establishment of the Bond Hill playground, which the association saw as an example of its commitment to the community's children.[59]

While most of the Association's efforts focused on improving conditions in Bond Hill, and, once the Depression hit, subsidizing efforts to help needy residents or monitoring the success of federal work projects undertaken in the community, the BHWA remained mindful of the larger city and the spirit of cooperation. It lent its support to Federated Civic Association initiatives such as the drive to "save the zoo." Concerned that the indebtedness of the Cincinnati Zoo would result in the city's loss of one of "its chief educational and amusement assets," the FCA rallied its constituent organizations to action. During the early 1930s the FCA's committee to save the zoo generated petitions and introduced resolutions to city council concerning the responsibility of the city to purchase and operate the zoo. The BHWA lent its support to the successful crusade and counted the purchase of the zoo by the city as one of its own achievements. In addition, the BHWA supported the Clifton Heights Welfare Association's interest in Bellevue Hill. The Clifton Heights association requested "the acquisition, by the Board of Park Commissioners of Bellevue Hill, in its entirety, for the purpose of annexation to the Park System of the City of Cincinnati and for the beautification of the barren unsightly slopes of said Bellevue Hill by the implantation of vines or shrubbery in order to rend said Hillside improved."[60] The BHWA believed that this project, while reflecting the desire of Clifton Heights' residents to improve their community, benefited the entire city by providing more park space and enhancing the city's hillside vistas. The BHWA issued a statement of support and saw itself as a partner in overall city development. It believed it had a role to play within both its local community and the city at large, and it acted upon that belief.

While the continued vitality of many neighborhood improvement associations during this period belied the notion that they were no longer catalysts for local activism or necessary agents of change in the years between

1920 and 1940, the emphasis on group, place, and distinctive qualities that informed the 1925 plan and the orientation of local officials toward managing the city promoted the very particularism that comprehensive planning was supposed to negate. The belief that groups, each possessing cultures that defined their particular worlds and whose locational experience shaped behavior, composed basic elements of the urban community highlighted the separatist tendencies inherent in the sorting process that characterized the development of the metropolitan community of the late nineteenth and early twentieth centuries. In the context of the worldview constructed by planners, informed by the insights of the Chicago sociologists, and acted upon by city officials, proper management would foster the necessary tolerance, intergroup respect, and larger civic identification deemed essential for the health of the metropolitan community. However, the emphasis on "distinctive groups," bound by place and manipulated through the use of "segregative planning and social welfare techniques"[61] by planners and city officials, could stimulate or enhance the very parochialism and intolerance this orientation to urban management was believed to counteract.

Not surprisingly, then, this approach, especially when coupled with the perceived need for local activism by neighborhood residents to address unmet needs, encouraged the more protectionist qualities often associated with neighborhood improvement associations. Defined as place-related groups that manifested distinctive ways of life, these neighborhood organizations acted to preserve and protect *their* special areas. Neighborhood improvement associations, ever mindful of their particular community concerns, could and did promote separatism and exclusion as well as integration and cooperation. The experience of the Price Hill Civic and Businessmen's Club illustrates both the integrative and the more protectionist aspects of these local associations during the interwar years.

Price Hill lay to the west of Cincinnati's downtown on the hillside closest to the Ohio River. Cincinnati merchant Evans Price bought up much of the land at the foot of the hill during the early nineteenth century. His son, Rees, subdivided the land and put the lots up for sale. By 1830 a small community existed, nestled along the lower part of the hillside. Rees's son, William, constructed an incline to transport people from the foot of the hill to the top, where they could enjoy a splendid view of the city as well as a number of resort-like amusements, and by the late 1870s the area became known as Price's, or more commonly, Price Hill.

Access to the hilltop stimulated interest in its possibilities for residential development. During the mid-1880s middle-class housing began to dot the hillside. Improved transportation increased with the influx of residents. When at the turn of the century the community located to the west of Price Hill sought annexation to Cincinnati in order to procure improved services, it became known as West Price Hill, and the eastern area associated with the incline, already part of the city, was called East Price Hill. By the 1920s, while increasing population in both sections often blurred the boundaries between the two, East and West Price Hillers saw themselves as separate from one another. A third division of the community, Lower Price Hill, emerged as well. Lower Price Hill was the more industrialized section that had grown up at the foot of the hill, while East and West Price Hill referred to the more residential areas along the upper hillside and hilltop.[62]

Despite the incline and an increase in the number of roads and streetcar lines to service the community, Price Hill residents believed the area lacked sufficient transportation links to Cincinnati's downtown. In the mid-1880s residents organized the Price Hill Improvement Association (PHIA) to push for more and improved transportation connections. Of particular concern was the need for a transportation link that allowed use during inclement weather when the surface lines running from the city through the Mill Creek Valley to the foot of the hill were flooded. Assisted by the Western Hills Improvement Association, drawn from members of various local associations in the western part of Cincinnati, the PHIA successfully pushed for the construction of the Eighth Street viaduct to link the relatively remote community directly to downtown.[63] Finished during the late fall of 1893, the viaduct opened for traffic in December of that year, making "travel to [the] western hills safer, speedier and pleasanter than to any other suburb of Cincinnati."[64]

The PHIA grew less active after the viaduct campaign, and by 1897 another organization, the Price Hill Businessmen's Club, emerged as the organization charged with the general betterment of the area. After a fitful beginning, the organization stabilized by 1915 as the Price Hill Civic and Businessmen's Club (PHC&BC) and stated its purpose as the "mutual benefit of its members [and] the general welfare of Price Hill and Cincinnati." The club joined the Federated Improvement Association in 1917. Publication of the club's newspaper, the *Price Hill Chirper*, began in 1919. PHC&BC focused its activities during the next decade on celebrations and parades, beautification, transportation, parks and playgrounds, streets and highways, and sewers.[65] It emerged as the major voice of the various Price Hill communities.

The club's initiatives and projects during much of the 1920s and 1930s were typical of improvement association activity during this period, as both the Westwood Civic Association and the Bond Hill Welfare Association pursued similar projects in their neighborhoods. The PHC&BC directed much of its attention toward transportation improvements. The club campaigned for new bus lines. It pressured the city to repave and resurface streets. With the help of the Federated Civic Association, it lobbied hard to secure and then monitor the progress of the erection of the Sixth Street viaduct. The organization received requests from other area improvement associations, such as the South Fairmount Improvement

Association, to cooperate on common traffic-related concerns, including the placement of new stop signs and new traffic lights. The club lent its support to local efforts to acquire more recreational space in Price Hill. As did the Bond Hill Welfare Association, the PHC&BC worked to secure and then monitor community projects using Works Progress Administration funds. At the same time, it supported the FCA's initiative to save the zoo and the Clifton Heights Welfare Association's interest in Bellevue Hill.[66]

During the 1930s, the Price Hill Civic and Businessmen's Club[67] exhibited a more protectionist attitude toward its community in addition to its role as champion for local needs and amenities. Like the Westwood Civic Association—which displayed this behavior as early as the late 1920s when it rallied to keep a milk distribution depot out the community and grew concerned about the movement of African Americans as well as those of marginal economic means into Westwood[68]—the PHC&BC attempted to stem the tide of "undesirables"[69] into Price Hill. Stressing the distinctiveness of its community, the Price Hill association argued that others not sharing the qualities that characterized those living on the Hill should be kept out.

Of particular concern to residents of Price Hill by the mid-1930s was the fate of the West End, an impoverished area composed primarily of African Americans that abutted the eastern border of the hill. As industry spread throughout the West End at the end of the nineteenth century, the area had lost its middle- and upper-class residents. Population density increased as the combination of labor needs during World War I and worsening social and economic conditions in the South stimulated a large-scale migration of blacks to northern cities. Cheap housing and job opportunities in the West End made the area an attractive destination for these migrants, and by 1925 approximately 80 percent of the city's African American population resided in this community. Housing conditions deteriorated, the health rate plummeted, crime rates soared, and the community appeared to be bursting at its seams by the 1930s.[70]

If this teeming population were going to spread beyond the boundaries of the West End, those communities with contiguous borders would immediately feel the impact of any spillover. By 1935 the minutes of the Price Hill Civic and Businessmen's Club included discussions of the black population in the West End, with members expressing concern about the possibility of "a Negro population coming up on the Hill." In the minutes for October 1, 1935, members noted the existence of "colored families" residing along the edge of the hill and indicated that they wanted "to forestall any mass migration of Negroes to the Hill." Some of those attending the meeting suggested that the club might want to "try to use moral suasion to keep property owners from renting to Negroes."[71]

When the federal government established programs to put the unemployed back to work as part of the New Deal, slum clearance and the construction of subsidized housing were among the many projects undertaken.

The Cincinnati Metropolitan Housing Authority (CMHA)[72] requested slum clearance and public housing monies from the Public Works Administration in December 1933. While the CMHA did not receive as much support as it desired, it was given enough to begin the process in selected parts of the West End. By 1936 appropriate property had been secured and construction begun on the city's first public housing project, Laurel Homes.[73]

The movement of blacks displaced by the construction of the project increased the population pressure on those communities bordering the West End, including Price Hill. By 1937 the PHC&BC had set up a vigilance committee to monitor the situation. In March of that year it raised questions about the "qualifications" of new families moving into "our neighborhood." It undertook a survey of local housing conditions and found "39 families of undesirables" in Price Hill. The committee assured the members that it saw as its central mission the prevention of such "undesirables" moving to Price Hill. By June the committee also indicated that it planned to double its efforts to "use moral suasion on persons planning to sell their property to undesirable purchasers, especially Negroes" and to watch for signs of "newcomers detrimental to high living standards, such as ha[d] always been the rule on Price Hill."[74]

The club remained concerned about slum clearance and its potential impact on Price Hill until distracted by the outbreak of World War II. Members generated numerous resolutions in favor of continued support from the federal government for slum clearance. Each resolution pointed out the proximity of the West End, almost always referred to as one of Cincinnati's "worst slum infested areas," to the community and called on the "Federal Government" to respond more vigorously to the city's need for public housing. Club members also expressed their opposition to the "'building of any (housing) project in any suburban district.'"[75] The club might want slum clearance and public housing, but not within its borders, for it would draw the very undesirables that caused so much alarm. Although protection was not the only goal of the Price Hill Civic and Businessmen's Club, those active in the organization clearly viewed their community as distinct from the West End and did not wish to share their living space with its residents. While the club might not have been as vigorous as similar groups in other cities in its efforts to keep out "undesirables,"[76] it saw the promotion of exclusion as part of its mandate.

The nation may have been in the grip of a neighborhood organization revolution in the 1960s and 1970s because of the intensity and omnipresence of the organizational frenzy in local communities. Organized activity on the neighborhood level, however, emerged as the "new city" of the late nineteenth century took shape. Residents of suburbs that hovered at the city's edge as well as those living in city neighborhoods organized to attend to the interests of their localities. Whether the emphasis was on social service delivery through settlement houses or campaigns for transportation, beautification, recreational amenities, sewer development, or protection, neighborhood-based organizations attempted to define local needs and translate them into political solutions. At times they worked alone; at other times they cooperated with similar groups across the city on projects that touched multiple communities. Leaders of these organizations saw their groups as building community and as integral players in the encouragement of civic loyalty. The most ubiquitous of these types of organizations, neighborhood improvement associations, appeared at the neighborhood party early and stayed late. They persisted, and in so doing, suggest that neighborhood activism survived even when such activism went out of favor in the years between 1920 and the late 1940s.

Neighborhood improvement associations endured because the communities in which people reside provide an important basis for collective action. As John Davis has argued in a recent study of collective action and the neighborhood, "[p]lace bound 'communities' act—sometimes out of a common interest in improving local safety, services, or amenity; sometimes out of a special interest in protecting local property values; sometimes because not to act is to acquiesce in the community's own destruction." Locality-based action does not necessarily mean that all parties have the same interests; different relationships to and uses of property in any given neighborhood will shape the limits of neighborhood mobilization.[77] The main point, however, is that it is very difficult to ignore the conditions in which one lives or the fact of place. As a result, it is not surprising that these neighborhood organizations persisted, even if they did not seem to fit within the world that the sociologists informed or the planners constructed between 1920 and the 1940s.

In particular, unmet needs on the neighborhood level under a system of managed care maintained local interest in improvement association activity. Some organizations, such as the Westwood Civic Association, became less active in the 1920s and 1930s under the expectation that comprehensive planning would deliver all the necessary improvements. Residents in other neighborhoods, including Bond Hill and Price Hill, believed it was important to remain vigilant and actively pursue the infrastructure needs of their communities. Cooperative activity continued under the aegis of the Federated Civic Association, although it often played a less central role in planning activities and possessed, perhaps, more clout as a civic booster organization. And finally, given the emphasis on homogeneity and group distinctions that guided city planning efforts during the interwar period, it is not surprising that neighborhood protection represents an important legacy of the first comprehensive planning era.

The scholarly community's propensity to see neighborhood organizing as part of progressive movements also has obscured the persistence of neighborhood activism in the years between 1920 and 1950. Those who situate the neighborhood movement's origins between 1890 and 1920, as well as those who place its emergence after either the 1940s or the 1960s, interpret the neighborhood movement only within the dominant two approaches to the study of community organizing, social work and political activist, each of which is perceived as within progressive parameters. Neighborhood improvement associations fall within an approach to the study of community organizing called neighborhood maintenance, which defines the community explicitly in residential terms. According to this approach, members of the upper or middle class, who are usually white, organize in order to fight for better services or to combat threats to property values or neighborhood homogeneity. The organizations are conservative, resisting rather than promoting progressive social action, and represent the dark side of neighborhood activism. If they survive at all, they do so only because their communities have not changed. They are, according to one study, an "anachronism in the neighborhood movement."[78]

However, if we accept the reality of locality-based organization and the fact that neighborhood residents do not always organize around and support progressive issues, we can learn more about the nature of the urban neighborhood. In addition, we can gain a deeper understanding of the public nature of place and what it means within the larger urban structure. And finally, if we better understand the historic neighborhood and how it has changed over time, it will be possible to better assess the state of neighborhood life and its relationship to today's urban community. The neighborhood movement did not drop from heaven in the 1960s or the 1940s or remain in suspended animation between 1920 and 1940. Instead, it grew out of the forces of urban change as well as the efforts of numerous communities to exert control over their environments since the emergence of the modern city in the late nineteenth century.

Notes

I wish to thank Loyola University Chicago for a Research Support Grant that funded part of the research for this essay; the staff of the Cincinnati Historical Society, especially Frances Forman and Anne B. Shepherd, for all their help and support; and my daughter, Grace, for her patience and good spirits during the final research phase of this project. An earlier version of this chapter was presented at the Seminar on the City, Cincinnati Historical Society, on November 9, 1994.

1. Stewart Dill McBride, "A Nation of Neighborhoods," series, *Christian Science Monitor*, September 9, 1977.

2. Milton Kotler, "The Purpose of Neighborhood Planning," *South Atlantic Urban Studies* 4 (1979): 27–31.

3. See, for example, John Clayton Thomas, *Between Citizen and City: Neigh-*

borhood Organizations and Urban Politics in Cincinnati (Lawrence: Univ. Press of Kansas, 1986), 3, and Michael R. Williams, Neighborhood Organizations: Seeds of a New Urban Life (Westport, CT: Greenwood Press, 1985), p. xi.

4. Frances Fox Piven and Richard A. Cloward, Poor People's Movements: Why They Succeed, How They Fail (New York: Pantheon, 1977), p. xiii.

5. Thomas, Between Citizen and City, 20–21, and Williams, Neighborhood Organizations, pp. 8, 72.

6. See, for example, Williams, Neighborhood Organizations, 29–30, 71; Robert Halpern, Rebuilding the Inner City: A History of Neighborhood Initiatives to Address Poverty in the United States (New York: Columbia University Press, 1995), pp. 22–44; Judith Ann Trolander, Professionalism and Social Change: From the Settlement House Movement to Neighborhood Centers, 1886 to the Present (New York: Columbia Univ. Press, 1987), 32–35; and Roy Lubove, The Professional Altruist: The Emergence of Social Work as a Career, 1880–1930 (New York: Atheneum, 1971), pp. 175–80. This analysis overlooks other types of social service delivery and/ or empowerment activities at the local level, such as Cincinnati's Mohawk Brighton Social Unit Organization, although its demise reflects, in part, this shift in professional orientation among neighborhood activists who were involved in social work–related efforts. See Patricia Mooney Melvin, The Organic City: Urban Definition and Neighborhood Organization, 1880–1920 (Lexington: Univ. Press of Kentucky, 1987), pp. 11–26.

7. See Zane L. Miller, "The Role and Concept of Neighborhood in American Cities," in Community Organization for Urban Social Change: A Historical Perspective, ed. Robert Fisher and Peter Romanofsky (Westport, CT: Greenwood Press, 1981), pp. 3–32; Zane L. Miller, "Pluralizing America: Walter Prescott Webb, Chicago School Sociology, and Cultural Regionalism," in Essays on Sunbelt Cities and Recent Urban America, ed. Robert B. Fairbanks and Kathleen Underwood (College Station: Texas A&M Press, 1990), pp. 162–65; Williams, Neighborhood Organizations, pp. 30–31; and John D. Fairfield, The Mysteries of the Great City: The Politics of Urban Design, 1877–1937 (Columbus: Ohio State University Press, 1993).

8. John Emmeus Davis, Contested Ground: Collective Action and the Urban Neighborhood (Ithaca: Cornell University Press, 1991), p. 6.

9. William H. Wilson suggests that neighborhood improvement associations were part of the late-nineteenth-century municipal improvement association movement that culminated in the formation of the American Civic Association. Municipal improvement, as Wilson points out, was a "descriptive yet marvelously elastic word," and it could, and did, mean virtually everything from the preservation of native plants to the construction of sanitary storm sewers. However, Wilson's willingness to collapse neighborhood improvement associations into this larger movement obscures the ways in which these organizations contributed to the city-building process of the early twentieth century. Neighborhood improvement associations sought to combine an interest in local improvements with the desire for citywide civic betterment and, in

a city without a plan, helped to provide direction for the development and improvement of the urban infrastructure. They share similarities to many of the municipal improvement initiatives but also possess many differences. Wilson, *The City Beautiful Movement* (Baltimore: Johns Hopkins University Press, 1989), pp. 35–50. For a discussion of the flaws in Wilson's argument on this issue see Patricia Mooney-Melvin, "Local Improvement Associations and the City-Building Process," paper presented at the New England Historical Association, April 1994.

10. Alexander von Hoffman, *Local Attachments: The Making of an American Urban Neighborhood, 1850 to 1920* (Baltimore: Johns Hopkins University Press, 1994), p. 168.

11. Kotler, "Purpose of Neighborhood Planning," p. 29.

12. See Kenneth A. Scherzer, *The Unbounded Community: Neighborhood Life and Social Structure in New York City, 1830–1875* (Durham: Duke University Press, 1992), for a discussion of a sense of neighborhood before the emergence of the new city of the late nineteenth century. Scherzer finds the existence of neighborhood-like associational identity early in the nineteenth century that ultimately began to acquire a more spatial presence as the century unfolded. For a more detailed explanation of the development of the new city see Melvin, *Organic City*, pp. 11–26, and Patricia Mooney Melvin, "The Neighborhood-City Relationship," in *American Urbanism: A Historiographical Review*, ed. Howard Gillette Jr. and Zane L. Miller (Westport, CT: Greenwood Press, 1987), pp. 257–70. David Schuyler, in *The New Urban Landscape: The Redefinition of City Form in Nineteenth-Century America* (Baltimore: Johns Hopkins University Press, 1986), also argues that a different conception of the city emerged in the late nineteenth century as the city ceased to resemble what Americans believed it to be earlier in the century. Harold L. Platt suggests as well that the process of urbanization in the late nineteenth century involved a "conceptual change" that resulted in the redefinition of the city into metropolitan terms. This redefinition reflected the transformation of urban space from the compact city of the early nineteenth century to the "fragmented patchwork of urban neighborhoods and suburban districts" that characterized the city at the end of the century. Platt, *City Building in the New South: The Growth of Public Services in Houston, Texas, 1830–1910* (Philadelphia: Temple University Press, 1983), pp. 184–208.

13. Cincinnati Bureau of Government Research, *A Survey Defining the Boundaries of the Cincinnati Region*, Report No. 43 (Cincinnati, 1943), pp. 6–8.

14. Joel A. Tarr, "From City to Suburb: The 'Moral' Influence of Transportation Technology," in *American Urban History: An Interpretive Reader With Commentaries*, 2d ed., ed. A. B. Callow (New York: Oxford University Press, 1973), p. 205.

15. See Zane L. Miller, "Boss Cox and the Municipal Reformers: Cincinnati Progressivism, 1880–1914" (Ph.D. diss., University of Chicago, 1966) for a fuller discussion of the Slums, Zone, and Hilltops breakdown for this period.

16. Zane L. Miller, *Boss Cox's Cincinnati: Urban Politics in the Progressive*

Era (New York: Oxford Univ. Press, 1968), pp. 46–55; Bond Hill Civic Association, *1892–1901 Minute Book,* Cincinnati Historical Society; John S. Snyder, "Suburb and Neighborhood: Hyde Park (Cincinnati, Ohio) 1877–1948," (M.A. thesis, University. of Cincinnati, 1981), p. 59; Westwood Improvement Association, *Minute Book,* February 4, 1896, Robert Brodbeck, Collection of Westwood and the Westwood Civic Association, Inc., 1865–1979, Cincinnati Historical Society.

17. Sidney D. Maxwell, *The Suburbs of Cincinnati* (Cincinnati, 1870; rep. New York: Arno Press, 1974), p. 139.

18. Lyle Koehler, *Westwood in Cincinnati: Community, Continuity, and Change* (Cincinnati, 1981), pp. 46–47, 60–62.

19. Hamilton County Research Foundation, *The Story of Annexation* (Cincinnati, 1955), p. 8, and Miller, *Boss Cox's Cincinnati,* pp. 107–8. The vote for annexation was 49,467 for to 4,467 against.

20. Cincinnati, Ohio, *Codification of Ordinances of the City of Cincinnati, 1911,* 8th supplement (Cincinnati, 1918), p. 130.

21. Koehler, *Westwood,* pp. 62, 81.

22. Placard: "Railroad!! Important Meeting for Decisive Action—Westwood, Cheviot and Dent Improvement Association," May 5, 1877, Robert Brodbeck, Collection of Westwood and the Westwood Civic Association, Inc., 1865–1979, Cincinnati Historical Society.

23. Westwood Improvement Association, *Minute Book,* February 4, 1896, and February 2, 1903.

24. Westwood Improvement Association, *Minute Book,* March 29, 1897.

25. State of Ohio, *General and Local Acts Passed and Joint Resolutions Adopted by the General Assembly, 1890* (Columbus), pp. 89–92.

26. West Cincinnati Business Association Company, Westwood Businessmen's Club, Westwood Improvement Association, and North Fairmount Improvement Association, *Opening of the Harrison Street Viaduct Souvenir* (Cincinnati, 1908), Cincinnati Historical Society, and Koehler, *Westwood,* p. 83.

27. West Cincinnati Business Association Company et al., *Opening,* and Koehler, *Westwood,* p. 84.

28. Westwood Improvement Association, *Minute Book,* August 3, 1908.

29. Federated Civic Association, *Thirtieth Anniversary Souvenir and History* (Cincinnati, 1937), p. 31.

30. *Civic News,* October 1911.

31. Ibid.

32. Miller, *Boss Cox's Cincinnati,* pp. 113–14, and Melvin, *Organic City,* pp. 11–26.

33. *Civic News,* February 1912.

34. Miller, *Boss Cox's Cincinnati,* p. 116.

35. In 1911 the WIA merged with the Westwood Businessmen's Club and the organization changed its name to the Westwood Civic Association. Westwood Improvement Association, *Minute Book,* February 11, 1911.

36. *Cincinnati Times-Star,* April 21 and November 17, 1911; January 10, 1912; *Commercial Tribune,* September 29, 1911; *Civic News,* November 1911; and *Twin City Journal,* February 23, 1912.

37. *Federated News,* April 1915.

38. Barbara M. Posadas, "Suburb Into Neighborhood: The Transformation of Urban Identity on Chicago's Periphery—Irving Park as a Case Study," *Journal of the Illinois State Historical Society* 76 (Autumn 1983): 174.

39. Piven and Cloward, *Poor People's Movements,* p. xiii.

40. See Joseph L. Arnold, "The Neighborhood and City Hall: The Origins of Neighborhood Associations in Baltimore, 1880–1911," *Journal of Urban History* 6 (November 1979): 3–30, for a discussion of neighborhood improvement organizations and the federation process in Baltimore.

41. Robert A. Woods, "The City and Its Local Community," in *The Neighborhood in Nation-Building,* ed. Robert A. Woods (Boston: Houghton Mifflin, 1923; rep. New York: Arno Press, 1970), p. 196. See Melvin, *Organic City,* 17–26, and Halpern, *Rebuilding the Inner City,* pp. 29–41, for a more detailed discussion of this issue.

42. Zane L. Miller, *Visions of Place: The City, Neighborhoods, Suburbs, and Cincinnati's Clifton, 1850–2000* (Columbus: Ohio State University Press, 2001), pp. 39–40.

43. These "competent communities" reflected Clarence Perry's notion of what constituted an appropriate neighborhood unit: business district, school, civic center, and recreational facilities. See Howard Gillette Jr., "The Evolution of Neighborhood Planning: From the Progressive Era to the 1949 Housing Act," *Journal of Urban History* 9 (August 1983): 421–44, and Christopher Silver, "Neighborhood Planning in Historical Perspective," *Journal of the American Planning Association* 51 (Spring 1985): 161–74, for a discussion of Perry's ideas about the neighborhood unit and its relationship to interwar city planning.

44. Woods, "The City," p. 196.

45. Harvey W. Zorbaugh, *The Gold Coast and the Slum: A Sociological Study of Chicago's Near North Side* (Chicago: University of Chicago Press, 1929), pp. 221–48.

46. Zane L. Miller and Bruce Tucker, *Changing Plans for American's Inner Cities: Cincinnati's Over-the-Rhine and Twentieth-Century Urbanism* (Columbus: Ohio State University Press, 1998), pp. 13–22; Zane L. Miller and Bruce Tucker, "The Revolt Against Cultural Determinism and the Meaning of Community Action: A View from Cincinnati," *Prospects* 16 (1990): 413–17; and Fairfield, *Mysteries of the Great City,* pp. 158–72. See Louis Wirth, "Urbanism as a Way of Life," *American Journal of Sociology* 44 (July 1938): 1–24, for the most developed articulation of Wirth's views on these issues, and Robert E. Park, "The Urban Community as a Spatial and Moral Order," in *The Urban Community,* ed. Ernest Burgess (Chicago: University of Chicago Press, 1926), pp. 3–11, for Park's discussion of primary and secondary relations.

47. Miller, *Visions of Place,* p. 44.

48. Davis, *Contested Ground*, pp. 6–7.

49. Federated Civic Association, *Annual Souvenir 1907–1926* (Cincinnati: Federated Civic Association, 1926) and *Thirtieth Anniversary Souvenir*, pp. 45–46.

50. By the 1890s the Marietta & Cincinnati Railroad had become part of the Baltimore & Ohio system.

51. Bond Hill was named after an early landowner who operated a sawmill on the property bought by the Cooperative Land and Building Association. Jean Singer, *A Hundred Years Ago . . .* (Cincinnati: Bond Hill Community Council, 1971), p. 2.

52. Geoffrey J. Giglierano and Deborah A. Overmyer, *The Bicentennial Guide to Greater Cincinnati: A Portrait of Two Hundred Years* (Cincinnati: Cincinnati Historical Society, 1988), p. 562.

53. Bond Hill Civic Association, *1829–1901 Minute Book*, 1892–94.

54. Giglierano and Overmyer, *Bicentennial Guide*, p. 562.

55. *Commercial Tribune*, January 20 and 21, 1911.

56. *Commercial Tribune*, March 11–October 28, 1911; *Civic News*, October–November, 1911.

57. *Citizens Bulletin*, February and November, 1916; *The Cincinnati Traction Company Dope Book*, Cincinnati Traction Company Records, 1858–1955, Cincinnati Historical Society; Federated Civic Association, *Thirtieth Anniversary Souvenir*, p. 47.

58. Giglierano and Overmyer, *Bicentennial Guide*, pp. 558–59, 562, and Office of Community Administration, *Bond Hill: Existing Conditions Study and Community Plan* (Cincinnati, 1977), pp. 6–12.

59. Bond Hill Civic Association, *1926–1936 Minute Book*, Cincinnati Historical Society, and Bond Hill Welfare Association, *Souvenir Program Dedicating Bond Hill Play Ground* (Cincinnati, 1935).

60. Bond Hill Civic Association, *1926–1936 Minute Book*; Federated Civic Association, *Thirtieth Anniversary Souvenir*, pp. 48–49, and Clifton Heights Welfare Association, "New Year's Greetings to the Members of the Clifton Heights Welfare Association," 1936–37, Cincinnati Historical Society.

61. Miller and Tucker, *Changing Plans*, pp. 10–13.

62. Giglierano and Overmyer, *Bicentennial Guide*, pp. 138–40.

63. Kelso Murdock and Ralph F. Diserrens, *Price Hill: Its Beauties and Advantages as a Place of Residence* (Cincinnati: Privately published, 1894), pp. 11–12; Cincinnati City Planning Commission, Price Hill Study Group, *Price Hill Existing Conditions Study* (Cincinnati, 1976), p. 9; and *Cincinnati Gazette.* March 6 and 8, 1890.

64. Murdock and Diserrens, *Price Hill*, pp. 5–7.

65. Price Hill Civic Club Papers, 1915–1920, Cincinnati Historical Society, and Federated Civic Association, *Thirtieth Anniversary Souvenir*, p. 63.

66. Price Hill Civic Club Papers, 1920–1940, Cincinnati Historical Society, and Federated Civic Association, *Thirtieth Anniversary Souvenir*, pp. 47, 63–64.

67. The Price Hill Civic and Businessmen's Club changed its name in 1939 to the Price Hill Civic Club.

68. Koehler, *Westwood,* pp. 103–4, 112–13, and *Western Hills Press,* June–July 1927.

69. Price Hill Civic Club Papers, 1930–40.

70. Giglierano and Overmyer, *Bicentennial Guide,* 102–4; Robert B. Fairbanks, *Making Better Citizens: Housing Reform and the Community Development Strategy in Cincinnati, 1890–1960* (Urbana: University of Illinois Press, 1988), pp. 63–75; Davis, *Contested Ground,* pp. 101–9.

71. Price Hill Civic Club Papers, October 1, 1935.

72. Created in the fall of 1933. See Fairbanks, *Making Better Citizens,* 75–88, on the drive to create this organization.

73. Ibid., 91–103, and Davis, *Contested Ground,* pp. 119–20.

74. Price Hill Civic Club Papers, March 3 and June 15, 1937.

75. Price Hill Civic Club Papers, 1938–40.

76. See Silver, "Neighborhood Planning," 164, and William M. Tuttle Jr. *Race Riot: Chicago in the Red Summer of 1919* (New York: Atheneum, 1970), pp. 173–80.

77. Davis, *Contested Ground,* pp. 5–7, 257–58, 307–10.

78. Thomas, Between *Citizen and City,* pp. 3–5, 40; Robert Fisher, *Let the People Decide: Neighborhood Organizing in America* (Boston: Twayne, 1984), pp. 73–75; and Robert Fisher, "'Be on the Lookout': Neighborhood Civic Clubs in Houston," *Houston Review* 6 (1984): 105–6. Fisher's work on neighborhood improvement associations represents one of the few studies to give them much attention as well as see them as an approach to organizing. Williams, *Neighborhood Organizations,* p. 72.

Chapter Six

Playing with Democracy: Municipal Recreation, Community Organizing, and Citizenship

ANDREA TUTTLE KORNBLUH

Today almost every American city, town, and suburb provides its citizens with public recreation centers, and we have come to think of such centers as necessary and highly desirable amenities. Housed in buildings owned by recreation commissions, the centers characteristically provide citizens with low-cost access to facilities such as swimming pools, basketball courts, and gymnasiums. The centers also provide a range of tax-supported organized programs, staffed by recreation professionals. These services range from summer day camps and after-school programs for children to exercise programs for senior citizens.

In the beginning of the recreation movement, "recreation center" referred not so much to a particular kind of physical space but to a particular kind of community organizing designed to actively involve citizens in shaping their communities. In the early days of the movement the "center" was the point from which recreation organizers moved into the community to organize it. Today the provision of public recreation services is a goal in and of itself, but between 1920 and 1950 the provision of recreation provided a vehicle for accomplishing a set of social goals that included racial and gender equity and training in democratic citizenship. During these years municipal governments saw themselves as the bulwarks of democracy. Training citizens in participatory democracy offered a strategy for uniting diverse groups of people, while ideas about an inclusive democracy served as an umbrella protecting the pursuit of a variety of reforms. Programs of training in democratic participation also provided a response to social critics who called for more radical change. An examination of the work of Cincinnati Community Service (1921–26) and the Cincinnati Recreation Commission (1927–50) reveals how recreation advocates took up the task of publicly funded community organizing. Cincinnati's initiatives during this period were not isolated events, but rather expressions of a national recreation movement. Although programs of municipal, tax-supported public recreation have received little attention from historians, there are insights to be gained from an examination of this widespread development.[1]

The leading national recreation organization in the first half of the twentieth century was the National Recreation Association (NRA). Founded in 1906 as the Playground Association of America with President Theodore Roosevelt as honorary president, this organization of social reformers included Luther H. Gulick, Henry Curtis, Jacob Riis, Joseph Lee, Jane Addams, and others in its early days. Rooted in the recreational work of social settlements such as Hull House, the recreation movement grew in the early twentieth century. With funding from the Russell Sage Foundation, the Playground Association of America undertook the organization of a national playground movement. The group changed its name to the Playground and Recreation Association of America in 1911, indicating the expansion of its interest from children's playgrounds to recreation facilities for youth and adults. According to NRA historian George Butler, the association's "emphasis upon the responsibility of the municipality to provide playgrounds and recreation centers helped to bring a general acceptance of the idea of public support." During World War I the Playground Association organized War Camp Community Service, which after the war reinvented itself as Community Service. In 1930 the organization became the National Recreation Association. The NRA employed field workers who traveled from city to city, meeting with recreation advocates and public officials and assisting in the creation of playgrounds and recreation programs. Through its various staff organizations, such as the Colored Workers Division, the NRA established connections among recreation workers across the country. Additionally, the NRA provided the recreation community with a variety of publications, including a monthly magazine to which staff members from around the country contributed articles.[2]

The NRA, while providing leadership for the public recreation movement, was not officially affiliated with any level of government. Recreation advocates, who enthusiastically endorsed programs of municipal public recreation, opposed any suggestions for formal federal government involvement in recreation. NRA supporters issued frequent declarations, especially in the 1930s and '40s, about the dangers of a national recreation program. National programs like those of Italy and Germany appeared to be undemocratic and unresponsive to the particular needs of local communities. Yet the NRA worked closely with the federal government during both world wars and actively sought connections with various New Deal programs such as the National Youth Administration (NYA) and the Works Progress Administration (WPA). Recreation advocates were willing to allow the federal programs to provide staff and funds for the expansion of recreation activities, but insisted that the direction of the work was to be determined by local communities. During the 1920s, '30s and '40s the NRA saw the local community as the only legitimate public body empowered to make decisions about recreation. Recreation advocates thought that democratic recreation programs rested on a close connection to local communities and citizens.

Public recreation's dramatic growth in the years after World War I can be attributed, in part, to a concern, widespread in the years between 1920 and 1950, about the future of liberal democracy in an uncertain political world. In those years Italian Fascists, German National Socialists, and Soviet Communists all used programs for the leisure-time activities of citizens to build support for the state and its ideology. The national movement for recreation in the United States, however, took the decentralized form of local organizing for democratic public recreation. The programs of athletics, music, drama, handcrafts, and community organizing provided countless Americans with an introduction to liberal ideas about democratic practice, racial and religious tolerance, gender equity, the role of government, and a communal sensibility that saw all citizens, despite the differences among them, as parts of a larger whole. Public recreation might be viewed as a massive program of cultural organizing that sought to shape an American culture comprised of diverse peoples and united by common beliefs and practices. Like its better-understood sister movement—city planning—which flourished in the same years, public recreation sought to structure the city. Both city planning and public recreation defined their tasks comprehensively and took as their project the whole city. Both assumed the city to be diverse. And both city planners and public recreation leaders thought that citizens needed the help of professionals in organizing the city. But rather than concentrating on the physical structure of the city, public recreation professionals sought to create a human relations infrastructure.

Americans interested in democracy in the early twentieth century began to see it as rooted in a particular kind of activity done in a special type of social and geographic space—a "social center." Reform-minded Americans such as Edward J. Ward, a University of Wisconsin expert in civic and social center development, called for the creation of a social center in every neighborhood. What Americans needed, Ward thought, was something akin to pure democracy as characterized by the New England town meeting. The social center plan called for the development of "a center of recreation, artistic, dramatic and musical expression, a local health office, employment bureau, and so on, as well as a center of democratic expression."[3]

Recreation advocates of the early twentieth century often saw democracy as linked to leisure and sought to find meaning and communal experience in the part of daily life that remained after meeting the commitments of work and family. Used in the right way, recreation reformers thought, leisure time served as an essential step in building democracy, since both involved a problem of choice and the exercise of freedom. Organized recreation provided, in a communal manner, freely chosen leisure-time activities for citizens. Recreation offered the best laboratory for the practice of democratic choice. This connection between leisure and democracy helps to explain why public recreation become so popular in the first half of the twentieth century. Tam Deering, who served as Cincinnati's director of public recreation in the 1930s and '40s, thought that citizenship became real through participation in neighborhood affairs. Citizens, he declared, "must be given some local responsibility of a tangible nature." He advocated the creation of a "neighborhood civic center" that would combine the school, branch library, and neighborhood park into "the ideal type of recreation center."[4]

The success of the neighborhood civic center, according to Deering, depended upon complete democracy, and the center needed to "provide an atmosphere, an attitude, a motive, conducive to the growth of a broad democratic spirit." Deering declared: "No individual, class or clique, no political brand of political or economic opinion can dominate it." In a successful center, Deering noted, "Everyone must be made to feel at home." Leaders needed to do more than direct the activities of the center; they needed to be community organizers "in whose minds and hearts the community exists." The aim of the leaders, Deering cautioned, "must not be to put over something, but to help each person or group to get access to the opportunity to express creatively what he or they have to express." The neighborhood civic center, he suggested, might well be the center for all social, recreational and educational activities of a community nature. Here neighborhood people of every age might recreate together and adults could discuss "their common neighborhood problems, including local improvements, educational, political, industrial, health and other matters."[5]

In the 1920s thousands of cities and towns across America created new municipal programs of tax-supported public recreation.[6] Unlike earlier public and private programs concerned with leisure activities, these new projects characteristically sought to serve all the citizens of the community—young and old, black and white, immigrant and native, male and female, city dwellers and suburbanites, poor and not-poor—and assumed that all citizens shared basic recreational needs that the local government had a responsibility to provide. Recreation advocates sought to provide specific programs for a variety of different groups of citizens, who were each assumed to have specific recreational needs. But programs of public recreation, based on a newly perceived need for municipalities to provide structured leisure-time activities for citizens, served a purpose larger than the satisfaction of individual needs. Recreational programs offered citizens a wide range of leisure-time facilities and expert recreation leaders; the programs also provided citizens with practical training in democracy.

This democracy of the 1920s differed in several significant ways from that of the earlier twentieth century. First, it was a democracy of open participation, rather than one of open political debate. This vision of democracy rested on the assumption that all citizens—black as well as white, female as well as male—needed to be involved, and that the success of democracy might be judged on how well the diverse citizens became part of the democratic system. In Cincinnati and across the country, public recreation sought to be comprehensive—to serve all citizens. The diverse characteristics mentioned were no longer differences of ideology, but physical differences—age, color, sex. For want of a better term, this might be called "partaker democracy." By the 1920s recreation advocates thought that the big political question had been settled—the United States was a liberal democracy, not a socialist or a fascist state. But for the United States to be a truly democratic community it would have to provide opportunities for all citizens and teach them how to get along and how to put the interests of the whole before those of the individual. Recreation advocates did not think they began with natural communities of people—they thought the community had to be built by citizens working and playing together.

Cincinnati Community Service (CCS), the predecessor to the Cincinnati Public Recreation Commission, began work during the First World War as part of the National Recreation Association's campaign to build local support for the war effort. Originally concerned with recreation for soldiers, CCS quickly expanded its work to include civilians. Once the war was over recreation advocates in Cincinnati, as in many other cities, converted War Camp Community Service into a new organization—Community Service, an agency supported by the Cincinnati Community Chest.

From the first year (1921) school-based community centers played a key role in the work of Cincinnati Community Service. The Cincinnati Board of Education had created a number of school-based social centers in the teens. Such centers appeared across the country in those years and constituted, Kevin Mattson has claimed, "the most important attempt to create a democratic public during the Progressive Era." In the early 1920s CCS took over responsibility for the centers and decided that successful centers would be both self-governing and partially self-supporting. For the first CCS center, Dyer School in the West End, CCS soon developed "a real spirit of community interest and co-operation." Based on that success, CCS took over direction of the community center programs at three more schools. Significantly, Community Service did not concentrate its effort on problem neighborhoods in the basin, but rather on geographically dispersed neighborhoods that were not in social or economic crisis but still seemed to suffer from a pervasive lack of "community," that is, a lack of coherent neighborliness and unity.[7]

CCS sought to provide a program that would allow the community to work together to solve common problems. Recreation leaders often described their program as comprehensive—designed to serve all the varied members of the community. But service for all was not organized in the same way. To serve black Cincinnatians CCS added a Department of Negro Recreation in 1922. This department combined in one unit all the recreation work done with Afro-Americans. Recreation organizing—in playgrounds, athletics, drama, music, and community centers serving the black community—was centralized in this CCS department.[8]

By 1926, in spite of the success of the privately funded Community Service program, or perhaps because of it, civic activists and social workers had come to the conclusion that the city needed a public recreation commission. Advocates of public recreation, led by Cincinnati Community Service, staffed a speakers bureau and conducted an educational campaign to prepare the public to endorse changes in the city charter, which would make a recreation commission possible. The park board, the board of education, and ninety-one other "Civic, Social, Patriotic, Fraternal and Religious" organizations passed resolutions supporting the creation of a municipal recreation body, and Cincinnati City Council unanimously passed an ordinance creating a Public Recreation Commission in May 1926. A successful campaign for a recreation levy allowed the city to inaugurate a recreation program in February 1927.[9]

The new Public Recreation Commission (PRC) divided its work into four departments, each headed by a supervisor: Municipal Athletics, Playgrounds and Playstreets, Negro Recreation, and Community Activities. The names suggest clearer functional divisions than existed and hide the fact that the basic organizing units were based not only on race but on age and sex. Municipal Athletics for example, served young white men. Playgrounds and Playstreets served white children. Community Activities covered white communities, including citizens of all ages and sexes, and women's and girls' work, as well as athletics, drama, storytelling, dance, and festivals. Negro Recreation handled all activities for Afro-Americans.

Negro Recreation, headed by Olympic star William DeHart Hubbard, and Community Activities, under the leadership of Mabel Vera Madden, formed the heart of the PRC's community organizing program. For the PRC, Afro-Americans and women and girls appeared to be particular sectors of the population in need of organization and of inclusion in the larger society. Hubbard led the work from 1927 until 1941, and Madden's term as supervisor lasted from 1929 to 1941. Both played crucial, formative roles in the work of the commission and in the vision of community organizing it adopted. Both Madden and Hubbard were recreation professionals, recognized on the national as well as the local level, and each participated in the national recreation movement. Each recorded detailed annual assessments of their work in community organizing. For both, the goal of community organizing was the creation of a group of self-governing citizens who actively created and pursued recreational programs. Both Madden and Hubbard used recreational issues as a tool for organizing the leadership of the Cincinnati community into interest groups promoting the cause of Afro-Americans and girls and women. And both Madden and Hubbard thought that for communities to be organized an outside expert—the PRC organizer—was necessary. Through a comparison of their careers and the work of their departments, a picture of recreational community organizing can be drawn.

In its first years of work, the PRC Department of Community Activities continued the CCS program of self-governing and partially self-supporting community centers in Cincinnati's public schools. The board of education provided school buildings for center use, asking only that the commission pay for light and heat charges on weekends. The commission provided an executive secretary to staff the white centers; DeHart Hubbard served in this role for the Afro-American centers. PRC community organizers such as Hubbard saw their task as not simply providing recreational opportunities, but as building democracy. "It is the belief of the Public Recreation Commission," wrote the director of PRC Community Activities in 1927, "that Democracy cannot be expected to seep down from governmental agencies, but that the science of learning and the practice of the art of living must be fostered in the smallest local community unit." That unit was the public schoolhouse. "[O]wned in common by all the people, the one building where all citizens have equal rights and may feel equally at home, the ultimate unit of democracy in every community, [it] is the one building that can be made the community home, club or capital." Using the school building for activities including "all the people of the community" would lead to "a better understanding between clashing constituent elements." Community center workers thus did not assume they served a hegemonic community, but rather that the center itself could help to create community out of disparate elements.[10]

For Hubbard, Cincinnati's black community was not monolithic but diverse. In choosing Hubbard to head its Department of Colored Work, the PRC selected one of the world's leading athletes, an honors graduate of the University of Michigan, an ardent supporter of social work, and a man with deep roots in Cincinnati's Afro-American community. Hubbard's centers served Cincinnati's segregated black community. Black citizens comprised about 7.5 percent of the city's population of 401,207 in 1920. Migration from the South had increased dramatically after 1915, and black Cincinnatians increasingly concentrated in one geographic area—the West End. By 1920, 57.2 percent of Afro-Americans lived in the West End; Walnut Hills held the next largest concentration of black residents. In these years black sociologist and social worker James Hathaway Robinson described Cincinnati as having "a southern racial relationship." Blacks, he said, faced discrimination in employment and in amusements. Blacks were not served in hotels, restaurants, and soda fountains, not admitted to movie theaters or private parks, or when admitted to theaters were segregated. In response to the increased migration, to the growth of segregation, and to an increased sense of group identity in the early 1920s, a number of separate black institutions developed in Cincinnati. Jennie Porter's Harriet Beecher Stowe School, an all-black public school in the West End, enrolled two thousand students by 1923. Artie Mathews, a classical ragtime pianist, founded the Cosmopolitan School of Music, a West End institution dedicated to the perpetuation and advancement of Negro art and music. Black musicians formed the Musicians Union of Cincinnati, Local 814. Mercy Hospital, designed to provide staff positions for black nurses and physicians, opened its doors in the West End. The Negro Civic Welfare Association, a predecessor to the Urban League, joined the city's Council of Social Agencies. The Public Recreation Commission, by establishing a Department of Colored Work, explicitly recognized that black citizens were part of the community, provided opportunities for black citizens and recreation leaders, and helped to create a growing racial segregation in the city.[11]

Two community centers for Afro-Americans were housed in Stowe (West End) and Douglass (Walnut Hills) public elementary schools and served what Hubbard referred to as the "predominantly colored districts." Under Hubbard's leadership these centers offered programs similar to those of the white centers—gym classes, swimming, indoor sports, dramatics, and choral and cultural activities. Total participation in indoor activities in 1928 totaled 12,982 people; outdoor participation in the playground, tennis, and baseball programs, including spectators, totaled 161,182. At this time Hubbard estimated the total black population to be 35,000 persons, so on average Hubbard's department served each member of the black community five times.[12]

Mabel Vera Madden, a child of working-class immigrants raised in a female-headed family, became the head of the newly renamed Department of Community Activities and Girls Work in 1929. In her first report on the department's work Madden stressed the "increased participation and interest of young business and industrial women in games and sports." Much of the work of her department, she noted, "has been experimental and of a pioneering nature." Perhaps not surprisingly, her interest and innovations centered on a new area—girls' work—rather than on the ongoing community center work, which was a continuation of the decade-long, school-based social center movement and took as its task the organization of all residents of the neighborhood. Or perhaps to Madden, as to Mary Beard and others, girls and women simply seemed to be the heart of the community.[13]

The PRC operated seven (white) self-governing and partially self-supporting school-based community centers in 1928: Hartwell, Kennedy-Silverton, Madisonville, Northside, Sands, South Cumminsville, and Windsor. The centers organized six dramatic groups and four orchestral groups. For children, Madden's department organized Boy Scout and Girl Scout troops, folk dancing classes, and play hours. At Hartwell Community Center, Madden announced, "the manual training class has been opened to women," suggesting the PRC saw women's roles as more than simply traditional.[14]

Madden called the community center movement in Cincinnati "an experiment in democracy" since the recreation commission sought "to afford the citizens of a given community an opportunity to work out in a small unit the method through which individuals and groups with nothing in common except the welfare of the youth of the community may work together to meet a common need." For Madden, the success of the centers was "in direct proportion to the amount of time and effort" expended by each center's volunteer board of directors. Residents of each community, elected by popular vote, formed a board and governed each community center. Madden praised those who served with the various boards. They made, she said, "unselfish and untiring efforts." In many cases neighborhood residents looked to these board members "for advice and guidance," and the boards "accepted the responsibility of providing wholesome, recreational activities for all the people in their neighborhood."[15]

Community organizing was not without problems. Sometimes the elected community center boards faced "neighborhood conditions beyond their control." Although Sands (a white school in the city's West End) had been home to one of the city's most successful community centers for the previous ten years, "the constantly changing population in the West End of the City" made it "impossible to conduct continuous activities," and the center closed. Madden's concerns about neighborhood organizing grew beyond that of organizing for a constantly changing population; by the end of the 1920s she expressed doubts about the whole project of neighborhood community centers. Private ownership of automobiles, public transportation, the telephone, and the radio, she reported, "have greatly increased the social horizon of people." Until recently, people had been "forced to remain in their own community to enjoy with their own immediate neighbors practically all their recreational activities." Now things had begun to change. "Interest groupings," Madden said, "are coming more and more to displace the old cohesive neighborhood groupings." For public recreation to be of "continuing service to the people," Madden suggested that its program must be adapted to changing needs. "People do not seem as vitally interested in purely neighborhood groups as in the past," she reported. "They now seek for recreation where they meet larger groups, even though they must travel a greater distance from their homes." She suggested the commission try concentrating many activities "in one or two down-town locations."[16]

Racial segregation and limited recreation activities for the black community pushed Hubbard to move beyond the school-based centers, while the "expanded social horizon" of white citizens caused Madden to think that these centers were no longer the best method for organizing. Although they arrived from different directions, by the early 1930s both Hubbard and Madden had decided that interest-based organizing would be the most useful form of community organizing for the PRC to undertake. Hubbard would spend the next decade organizing Cincinnati's black citizens, while Madden turned her attention to women and girls.

Hubbard sought to use recreation to organize the entire Afro-American community. Working with the Negro Civic Welfare Association, in 1929 Hubbard began work to organize a "Recreation Council of leading citizens" to help "promote recreation among the colored people." Such a council, Hubbard hoped, would help ensure that "all classes and groups of people will be reached, and the program really become all-inclusive." In his 1930 report Hubbard suggested that a recreation survey and "organization of the citizens by the representative of the National Recreation Association" be done as soon as possible. "There is," he noted, "an awakening recreation consciousness among the leaders of the Colored people and the coming of a National worker will have a much more stimulating and beneficial effect than could be achieved by any local agency."[17]

But the black community was divided, and Hubbard failed to enlist the support of significant individuals, including Jennie Porter, principal of the Stowe School in the West End, who refused to work with the PRC.[18] Hubbard tried again in 1932 to create a citywide organization of influential black citizens in support of public recreation; this time he had help from both the new director of public recreation and the National Recreation Association. In March 1932, the Colored Workers of the NRA held a conference in Cincinnati. At the conclusion of the conference Ernest T. Attwell, NRA field secretary for "colored work," work stayed in Cincinnati to organize and analyze a community survey of the recreational opportunities available to black Cincinnatians. The survey provided an outside expert's assessment of the recreational needs of the entire black community and served as an important tool for improving black public recreation. Attwell's visit demonstrated that recreation leaders on both the local and the national level had made a national priority of organizing black citizens. In Cincinnati Tam Deering, who became director of recreation early in 1932, had as one of his first concerns the development of work in the black community.[19]

The leaders of the newly organized Citizens' Recreation Council of Cincinnati, Ohio (W. N. Lovelace, R. P. McClain, M.D., and Hazel Jean Lucas), wrote to the NRA expressing their appreciation for Attwell's work. "Words fail to express the appreciation of our citizens of Cincinnati for the inestimable service rendered us by your Mr. E. T. Attwell," they wrote. His "devoted and untiring efforts won for him the gratitude and friendships of all our forward thinking people." His visit "gained countless new allies to the cause of Public Recreation" and had been instrumental in the organization of the Citizens' Recreation Council, which was "already making itself felt in the recreation life of the city." The new Cincinnati group "earnestly and sincerely" thanked the NRA for Attwell's visit and promised "our cooperation upon any visit to our city in the future."[20] The following year, 1933, Hubbard established three new recreation centers that were projects of the community center committee of the Citizens' Recreation Council.

In his annual reports Hubbard discussed the problems his department faced as a result of the racial situation in the city and suggested how recreational community organizing offered a solution. The "masses of the Negro citizens of this city," he said, constituted a group that was "marginal, socially and economically." Black citizens lived in the oldest houses in the city, in the most congested neighborhoods, "with the basest fraction of modern conveniences," and a severe lack of open public space. In the congested black neighborhoods the death rate was 22 per thousand, compared with 15.7 per thousand for the city as a whole. "Crime and delinquency, the by-product of unfavorable health, housing and recreational opportunities, showed an even greater disproportion detrimental to the Negro group," Hubbard declared. "Fortunately, we are possessed of a Recreation Commission, a Recreation Director, and a group of recreationally minded citizens in the form of a Citizens' Recreation Council, who appreciate this problem, and who are making every effort to help improve conditions, through a recreation program that will, in the end, closely approach the adequate." Although impatient with the "seemingly slow progress toward their ultimate solution," Hubbard said, "large strides forward have been made." Public recreation, he believed, clearly offered a route to racial equity.[21]

With the assistance of the Citizens' Recreation Council a new recreation center opened in the West End. The C&O Center, a building with a large number of rooms well-suited for community use, allowed the Department of Colored Work to place even more emphasis on community organization. The C&O Center had originally been a railroad building, on land belonging to the C&O Railroad, and was located near the new Union Terminal. The recreation commission brought a special community organizer, Ethel R. Clark, from San Francisco to Cincinnati to head the C&O project. Her goal was "the integration of the constituent part of this community" and "the creation of a common interest in the common welfare through the instrument of recreation."[22]

Hubbard saw his department's community organizing as building democracy. "Nazi Germany, Fascist Italy, and Communistic Russia," Hubbard wrote in 1935, "are setting a goal for the United States in extending the benefits of recreation." "Each of these countries," he continued, "is enforcing positive measures that bring the individual to recreation rather than waiting for the individual to find his own way to an avocation." "America," Hubbard declared, "does it differently." Democratic Americans, unlike totalitarians, allowed citizens to plan and organize their own recreation. In 1936 the name of Hubbard's department changed from the Department of Colored Work to the Division of Work with Colored Citizens, another indication of the idea that recreation provided training for democracy and citizenship and the importance of involving black Cincinnatians in that training. As NRA secretary Howard Braucher declared in 1936, "To us active participation in our government, national, state and local, or at least the right to so participate, is part of abundant living, a form of recreation if you will." "Something is taken away from us," Braucher continued, "we are no longer complete, fully members, if we don't participate." Self-training for democracy thus constituted a key task of recreation workers. As Braucher declared in 1936, "The recreation movement has a vital part to perform in buttressing democracy. . . . its methods should be those that build democracy."[23]

Although Braucher, Hubbard, and other American recreation advocates often pointed to the difference between top-down national recreation programs common in fascist countries and the grass-roots, community-based model of the NRA, public recreation programs in the United States benefited greatly from New Deal programs such as the National Youth Administration and the Works Progress Administration. These programs provided funds for both recreational staff and laborers to construct facilities. As was characteristic of New Deal programs, the decisions about how to use the federal assistance provided to recreation agencies were left to local public recreation bodies. Federal assistance allowed Hubbard's department to conduct its first year-round program in 1936. Additional staff, 79 people provided by the WPA and 110 funded by the NYA, allowed the department to achieve record attendance levels: 518,266 citizens.[24]

The NYA and WPA staff were crucial to the extension of community organizing, but the PRC continued to depend heavily on the efforts of volunteer groups. A volunteer dance board, composed of young people— including many university students—organized weekly dances. The board had full responsibility for the dances, both financing the events and monitoring the conduct of the dancers, who were neighborhood residents between the ages of sixteen and twenty-six. The Race Relations Committee of the Woman's City Club outfitted a smoking lounge in the basement of the C&O Center. The Committee on Children's Dramatics, a group composed of mothers from the immediate neighborhood of the center, financed the cost of all the materials used in the children's plays. The outreach work of the center formed a basic part of the program; community organizing led the list of Ethel R. Clark's goals for 1937.[25]

Hubbard's division reported progress in democratic organizing. Sinton Park, for example, had developed a "democratic playground government" led by the Playground Youth Council, "a group of children who assisted with discipline and the promotion of the playground program." The Douglass School Center had a "very able Community Center Council." The experimental C&O Center continued its program to help the PRC study "the possibility of creating more closely knit communities through recreation programs." Hubbard thought that the finest achievement of the year was the construction of an old-fashioned barbecue pit. Built by a group of neighborhood men, the pit construction at the C&O Center demonstrated a new level of commitment to the center by neighborhood residents.[26]

DeHart Hubbard left the PRC to work with the Cincinnati Metropolitan Housing Authority and Valley Homes in 1941; Ethel R. Clark took over his position as head of the Division of Work with Colored Citizens. Hubbard's departure happened at a time when the C&O Center, the heart of the community organizing effort, faced a major crisis. The center had been created on land belonging to the Chesapeake and Ohio Railroad Company. In 1941 the railroad erected a dirt-filled spur track across the center's play area, making the grounds "totally unsuitable for adults during the entire summer." Other centers suffered as well. The community center at Douglass School was discontinued due to "inadequate staff and shortage of funds with which to employ capable personnel." The curtailment of the WPA program in 1942 resulted in cutbacks in the PRC program. At the same time, PRC civil service workers left the city agency for the armed forces and work in the defense industries.[27]

Still Clark found success in her division's community organizing program. "One of the finest evidences of awakened social consciousness at our largest basin play area," she reported in 1942, "was a petition, initiated by parents themselves, requesting that traffic control devices be set up for the protection of children and other pedestrians in the vicinity of the C&O Playground on Fourth Street." Since one of the major goals of the playleaders had been "acceptance of social responsibility by that community," the community-initiated petition "spoke volumes." The community organized itself, and city council responded to its demands: a city traffic study resulted in the painting of a pedestrian walk, the erection of crosswalk signs, the elimination of parking, the creation of a speed check zone, and the painting of a double white city line.[28]

The most significant program Madden developed was the annual city-wide Girls' Week, which she initiated in 1930 and which continued, although in changed form, until 1977. Just as Hubbard had organized an advisory council of prominent black citizens to aid him in his work, so Madden created a community-wide organization to support her efforts for Girls' Week. The Girls' Week Advisory Council consisted of a fifteen-member volunteer agency comprised of prominent women, and it provided a forum for networking among women's organizations as well as support for girls' recreation. This group provided an opportunity for women of various organizations to jointly pursue issues related to their interests.[29]

Madden followed the NRA guidelines for organizing women's and girls' work suggested by NRA field secretary Ethel Bowers. The NRA viewed work with girls as a crucial area and organized regular discussions of the topic at its annual conventions. Bowers suggested calling together "a group of influential and intelligent lay women" and presenting them with the problem of how best to "promote the interests of women and girls." Madden recruited the following women's groups to participate: the Federation of Mothers' Clubs, the Business Women's Club, the Catholic Women's Club, the Rockdale Avenue Temple Sisterhood, the Woman's Rotary Club, the Council of Jewish Women, St. William's PTA, B'nai B'rith, the Junior Business Women's Club, the Catholic PTA Federation, St. Mary's Mother's Club, Woman's City Club, Daughters of Isabella, Virginia Asher Hamilton County PTA, Cincinnati Teachers Association, the Girl Scouts, the Campfire Girls, and the Girl Reserves.[30]

Madden saw her work as a possible national model and reported on Girls' Week in an article in *Recreation* in 1933. Girls' Week, she said, drew its inspiration from the already existing national program of Boys' Week. Madden believed that while boys had plenty of recreational activities, girls enjoyed only a few, and those were provided by private agencies. Cincinnati women were not immediately responsive to her invitation when she asked prominent citizens to sit on the first Girls' Week Advisory Council in 1930; but they soon warmed to the task. The objective of Girls' Week, as described in the original announcement in 1933, read as follows: "To concentrate attention of the people of the city on the various activities of girls; to point out to the citizens how it is possible for them to make the lives of girls bigger, finer and more useful, and to demonstrate to the girls how it is possible to lead these finer, more interesting and more useful lives." The program called for each day of the week to be dedicated to a particular theme.[31]

Monday, for example, addressed "The Girl and her Health," and the Women's Medical Association conducted physical examinations for girls in the high school. A good posture competition was held, and each high school had a display titled "The American Girl's Beauty Products." But rather than lipstick or powder, the display, arranged on a vanity table, featured carrots, milk, tomatoes, and other healthy foods. On Tuesday the "Girl and her Work" program, sponsored by the Business and Professional Women's Club, provided girls with information on various occupations. All high school and eighth-grade girls in the city received bulletins containing reference material on vocations, including educational requirements and salary schedules.[32]

Girls' Week celebrated both civic responsibility and the development of domestic skills. Wednesday's theme was "The Girl and Her City," and the day was titled "Civic Responsibility Day." On this day in 1933 four hundred girls, drawn from ninety-six schools, both public and parochial, met and worked with various civic and governmental officials. "All important civic and governmental positions," Madden noted, "were filled by girls."

The "Girl and Her Home" committee chose to celebrate that theme on Thursday by holding a hobby fair in which more than two thousand girls exhibited their hobbies. The work, as cataloged by Madden, included "embroidery, art work, tie and dye, original music compositions, poetry, short stories, photography, dolls, collections, flowers, lamps, sewing . . . [and] pies, cakes, candies, and many other delicacies." Hobbies were viewed by the fair's organizing committee as aiding in the social achievements of girls by "stimulating the feeling of individual achievement" and building friendship among girls with common interests, as well as "providing an escape from mechanical routine."[33]

Schoolgirls, working girls, and girls living in institutions such as orphanages were all included in Girls' Week festivities. To mark "The Girl and Her Recreation" on Friday, five hundred high school girls attended athletic play days and girls working in industry had a supper and an athletic play night. Mothers and daughters attended a joint luncheon in their honor on Saturday. For this event unmarried women and married women without their own daughters "were urged to adopt for this occasion girls living in the orphanages and other institutions." To celebrate the "Girl and Her Church" on Sunday, the committee requested that "every minister, rabbi and priest in the city" devote his sermon to "some subject connected with problems of girls."[34]

The Public Recreation Commission, Madden reported to readers of *Recreation*, sponsored Girls' Week "in cooperation with all the public and private organizations in the city interested in the welfare of girls." The funding for Girls' Week, she noted, "came exclusively from women and women's organizations." Although the actual events took only seven days, Girls' Week organizers saw the week as "the climax of a year's work in the interest of girls." Civic Responsibility Day, for example, was valuable since it gave girls "a general idea of the complex problems in government." Madden's program seemed to be having success in this area, for one girl who spent a day in the traffic department commented, "I think I have received a picture of the city as a whole and in the future when anything goes wrong in our neighborhood or on our street, I will remember we are just a very small part, and instead of complaining I will try to help." The sponsors of Girls' Week, Madden declared, "tried to awaken in the girls the idea that every citizen is responsible for the good government of the city and efficiency or inefficiency in government depends, in the last analysis, on the watchfulness or indifference of the individual voter."[35]

If Girls' Week sought to make girls better citizens, it also provided a way to organize women. In a report on the 1938 Girls' Week Madden explained that its significance lay in the fact that the work "refutes the old saws about women being jealous of each other, about women not being able to work together, and not being able to take orders from one another. . . . [T]he good humor, the sportsmanship and the willingness of everyone to subject her interest and ideas to the common good, that is, the best interest of the girls of the city, has been a real inspiration to me."[36] To Madden, the differences among women could be overcome when they joined together in pursuit of a larger goal.

By the late 1940s the vision of democracy promoted by Girls' Week began to change in form. In the area of race relations, for example, the work moved from the inclusion of groups of black girls in citywide events to racial integration. The Girls' Week Advisory Council decided to turn over the actual running of Girls' Week to girls. This trend toward gradually transferring the responsibility for the activities to girls themselves first appeared in the early 1940s. By the late 1940s the toastmistress of the Mothers-Daughters Luncheon was a student chosen by the girls, committee reports at the luncheon were given by the girl members of the committees, and girls themselves furnished the entertainment. Perhaps most notably, by the 1950s the girls of Girls' Week had begun to talk openly about prejudice and discrimination against women. For the "Girl and Her City" day in 1956 Cincinnati High School girls "shouldered the city fathers out of the way and took over the helm of this thriving metropolis." Doreen Spackman, a senior at Western Hills High School, served as mayor for the day. The *Cincinnati Post* (in an article by a girl reporter specially selected to cover Girls' Week) quoted Spackman as declaring: "From now on I want to hear people say her honor instead of his honor when they talk of the mayor . . . and I want to see women governors, senators, ambassadors—and women presidents." "It is just prejudice now," she continued, "that holds women back from many of these political offices." Spackman, the *Post* reporter noted, received more first-choice votes than any previous girl mayor candidate.[37] A different era had begun.

There are few physical artifacts of the community organizing work conducted by the Public Recreation Commission in the years from 1920 to 1950. The ubiquitous centers, which we have come to associate with public recreation, came into existence in the 1950s in the post-World War II wave of recreation construction. By then recreation centers had become places individuals went for leisure-time activities—not centers from which professional organizers went out into the community. But the earlier work laid the basis for continued community support of the public leisure-time infrastructure that we now enjoy. And the organizing efforts of recreation professionals shaped the human interactions of the city for years to come.

Recreation organizers such as Hubbard and Madden saw their task as providing more than individual leisure-time activities; they were creating active citizens, partakers in democracy. Recreation advocates saw democracy as being based among the people at the grass-roots level. In the words of Tam Deering, the people need the assistance of experts "in whose hearts and minds the community exists." But Madden and Hubbard never doubted that citizens had the potential to become players in the game of democracy, and they carefully monitored, recorded, and promoted those examples of citizen activism that came out of recreational organizing.

American public recreation advocates in the years from 1920 to 1950 were acutely conscious of the world situation, the role of democracy internationally, and the connection of recreation to the nation state. They thought they had developed an approach to recreation that promoted democracy independently of the state. Aided by the National Recreation Association and New Deal programs, recreational organizers worked at the grass-roots level. Local training in citizenship, provided through recreation programs, might use government resources, but they were not top-down organizations. Instead, recreation programs used local organizing to allow groups of citizens to choose their own leisure-time activities. And this choice, this partaking, seemed to be a crucial part of democratic training.

Hubbard and Madden took as their tasks integrating into the civic landscape those Cincinnatians previously left behind—Afro-Americans and women and girls. The results of the efforts to shape the human relations landscape through recreational organizing in the 1920s, '30s, and '40s might yet be discovered in the unfolding of the Cincinnati civil rights movement in the 1950s and '60s and in the women's movement of the 1960s and '70s. Partaker democracy of the 1920s, '30s, and '40s, in which previously marginalized groups were organized and encouraged to become part of the larger civic community, was replaced by calls for participatory democracy of students and civil rights workers who sought not only to be part of the social system, but to change it.

Notes

1. Historians have generally ignored the public recreation movement, but recreation professionals such as George D. Butler recorded the insider's perspective on the movement in books such as *Pioneers in Public Recreation* (Minneapolis: Burgess, 1965). See also Elizabeth Halsey, *The Development of Public Recreation in Metropolitan Chicago* (Chicago: Chicago Recreation Commission, 1949), and Reynold Edgar Carlson, Theodore R. Deppe, and Janet R. MacLean, *Recreation in American Life*, 2d ed., (Belmont, CA: Wadsworth, 1972). Urban historians have shown little interest in the topic; there are no monographs on the history of municipal public recreation, although two recent dissertations suggest this may change. See Cheryl L. Jordan, "The Evolution of the Baltimore Bureau of Recreation, 1940–1988" (Ph.D. thesis, University of Maryland, 1993), and Randolph Stephen Delehanty, "San Francisco Parks and Playgrounds, 1839–1990: The History of a Public Good in One North American City" (Ph.D. thesis, Harvard University, 1992). The National Recreation Association published a monthly magazine during these years. Titled first *Playground* (1907–29), then *Playground and Recreation* (1929–30), and finally *Recreation* (1931–65), the periodical

regularly included reports on municipal recreation programs across the country. The Cincinnati Recreation Commission published annual reports on its work. These can be found at the Public Library of Cincinnati and Hamilton County. Many of the papers of the National Recreation Association from the early years are in the Social Welfare History Archives of the University of Minnesota.

2. George D. Butler, *Introduction to Community Recreation* (New York: McGraw-Hill, 1967), pp. 85–86, 87.

3. Edward J. Ward, ed., *The Social Center* (New York: D. Appleton, 1913), pp. 3, 38–39, 74.

4. Tam Deering, "Neighborhood Recreation Centers," *Playground* (March 1926): 665–67.

5. Deering, "Neighborhood Recreation Centers," p. 667.

6. Just fourteen American cities provided supervised play facilities in 1900; fifty years later more than a thousand municipalities supported public recreation programs. For more on the growth of public recreation see Chas. E. Doell and Gerald B. Fitzgerald, *A Brief History of Parks and Recreation in the United States* (Chicago: Athletic Institute, 1954), pp. 58, 63; Howard Braucher, "The Fortieth Year of the National Recreation Association Begins April 12, 1945," *Recreation* (April 1945): 1.

7. Kevin Mattson, *Creating a Democratic Public: The Struggle for Urban Participatory Democracy During the Progressive Era* (University Park: Penn State University Press, 1998), p. 48 and chap. 3 in general. Mattson sees this movement as ending in 1917, but Cincinnati was not the only city in which the school-based centers became arms of new democratic recreation programs.

8. "A Report of Cincinnati Community Service for 1921," *Woman's City Club Bulletin* (May 1922): 13–15. Woman's City Club Papers, Cincinnati Historical Society.

9. "Public Recreation Committee," *Woman's City Club Bulletin* (May 1926): 14–15. Andrea Tuttle Kornbluh, "The Bowl of Promise: Cincinnati Social Welfare Planners, Cultural Pluralism and the Metropolitan Community, 1911–1952" (Ph.D. thesis, University of Cincinnati, 1988), pp. 349–51.

10. No comprehensive biography of William DeHart Hubbard exists. However, see Ralph W. Bullock, *In Spite of Handicaps: Brief Biographical Sketches With Discussion Outlines of Outstanding Negroes Now Living Who Are Achieving Distinction in Various Lines of Endeavor* (New York: Association Press, 1927), pp. 59–66, for a discussion of Hubbard's early life and Olympic success. *Annual Report of the Public Recreation Commission* (1927), p. 18.

11. Lyle Koehler, *Cincinnati's Black Peoples: A Chronology and Bibliography* (Cincinnati: Cincinnati Arts Consortium, 1988), pp. 114–21; Kornbluh, "Bowl of Promise," p. 217.

12. *Annual Report of the Public Recreation Commission* (1927), p. 23; (1928), pp. 32, 33.

13. The information on Madden's background is drawn from city directo-

ries and the federal census. See also *Cincinnati Enquirer*, 7 March 1942, 20 April 1956.

14. *Annual Report of the Public Recreation Commission* (1928), pp. 38, 39.

15. Mabel V. Madden, "Report of the Department of Community Activities and Girls' Work," *Annual Report of the Public Recreation Commission* (1929), pp. 28, 29.

16. *Annual Report of the Public Recreation Commission* (1930), p. 30.

17. *Annual Report of the Public Recreation Commission* (1929), p. 50; (1930), p. 59. Tam Deering to Howard S. Braucher, 18 April 1932. National Recreation Association Papers, box 27, folder "Colored Work." Social Welfare History Archives, University of Minnesota.

18. Deering to Braucher.

19. Ibid.

20. Citizens' Recreation Council of Cincinnati, Ohio, to Mr. Charles E. Reed (n.d.) National Recreation Association Papers, box 27, folder "Colored Work." Social Welfare History Archives, University of Minnesota.

21. *Annual Report of the Public Recreation Commission* (1935), pp. 35, 36.

22. Ibid., p. 38.

23. Ibid., p. 41; Howard Braucher, "Recreation Workers and the Preservation and Development of Democracy," *Recreation* 30 (September 1936): 281.

24. *Annual Report of the Public Recreation Commission* (1936), pp. 31, 32.

25. Ibid., p. 35.

26. *Annual Report of the Public Recreation Commission* (1937), pp. 40–42.

27. *Annual Report of the Public Recreation Commission* (1941), p. 57; p. 27.

28. *Annual Report of the Public Recreation Commission* (1942), p. 27.

29. There is not a lot of historical work on American girls in the 1920s, '30s, and '40s, but one recent collection suggests this may be changing. See Sherrie A. Inness, ed., *Delinquents and Debutantes: Twentieth Century American Girls' Cultures* (New York: New York University Press, 1998).

30. See, for example, "How to Provide Recreation more adequately for Women and Girls," *Recreation* 28 (December 1934): 439–40, and "Clubs for Girls and Women," *Recreation* 29 (November 1935): 416. Mabel Madden, "Girls' Week—A Challenge," *Recreation* (February 1933): 536–38. "Girls' Week History." Girls' Week Advisory Council Records, box 6, folder 2. Cincinnati Historical Society. Ethel Bowers, "Centers for Girls," *Recreation* 33 (August 1939): 289.

31. Madden, "Girls' Week—A Challenge," p. 536.

32. Ibid., pp. 536–37.

33. Ibid., p. 537.

34. Ibid..

35. Ibid., p. 538.

36. "Girls' Week History."

37. Ibid.; *Cincinnati Post*, 8 March 1956.

Chapter Seven

Making History: The Search for Civic and Cultural Identity in an American New Town, 1940–1980

BRADLEY D. CROSS

Uncharitable observers might accuse the residents of Mariemont of changing their community into a miniature theme park for themselves in the last half of the twentieth century. This community, on Cincinnati's eastern periphery, sought out distinct political sovereignty, created a cast of historical characters, and shaped its built environment to evoke a nostalgic past. New Urbanists at the end of the twentieth century found Mariemont a compelling example of good planning, but what was at stake in Mariemont's transformation? Mariemonters, by midcentury, used history to transform the meaning of their community as part of their search for individual cultural identity. This new identity emerged during the decades between 1940 and 1980, punctuated originally by the creation of a colonial New England-styled civic assembly, and culminated in Mariemonters' application for inclusion of their community in the National Register of Historic Places.[1]

What compelled this fifty-year-old community to seek such a visible indicator of legitimate historical status when many of its neighboring Cincinnati communities could boast of longer histories? Why was oldness and attaining National Register status so important to this new town? And what was wrong with Mariemonters' former identity? This essay argues that the people of Mariemont constructed their own sense of community and culture from nostalgic and historical meanings they associated with their neighborhood, which grew out of the process of Mariemonters' defining their individual and community identities. In searching for a new cultural identity, their particular conception of the past proved plastic as they imagined their community to be a piece of the "Old World" in a new town.

Mariemont began as a project of Cincinnati philanthropist Mary Emery to memorialize her deceased husband, and was one of her many projects designed to bring reform and urban regeneration to her adopted city of Cincinnati. Emery hired John Nolen, one of the most influential American town planners of the early twentieth century, to design this leafy American "garden city."[2] Nolen conceived of Mariemont as an "interpretation of modern planning principles applied to a small community to produce local happiness," and touted it as a "National Exemplar."[3] To him, Mariemont represented the transplantation of the English garden city to the United States, "but put on a business basis in accordance with American Ideas."[4] Originally Mary Emery and the Mariemont Company (a private development corporation created to construct the community), and by the 1920s the Thomas J. Emery Memorial (a trust Mary Emery devised in the name of her dead husband), controlled all aspects of the model town. This was top-down planning initiated by the efforts of one of Cincinnati's wealthiest citizens, designed by a team of expert planners, architects, and engineers, and managed by a board of directors. Ostensibly modeled on the English garden cities of Letchworth and Welwyn, Mariemont's architecture reflected styles in vogue in the United States by the 1920s: Tudor half-timber, Georgian, and colonial vernacular.

For its first twenty years, Mariemont functioned as a sort of not-for-profit, philanthropic company town. Its extensive scale subjected it to the designs of Emery and her development company (a corporation with an appointed board of directors that included prominent real estate developers, politicians, and family friends of Emery), and its location outside the metropolitan boundaries of the city of Cincinnati provided no other means of local government. As an unincorporated entity Mariemont was the creature of the Mariemont Company, and by 1927 the Emery Memorial took over exclusive guidance of the community following Mary Emery's death.

Although Mariemont had been carefully designed by experts and had been under the management of a private corporation for the first two decades of its existence, in the 1940s a local grass-roots democratic movement emerged in the bucolic new town.[5] Until that time, Mariemonters saw themselves as suburban pioneers living in a modern and well-appointed planned community.[6] If anything, they looked to the future rather than to the past.[7] But a wave of annexation attempts by Cincinnati in the late 1930s and early 1940s forced Mariemonters to define their community's relationship to the city.

The Struggle for Municipal Sovereignty

Mariemont, by 1941, either had to accept annexation by Cincinnati or incorporate as a village. John Nolen and his engineers designed

Mariemont as a self-sufficient small town, yet it possessed strong ties to Cincinnati. Mariemont had its own hospital, steam-heating facility, and an array of local utilities, and the plans called for a modest collection of local light-industrial and commercial businesses. But many of Mariemont's residents worked in Cincinnati. Nolen himself had not addressed the political structure of Mariemont, saying only that "adequate provision will be made for the proper maintenance of the property as a complete town or suburb."[8] This question of community governance moved into center stage during the 1940s as residents confronted the issue of political association. Was Mariemont to be a suburb within Cincinnati, or was it a discrete and sovereign community?

In the process of deciding the annexation debate Mariemonters defined new identities for themselves and the community. A grass-roots movement emerged that asked what relationship residents had to the Thomas J. Emery Memorial; what role Mariemont's own history would play in any decision to incorporate as a village; and what basis the community had for justifying resistance to the perceived encroachment of Cincinnati.

Mariemont residents had something to gain by joining Cincinnati. The city could provide Mariemont with a growing network of public transportation and municipal services, such as waste collection, police and fire protection, and street lighting.[9] As residents of Cincinnati, upwardly mobile Mariemonters would qualify for greatly reduced tuition rates at the University of Cincinnati.[10] Furthermore, Cincinnati gave Mariemonters a sense of belonging to the larger civic community of the metropolis. Of course, by annexing Mariemont, Cincinnati would benefit from an increased tax base, one of the driving forces behind such annexation campaigns.[11] The residents of the new town had something to lose if they did not agree to be annexed, since the city of Cincinnati threatened to revoke such municipal services as sewage and fire protection from Mariemont.[12]

Any successful annexation bid by Cincinnati depended upon building a consensus among the various constituencies within Mariemont. The Emery Memorial initiated a discussion of annexation and remained a principal constituent in the bid for inclusion in Cincinnati. The Memorial operated since the mid-1920s as a kind of de facto local government because it owned the public spaces, controlled the sale of lands, maintained public amenities, and offered steam-heating services to the suburb. In effect, the Emery Memorial had taken over the original development company that had been assigned the task of building and coordinating the Mariemont project.[13] The interests of the Memorial spanned an impressive array of investments, charities, and real estate holdings far beyond Mariemont itself, although Mariemont remained an important example of the Memorial's activities. By the late 1930s, the Memorial had expressed an interest in withdrawing from the daily management of Mariemont in favor of a more limited investment role. Cincinnati offered the Emery Memorial great financial incentive in 1941 by paying nearly half a million dollars for the community's steam-heating station. Mariemonters demonstrated their outrage upon learning that the Memorial had accepted the city's offer without any consultation with the townspeople. Faced with such public outcry, the Memorial withdrew its acceptance of the offer and repaid the city.[14]

Even before the scandal, Mariemont residents showed their concern by organizing the Mariemont Civic Association (1939), which emerged as "an open forum for the discussion of all questions affecting the interests of the citizens of the community."[15] It represented a grass-roots resistance to the preliminary discussions of uniting the unincorporated new town of Mariemont with metropolitan Cincinnati. Put more pragmatically, the Mariemont Civic Association primarily represented private property owners from within the Mariemont community, and it challenged the authority of the Emery Memorial to make decisions over the future status of its local governance and municipal status.

Cincinnati City Council's committee on annexation and boundaries introduced an ordinance "declaring intent to annex the area of Mariemont, Homewood, Fairfax and Indian View Subdivisions" on 26 February 1941.[16] With this action the metropolitan government of the city of Cincinnati sought to expand eastward beyond its present corporate boundaries. It also brought into focus the future political status of Mariemont, forcing a decision among the members of the Emery Memorial and the Mariemont Civic Association.

Mariemont would either incorporate in order to fight off Cincinnati's annexation bid, or it would have to ask the county commissioners to hold a hearing of Mariemont citizens and rely on the commission's authority to defeat the city's annexation attempt. A municipality had the power to annex adjacent unincorporated areas by petition of the residents in the territory under consideration, but county commissioners had to supervise the processes of incorporation and annexation.[17] Municipal incorporation in the status of village could be granted to communities of less than five thousand people.[18] Furthermore, the decision by any unincorporated area to accept a petition of annexation by a neighboring municipality depended upon a process of public hearings and input from freeholders within the prescribed unincorporated territory.[19] This process demanded that the majority of freeholders within the territory proposed for annexation agree to it. The process of incorporation similarly depended upon the majority consent of electors (not necessarily freeholders) within the designated territory, but it had to be initiated through petition to the county commissioners by at least thirty electors, the majority of whom had to be freeholders. The petition to incorporate included the process of holding an election to determine the will of the majority of electors. Township trustees verified the status of the electorate and ordered the election within fifteen days of receiving the petition. If a majority of electors voted for incorporation, the village acquired municipal status. The county commissioners maintained oversight of such an election for incorporation, and had the final decision.

As it turned out the Mariemont Civic Association championed the idea of incorporation. This strategy would at once fend off annexation by Cincinnati and cede control of the community from the Thomas J. Emery Memorial into the hands of Mariemonters. Less than a week after the Cincinnati City Council passed the ordinance to annex Mariemont, the civic association initiated a pair of public meetings, one aimed at discussing the community's responses to annexation and the other to debate the prospects of incorporation. The civic association appointed a governmental status committee to arrange these meetings and invite discussion of the subjects at hand. At the association's regular March meeting in 1941, speakers representing the city of Cincinnati made their case for annexation before an assembly of more than four hundred Mariemonters. Just more than two weeks after the annexation meeting the civic association held a second, special meeting to discuss the issue of incorporation. Speakers for this meeting of more than three hundred people included Roy Elliott, the mayor of adjacent Amberley Village,[20] as well as Columbia Township trustee Boyd Jordan.[21]

Governmental status committee member John Reid expressed concern to his fellow committee member Harry Mohlman[22] over the pressure some Mariemont residents felt in coming to a decision over annexation and incorporation. Three days after the first meeting, and with less than two weeks before the discussion on incorporation, Reid wrote:"[M]any Mariemonters are upset by the feeling on the part of some of the residents that apparently Mariemont is forced to do one of two things, either stand for annexation or incorporate. I know that many of the residents have asked me if it were necessary to do one of those two things and I have told them that we do not have to do anything and I believe that this should be made very clear to the residents at the next meeting."[23] In Reid's opinion, the question was not clear cut. Nonetheless, he predicted that Mariemont residents would reject the annexation bid of Cincinnati and remain an unincorporated entity. Reid explained this opinion by arguing that "people moved into Mariemont . . . to find a community atmosphere as it has and would have, no doubt, gone somewhere else if they had wanted something different."[24] For Reid, Mariemont was neither a part of the metropolis of Cincinnati nor to be defined by its own municipal incorporation. It was a creature of the Emery Memorial, which in his view still had "some duties and responsibility in maintaining Mariemont as was originally intended."[25]

The prospect of financial burden stemming from the costs of acquiring and maintaining public services from the city of Cincinnati and the Emery Memorial concerned Mariemonters, too. The governmental status committee, urged by Reid, investigated the economics of incorporation in order to present Mariemonters with a "very clear picture . . . of what the cost would be of incorporation." Reid also proposed to have present at the special meeting called to debate Mariemont's incorporation officials from the recently incorporated village of Amberley, "plus anyone else who can give us any worthwhile information on the cost of incorporation and the problems connected therewith."[26]

Independence had a price. The annual costs, calculated by the Cincinnati city manager in 1941, ran about $67,300 per year just to maintain street lighting, traffic signs, street maintenance, waste collection, parklands, and fire and police protection. C. O. Sherrill, the city manager, estimated one-time costs for the purchase of the existing public works and the costs of immediate necessary modernization improvements at $475,800.[27] One estimate of the cost of incorporation on property taxes projected that the tax rate would rise from the present (1941) value of $16 per $1,000 to about $19.50 per $1,000 valuation.[28]

Concerns over Mariemont's identity also contributed to the debate on incorporation. The *Mariemont Messenger* played host to indirect debates over the inseparable issues of annexation and incorporation, each side arguing that it supported the preservation of Mariemont's character. The committee for incorporation urged Mariemonters to vote for incorporation so their community would "retain its distinctive individuality."[29] Two governmental status committee members noted that "the best interests of the residents of Mariemont can be served by annexing to Cincinnati," but denied that they were trying to persuade Mariemonters to vote one way or the other.

Still stinging from the rebuke it suffered when Mariemonters cried out against the half-million-dollar deal it made with Cincinnati for the steam-heating facility, the Emery Memorial added its voice to Mariemont's civic groups by pushing for a decision either to annex or incorporate. It cautioned Mariemonters that "as long as the community remains unincorporated, it is subject to being broken up and inadequately protected by the activities of representatives of other areas."[30] However, in the local community newspaper the committee for incorporation allied itself with the Memorial, citing the cautioning it gave to Mariemonters as tacit support for its cause and offering seven reasons for incorporation, most of which appealed to a sense of fear about annexation. It also argued that anxiety could be put to rest by gaining local political control founded upon a shared sense of community history and common identity. Merging with Cincinnati in an annexation agreement, the committee claimed, would threaten "the present high standards of our schools—THE SCHOOLS WE HAVE FOUGHT TO ESTABLISH. . . . We believe incorporation will enable us better to retain the reins of government in the uncertain years to come; that as a small community, where public opinion can be tested readily, we can more quickly make needed adjustments."[31] Not surprisingly, given the straw vote taken on 19 March 1941 at a special meeting of the Mariemont Civic Association, the vote to incorporate succeeded 522 to 286 on 14 April 1941.[32]

Incorporation brought with it the necessity to form a municipal government. With a population of more than two thousand, Mariemont qualified as a village under the Ohio statues.[33] Government of the new village of Mariemont fell under the aegis of Columbia Township trustees until the village could elect its own officers.[34] Also, the Emery Memorial agreed to supply the village "with fire protection and other public services until accrued village taxes were sufficient to enable the village to assume these responsibilities."[35]

But what kind of government would the village adopt? The Mariemont Civic Association called for a town meeting at which the future of Mariemont's government would be debated, and out of this process came the Mariemont nonpartisan citizens committee. This committee presented a plan at a meeting on 19 May 1941 that divided the village into six geographical districts and outlined village offices. The meeting also sought nominations for the executive offices and potential representatives from the six geographical districts.[36] Hamilton County, however, determined the district boundaries.[37]

Mariemonters initially decided to name their government the Mariemont Town Meeting and adopted a constitution "to foster good government for the Village of Mariemont . . . [and that] provided that the executive committee of 22 should include the chairman, secretary, [town] crier, treasurer, and three representatives from each of six districts."[38] Ultimately the town meeting separated from the municipal government of the village of Mariemont by concerning itself with the selection process of candidates to be elected to the village government assembly in a kind of primary process and ensuring that elections for the village of Mariemont offered representatives from all areas of the village, including lower-income renters living in apartments as well as owners of the larger homes adjacent to Mariemont's scenic parks and vistas. There was a representative in village government for about every 111 residents.[39]

It was not direct democracy, but this new form of government stood in stark contrast to the rule of the Emery Memorial that once made all the principal decisions affecting the community through its board of directors (almost none of whom lived in Mariemont itself). This grass-roots control of civic government offered Mariemonters independence and the opportunity to assert their wishes about the future of the community. But this assertion also relied on a particular conception of Mariemont's own history. The incorporated village of Mariemont came about in an attempt to maintain aspects of its past as a distinct entity outside of the control of metropolitan Cincinnati.

Public Ritual and Civic Identity

Arguing that their community was built on a tradition of independence from Cincinnati, Mariemonters sought to preserve their community by making it a sovereign political entity. But instead of preserving Mariemont as it had been, the process of seeking incorporation changed the identity and meaning of Mariemont and created a new kind of civic discourse. No longer under the political control of the Emery Memorial, Mariemonters searched for a way to govern themselves that reflected the more democratic and participatory tack they took in countering Cincinnati's annexation bid.

Mariemont's emerging new identity is demonstrated in the way it named and performed nascent civic functions, drawing on popular conceptions of America's democratic origins. For example, the decision to name Mariemont's original municipal government the Town Meeting came at a mass gathering of Mariemont residents at which the nonpartisan citizens committee solicited opinions on the future of the village government. Mrs. E. Marie Hawk Jordan commented to her husband, Boyd Jordan, "[W]hy don't we call it the Town Meeting like they did in New England in the olden days?" Mr. Jordan rose to his feet and suggested what his wife had said. The assembly adopted the name.[40]

The designation "town meeting" resonated with Mariemonters because it acknowledged their grass-roots movement toward governing their own community. It also offered Mariemonters an historical antecedent upon which they could hang justifications for their actions. More conservative members of the community who had opposed incorporation could take solace in the fact their new municipal body sought an identity akin to colonial assemblies in the American past. This naming of the municipal assembly was not predicated on the actual history of town meetings in New England of the seventeenth and eighteenth centuries, and certainly not on the history of the Ohio Valley. Rather, it evoked a popular conception of an era past, one that suggested harmonious, participatory democratic assembly that gave rise to the American movement for independence.[41] Perhaps this sense of historical imagination was informed by the expansion and flourishing of reconstructed historical sites, such as Colonial Williamsburg and Old Sturbridge Village in the 1940s.[42] Whatever the specific source of inspiration for naming the town meeting, Mariemonters understood the historical allusion.

Now that Mariemont had legal, geographical boundaries and the municipal sovereignty to enforce them, Mariemonters created their "imagined" community with a carefully selected set of historical signifiers.[43] They used public civic ritual to represent the ideals for which the simultaneously "new" and "historical" Mariemont stood. Mariemont's constitution outlined a list of civic offices, including those one expected to see in any American village assembly: chairman, secretary, treasurer, and councilors. But Mariemonters also made provision for a town crier and a marshal, investing these two offices with symbolic meaning.

The town crier stood as the most ceremonial and ritualistic of the village's public offices. The idea for a town crier emerged at the same mass meeting as had the idea of naming the village assembly after the New England town meeting. Mrs. E. Marie Hawk Jordan recounted: "We had a man in charge of the meeting that night who came in and I said to Boyd, 'Why can't we call him the Town Crier?' so Boyd stood up and said that at the same time that we called it the Town Meeting, and they did that. So we had a town crier as they had in early New England days."[44]

Initially the town crier had little more duty than calling town meetings to order and introducing speakers or officials. The first Mariemont town crier, Bob Taylor, rang his bell in May 1941 to call to order an organizational meeting for the election of the executive for the new village government.[45] Apart from the hand bell, there was little to distinguish the town crier from other village officeholders.

The office of town crier became increasingly more active by the 1950s and included the duties of leading community parades and participating in official civic occasions. Ralph Smith became the second town crier in 1959 and held the position until his death in 1995.[46] Mr. Smith quickly transformed the role by adding an elaborate costume and expanding his public activity.[47] Modeled explicitly on the dress of a colonial gentleman, Smith's costume included a white wig, red velvet jacket, black brocade waistcoat, black velvet breeches, and custom-made shoe buckles forged by the blacksmith at Colonial Williamsburg itself.[48] This town crier took the role to heart, researching the history of town criers, traveling to participate in international town crier competitions, and duplicating some of the traditional practices and ceremonies performed by the town crier at Colonial Williamsburg.[49] No longer would the civic process in Mariemont be a sedate and drab affair. The crier opened all town meetings, announced the results of elections held within the community, led parades, read aloud proclamations from the mayor, officiated as a master of ceremonies for civic celebrations, and made appearances on other civic occasions.[50]

The town meeting and the town crier signaled a break with the arbitrary decision making process the residents of Mariemont had been subject to under the private Mariemont Company and then the Thomas J. Emery Memorial. Incorporation of the village had not only allowed greater political autonomy and made Mariemont safe from annexation, it had offered Mariemont residents the opportunity to create a cultural and political language for self-determination. In their custodian of civic ceremony, the town crier, Mariemonters saw the personification of their historical imaginations. To live in Mariemont was to live in a special place offering a consciously historical, imagined civic atmosphere.

The town crier gave Mariemont a brand of ritualized public theater that evoked a nostalgic, idealized portrait of America's past, one in which community was associated with face-to-face interaction. In pseudocolonial pageantry residents celebrated a past that had nothing to do with Mariemont's origins as a garden city social reform project of the 1920s, or even the history of the Ohio Valley. Yet their version of colonial America featured and reinforced the themes of the close, closed community, with elements of small-scale village life. Mariemonters chose to imbue their village government with these meanings as they sought an identity for themselves.

The highest office of law enforcement in Mariemont, the village marshal, also evoked a sense of the past. Like the town crier, the marshal rendered a deliberately historical profile on Mariemont's increasingly anachronistic public stage. Dressed in a self-described "costume" rather than uniform, the marshal appeared in a bobby-like helmet, carried "an over-sized mace" and a kerosene lantern (in an era of battery-powered flashlights!), and had a large tin-star badge pinned to his chest.[51] The *Mariemont Messenger* reported that marshal "Chris [Robisch] won't have any trouble catching criminals with this outfit; they'll probably faint when they see him coming."[52] While the *Messenger* jested at the appearance of the village marshal, it and the community took his law enforcement seriously. The *Messenger* faithfully reported and celebrated the incidents of police intervention in the affairs of the village, from handing out speeding tickets to chasing and apprehending thieves. While there was no specific historical period rendered in the marshal's costume, it was certainly intended to represent some earlier era when cops carried maces, and lanterns instead of flashlights. Mariemont's marshal seemed a fusion of night watchman, Old West sheriff, and London bobby.

Civic ritual demonstrated Mariemonters' emerging conception of their own identity, one in which choosing historical symbols allowed them to create new meanings in the community they sought to define for themselves. Independent of both the Emery Memorial and the city of Cincinnati, Mariemonters began designing public roles in their government and law enforcement that offered them a chance to enter into a discourse about their civic identity. Mariemont became a platform for pursuing a particular life style that residents chose and enhanced by employing specific elements of public civic ritual. Nostalgic historical symbolism created a sense of intimate and peaceful community regained—the New England town meeting convened by a town crier who delivered news in a face-to-face society, and the village marshal who proudly displayed his tin star.

Mariemonters also took control of their built environment with an eye to historical imagery. Just as some civic officials clothed themselves in historical garments, Mariemonters often dressed their buildings in period costume. Mariemonters saw their community as a place in which they could express a self-constructed identity based on English and historical references. While the town meeting found its conceptual origins in Mariemonters' perception of colonial New England village assemblies, the collective community identity became increasingly English by the 1950s and 1960s.[53]

The village government created the Mariemont Planning Commission shortly after incorporation in 1941 to shape the territory's physical form. The planning commission, comprised of village residents where possible, began with five members: the mayor, one council representative, an electrical engineer, an investment counselor, and a builder-contractor.[54] Even though John Nolen planned Mariemont with discrete functional areas that provided for separate industrial, commercial, and residential spaces as early as the 1920s, there had been no formal zoning regulations, and there was no legal means of compelling particular land use within the boundaries of the community. The Mariemont Company and the Emery Memorial guided land use activities up to 1941. With incorporation and the gradual transition of public land ownership from the Emery Memorial to the village corporation, zoning regulations offered Mariemonters a way of deciding how land would be used in the future.[55] The planning commission consulted the public as it zoned their municipal landscape to ensure that all future construction in Mariemont would conform to designated land uses and building and architectural style codes.[56] Shortly after the preliminary zoning of Mariemont the village government convened a planning and zoning committee to create a building code in cooperation with the planning commission.[57] Mariemont residents decided the future of their built environment by establishing construction and planning guidelines as soon as possible.

Architectural provisions for the maintenance of Mariemont as a pseudo-colonial or romantic English village emerged in some of the earliest decisions by the planning commission and its consulting architect. The village applied tight architectural style controls to new construction in the community, but perhaps it gave the closest scrutiny to commercial development at the heart of the village. Articles about the village began to appear that painted the community as a piece of "Old England."[58] Mariemont's own perception of itself as an English village in America was echoed in advertising and articles in the community's *Messenger* newspaper.[59] A new Kroger supermarket that opened in Mariemont in 1953 adopted an exterior of Tudor half-timber. Advertising copy in the *Cincinnati Post* asked readers to come "see a store that successfully combines the finest, most modern conveniences with the old English charm and rustic beauty at one of our finest residential areas. It's the store that's 'Made for Mariemont.'"[60] The stucco and dark wood evoked, but did not reconstruct, sixteenth-and seventeenth-century building styles common in England. This large modern supermarket fused the commercial function of the particularly American phenomenon of the supermarket with reference to an English historical style of architecture. Another fusion of modern function and historical style came with the construction of Central Trust Company's drive-in teller facility. The drive-in customer entered one of three lanes covered by a canopy that adjoined a small outbuilding. Here the automobile age met the Middle Ages, since Central Trust clad its drive-in with stucco and darkly stained half-timber.[61] The Tudor motifs of the new supermarket and other additions to the village core evoked an imagined sense of history, but did not attempt to deceive people into thinking the buildings were authentic. It would have been historically impossible.

Admittedly, the new buildings at the "village centre" reflected the Tudor revival buildings Mary Emery preferred for her initial version of Mariemont, but the deliberate decision to extend this style to include most new construction was also informed by an increasing association of historical "Englishness" with Mariemont. This identity found further demonstration when the Mariemont Inn sought a bus to shuttle guests around town or for use at special occasions. It acquired in 1967 an authentic double-decker London Transport omnibus designated RLH #41.[62]

Discovering a "Real" History

During the 1940s and 1950s Mariemonters looked to external sources for historical inspiration, the substance of which had no relation to Mariemont's actual history. However, in the decades following, Mariemonters looked inside their community for inspiration and found much to celebrate in its actual history. Mariemont began as a garden city adapted to American ideas, a feature that took on new importance by the 1960s and 1970s as Mariemonters continued to use history as a means of creating their identity. The fact that Mariemont stood as the first American example of garden city planning[63] became more important than the planning ideas that undergirded the community's original design. Publications from village residents on the history of Mariemont celebrated the community as a "national exemplar" of good design and cataloged the construction of various phases of the village.[64] Yet nowhere in their fight against annexation by Cincinnati nor their movement to incorporate had Mariemonters cited the historical fact of their community's garden city origins to justify independence. Only when combined with an increasingly historical sensibility, overlaid by a newfound Englishness, did Mariemonters celebrate their garden city roots. Mariemonters forged a collective identity out of local history and appropriated cultural symbols. In effect, Mariemont became a pleasant English village on the outskirts of an American rust-belt metropolis.

The village assembly, on the fiftieth anniversary of Mariemont's opening, revised its municipal bylaws to reflect an emerging historical purpose in its role. The municipal government declared:"The general purposes of this organization shall be to encourage, support and develop the educational, cultural, civic, *historical* [author's emphasis] and social welfare activities of the Village of Mariemont, Ohio . . . and thereby render a community-wide service to all its residents."[65] The promotion of historical activities within Mariemont took on an increased educational and civic role by the 1970s, and history still served Mariemonters in their search for cultural identity. The village government and town meeting provided residents with instances of historical imagination in the personas of the town crier and the marshal, but this new emphasis on historical activity suggested a qualitatively different kind of history. This history needed to be legitimate and verifiable, rather than conjured and imagined, since it carried an educational purpose.

Mariemonters went a step further in implicating history as part of their search for cultural and civic identity when the village applied for inclusion on the National Register of Historic Places. Mariemont's garden city origins served as the primary justification for its petition. Amateur village historians reframed Mary Emery and John Nolen's modernist vision of the model workers' community into a celebration of Mariemont as an historical artifact. Mariemont's application to the National Register depended on the community to fulfill the criteria laid out in the National Historic Preservation Act of 1966. Mariemont qualified on this basis:

> The quality of significance in American history, architecture, archeology, engineering, and culture is present in districts, sites, buildings, structures, and objects that possess integrity of location, design, setting, materials, workmanship, feeling, and association, and:

> . . . type, period, or method of construction, or that represent the work of a master, or that possess high artistic values, or that represent a significant and distinguishable entity whose components may lack individual distinction."[66]

Mariemont was only about forty years old in 1966, and the National Historic Preservation Act required any subject for consideration to be at least fifty years in age. Mariemont made ready its application for inclusion on the National Register by 1978.[67]

Mariemont's application to the National Register made no mention of the office of town crier, the marshal's costume, or the double-decker bus. Instead the village emphasized its concrete historical origins by making clear the connections with the nationally prominent town planner John Nolen, Mary Emery's philanthropic social mission, and Mariemont's roots as a garden city project. This brought about a carefully documented, authenticated, and legitimized historical identity for the community, changing its meaning yet again. No longer would vague historical allusions serve Mariemonters' needs. They required a "real" history constructed from Mariemont's own verifiable past instead of a pastiche of historical symbols taken from a popular conception of the past.

The move toward integrating a new sense of history based on the community as historical artifact prompted the creation of the Mariemont

Preservation Foundation within a year of the village's attaining National Historic District status.[68] The preservation foundation initiated the collection and preservation of a community archives and oversaw the maintenance of the village in order to keep its place as a qualified member of the National Register of Historic Places. Mariemonters continued to pursue architectural regulation and historical research into their past as important contributions in their efforts to redefine their community as a National Historic District. In their search for a chosen life style Mariemonters replaced the public theater of a historically inspired motif with an explicit civic mission of cataloging their past and preserving it for their future.

By "making history," whether imagined or documented, Mariemonters made sense of their civic and cultural identities. In a grass-roots effort to influence their urban environment the people of Mariemont redefined the nature of their community, transforming it into a place where they actively pursued a chosen life style. Mariemonters' self-constructed cultural landscape emerged with their political sovereignty and gave them the opportunity to search for, define, and express new meanings for their community. Ultimately Mariemont rejected an identity that would have included it in metropolitan Cincinnati. Mariemonters instead favored a set of identities that depended upon the use of history to make their culture specific to them. Mariemonters recreated their community primarily for themselves, and it served them in a search for political and cultural identity. As for the larger metropolis of Cincinnati, it could count Mariemont among its more colorful neighbors, but it couldn't count it among its own neighborhoods.

Notes

The author wishes to thank Janet Setchell, archivist and executive secretary of the Mariemont Preservation Foundation; the honors seminar "Topics in North American History," 1999–2000, at St. Thomas University for commenting on a draft of this essay; and Christine Cook Cross for carefully reading, editing, and suggesting improvements to the manuscript.

1. Letter from W. R. Knoble, president of village assembly, to "Organization Representatives," 28 March 1978. Mariemont achieved National Register of Historic Places status on 24 July 1979. Chronological files, Mariemont Preservation Foundation Archives (hereafter MPF).

2. A garden city, according to Ebenezer Howard's *Garden Cities of Tomorrow: A Peaceful Path to Real Reform* (London: Swan, 1902), consisted of a self-contained walking town complete with industry and recreational facilities, to house no more than thirty thousand inhabitants, with discrete land use according to function, surrounded by a permanent green belt to be reserved for rural and wilderness purposes. For a more complete discussion of the changing

definitions and uses of the garden city in a comparative international framework, see Bradley D. Cross, "New Jerusalems for a New World: The Garden City Idea in Modern Planning Thought and Practice in Britain, Canada, and the United States, 1900–1970" (Ph.D. dissertation, University of Cincinnati, 1997).

3. John Nolen, Appendix 1, *General Plan, Mariemont: a New Town* (Cambridge, MA: Town Planning Associates, 1921), MPF.

4. Nolen, *General Plan* . For land ownership in the conception of the English garden city idea, see Ebenezer Howard, *Garden Cities of Tomorrow* (Powys, Wales: Attic Books, rep. 1993).

5. Zane Miller identified this tendency toward citizen participation in community planning in the work of Louis Wirth, a University of Chicago sociologist and urbanist of the 1930s and 1940s. Miller uses the term "maximum feasible participation" to denote the democratic nature of such grass-roots efforts in the context of community planning. Miller, "Pluralism, Chicago School Style," *Journal of Urban History* 18 (May 1992): 251–80.

6. "Pioneers," *Mariemont Messenger* , 9 September 1926, p. 2.

7. J. Walter Thompson, "News Bulletin Describing Mariemont, the New Town" (Mariemont: Mariemont Company, 1926), PVA.994.08.008, MPF. "A New Suburb, Scientifically Planned, a Marvel in Construction, Beauty and Appointment," *Suburban Life,* September 1926, pp. 10–11.

8. Nolen, *General Plan.*

9. *Report of the Governmental Status Committee at the Regular Meeting of the Mariemont Civic Association, Monday, April 7, 1941,* p. 4, RA.992.01.044, MPF.

10. City manager, *Cincinnati Yearbook, 1942: The Annual Report of the City Manager of the City of Cincinnati* (Cincinnati: 1942). Letter from Norman P. Auburn (acting dean) to Harry J. Mohlman (member of Mariemont Governmental Status Committee), 18 March 1941, Exhibit 6, *Report of the Governmental Status Committee at the Regular Meeting of the Mariemont Civic Association, 7 April 1941,* p. 15.

11. Roger Hansen, "Invitation to Annexation: Metropolitan Fragmentation and Community in Cincinnati and Houston, 1920–1980" (Ph.D. dissertation, University of Cincinnati, 1998).

12. "Little Miami Sanitary System", entry from 19 June 1940. Thomas J. Emery Memorial Minute Book, vol. 2, 3 February 1936, 11 August 1941, p. 180, MPF.

13 "Historical Background," *Report of the Governmental Status Committee.*

14. *Minute Book, Thomas J. Emery Memorial* (1939–41), MPF.

15. "Foreword," *Report of the Governmental Status Committee.*

16. "The Problem," *Report of the Governmental Status Committee.*

17. *Ohio Code of Statues,* sec. 3516–21, 3526–30, 3547–49, 3558–61.

18. *Constitution of the State of Ohio,* art. 18, sec. 2.

19. "The Problem."

20. Letter from John A. Reid to Harry Mohlman, 6 March 1941, Chronological files, MPF.

21. "Foreword," *Report of the Governmental Status Committee. Cincinnati Enquirer,* 4 March and 20 March 1941.

22. Mohlman headed the governmental status committee. "Five Villages," *Cincinnati Enquirer,* April 1941, Chronological files, NEA.992.01.011, MPF.

23. Letter from John A. Reid to Harry Mohlman, 6 March 1941, MPF.

24. Ibid.

25. Ibid.

26. Ibid.

27. C. O. Sherrill, city manager, "Report of Incorporation Costs" (condensed), in "Annexation," *Report of the Governmental Status Committee.*

28. Tax estimate given by Harry Mohlman, Governmental Status Committee. "Mariemont Vote on Incorporation Probable April 7," *Cincinnati Enquirer,* 29 March 1941.

29. *Mariemont Messenger,* 11 April 1941, p. 3.

30. Ibid.

31. Ibid.

32. "Mariemont Likely to Wait Until Fall to Elect Officers: Incorporation is Approved," probably from *Cincinnati Enquirer,* 15 April 1941. Chronological files, 1941, NEA.992.02.015, MPF. Fred Rutherford, "Municipal Spirit in Mariemont" (Mariemont Preservation Foundation, 16 July 1998), p. 3. "Civic Body Favors Incorporation, Straw Vote Taken at Mariemont," probably from *Cincinnati Enquirer,* March 1941, Chronological files, 1941, MPF.

33. A census performed at the time of incorporation counted 2,444 residents of Mariemont, with 43 percent categorized as homeowners. "Interesting Sidelights on Mariemont Census," *Mariemont Messenger,* 16 January 1942, p. 3, MPF.

34. "Proposed Charter for Mariemont," *Cincinnati Times-Star,* 30 July 1941, p. 8:3.

35. "Incorporation is Favored By Residents of Five Areas In and Around Mariemont," *Cincinnati Enquirer,* 15 April 1941, E. Boyd Jordan Scrapbook, NEA.992.01.012, MPF.

36. "Mariemont to Hold Mass Meeting Monday to Organize Non-Partisan Citizens Group," *Eastern Hills Journal,* 19 May 1941, p. 1.

37. "Transcript of Oral History Interview, Mrs. E. (Marie Hawk) Jordan." Interviewed by Lois Ralston, 1984, Oral history tape 2, MPF.

38. "Constitution Adopted," *Mariemont Messenger,* 23 May 1941, p. 6.

39. "Interesting Sidelights on Mariemont Census."

40. "Transcript of Oral History Interview, Mrs. E. (Marie Hawk) Jordan," p. 10.

41. Jack P. Greene and J. R. Pole, "Reconstructing British-American Colonial History: An Introduction," *Colonial British America: Essays in the New History of the Early Modern Era* (Baltimore: Johns Hopkins University Press, 1984), p. 2.

42. David Hamer, *History in Urban Places: The Historic Districts of the United States* (Columbus: Ohio State University Press, 1998), p. 3. The author cites attendance statistics indicating a increase from 4,047 in 1932 to 210,824 in 1941,

the same year Mariemont incorporated and sought a name for its new municipal government.

43. Benedict Anderson, *Imagined Communities: Reflections on the Origin and Spread of Nationalism* (London: Verso, 1983), pp. 15–16.

44. "Transcript of Oral History Interview, Mrs. E. (Marie Hawk) Jordan," p. 10.

45. "Town Crier With His Bell to Feature Village Meeting: Call of 'Hear Ye, Hear Ye' to Summon Mariemont Residents to Order for Consideration of Candidates," probably from *Cincinnati Times-Star*, 20 May 1941. E. Boyd Jordan Scrapbook, IG.MTM.1.941.5, MPF.

46. "Town Loses Legend," *Cincinnati Enquirer*, 2 August 1995, p. A1.

47. Fig. 1. Ralph Smith as Mariemont Town Crier, MPF. Mr. Smith's town crier uniform is also archived at the MPF.

48. "Transcript of talk, given by the Madisonville Monday Club, by Ralph Smith on the History of the Town Crier of the Village of Mariemont," p. 1. Taped 6 January 1986, registration no. OHA.008, MPF.

49. Ibid.

50. "Mariemont's Town Crier," *Enquirer Magazine*, 1 June 1969. Warren Wright Parks, *The Mariemont Story: A National Exemplar in Town Planning* (Cincinnati: Creative Writers and Publishers, 1967), p. 154.

51. Fig. 2. Photograph of Chris Robisch, marshal, MPF.

52. "New Village Marshal Goes to Work," *Mariemont Messenger*, 11 July 1941, p. 1.

53. Typical of its increasingly English affinity was the Kiwanis Club of Mariemont's charter night program in 1966 that opened with the singing of "America" and "God Save the Queen." See program, *Kiwanis Club Charter Night*, 19 February 1966, IOK.1.966.2, MPF.

54. "Planning Commission Appointed by Mariemont Mayor," *Mariemont Messenger*, 19 September 1941, p. 1.

55. *Building Zone Map of Village of Mariemont, Hamilton County, Ohio* (Mariemont: Village Planning Commission, 10 January 1942), MPF.

56. "Public Hearing—Interim Zoning Ordinance," *Mariemont Messenger*, 25 July 1941, p. 3.

57. *Building Code of the Village of Mariemont.*

58. "Old English Village Created, Mrs. Mary Emery's Model Town," *Cincinnati Times-Star*, 20 January 1951, p. 13.

59. A striking example of the interest in Englishness by Mariemonters is a commemorative article/advertisement for the Boy Scouts of America that told the story of an American helped by a Boy Scout to find his way on a foggy London night. The man apparently was so grateful for this act of kindness that he founded the Boy Scouts of America. *Mariemont Messenger*, 4 February 1949, p. 2.

60. *Cincinnati Post*, 12 May 1953, pp. 4–5.

61. "Central's Newest Drive-In," *Eastern Hills Journal*, 10 September 1969. Chronological files, EHJ.969.9.10, MPF.

62. Mariemont Inn promotional literature, probably 1968, MPF.

63. Cross, "New Jerusalems for a New World."

64. Parks, *Mariemont Story.*

65. *Bylaws,* Mariemont Village Assembly, October, 1975, p. 1.

66. Hamer, *History in Urban Places,* appendix.

67. The application by Mariemont to the National Register of Historic Places and the companion architectural inventory is on file in the MPF. Local newspapers covered the community's application. "Mariemont Hails Historic Status Bid," *Cincinnati Post,* 24 March 1978, p. 13. "Mariemonters Back Historic Status Bid," *Cincinnati Enquirer,* 5 May 1978, p. B2.

68. "Mariemont on Historic Register," *Cincinnati Enquirer,* 2 August 1979, p. C2. "Mariemont Placed on Historic Register," *Cincinnati Post,* 2 August 1979, p. 16. The Mariemont Preservation Foundation began in 1980.

Chapter Eight

Giving Meaning to Democracy: The Development of the Fair Housing Movement in Cincinnati, 1945–1970

CHARLES F. CASEY-LEININGER

Massive and decaying African American inner-city neighborhoods re-main among the most visible reminders of the continuing failure to obtain racial justice in the United States. The period of twenty-five or so years after World War II is especially crucial to understanding the growth and persis-tence of these involuntarily segregated communities, since it was then that they mushroomed to unprecedented size. This is also an important period in understanding these communities because it was then that the civil rights movement achieved a string of legal victories that sought to eliminate invol-untary racial residential segregation. These victories began with *Shelly v. Kraemer* (1948), which banned racially restrictive covenants, and culmi-nated with the Fair Housing Act of 1968 and *Jones v. Mayer* (1968), which together banned virtually all racial discrimination in real estate transac-tions. These victories failed, however, to achieve their goals.[1]

The story of the struggle against involuntary residential segregation in Cincinnati does much to illustrate both why the fair housing wing of the civil rights movement achieved its victories and why American cities remain highly segregated. Ironically, a portion of the story involves the invocation of the right of self-determination, which has been so ably cham-pioned by civil rights activists but used by others to effectively perpetuate residential segregation. The struggle for individual freedom contributed materially to the creation of Housing Opportunities Made Equal, a Cincin-nati organization devoted to helping African Americans gain access to the housing of their choice, and to the passage of state open housing legislation in Ohio. Opponents of open housing, however, found it possible to under-mine efforts to create housing choices for blacks by arguing that neighborhood residents had the right to determine the character of their communities, an argument that resonated across both class and color lines.

Cincinnati's first large-scale residential concentration of African Americans took shape around the turn of the century in the city's old West End adjacent to the central business district. By 1940, 64 percent of Cincinnati's black population lived in that neighborhood's decaying housing, an area then 74 percent black. Following World War II massive racial population shifts changed the face of the Cincinnati metropolitan area. Between 1940 and 1960 the black population in Cincinnati increased from 55,600 (12 percent) to 108,800 (22 percent), with 64 percent (69,200) of the city's blacks now living outside the West End in expanding racially segregated communities.[2]

This massive shift resulted from a number of circumstances in addition to the large increase in black population. The inability of the city to provide adequate relocation housing for the large numbers of African Americans displaced from the West End by slum clearance starting in the mid-1950s exacerbated an already existing housing shortage for black Cincinnatians. This shortage had resulted from severe housing discrimination and little new residential construction during the Depression and World War II. Real estate brokers of both races took advantage of this situation by encouraging whites, through a variety of means, to move out of areas adjacent to African American neighborhoods. As a consequence, many neighborhoods changed rapidly from white to black, sometimes within a matter of months, as whites fled to the new suburbs on the urban fringe.

But even this rapid racial change failed to provide an adequate supply of black housing. Consequently those selling or renting to blacks could charge inflated prices. Under these circumstances, housing stock in new black neighborhoods often deteriorated as both absentee landlords—under little pressure to compete for tenants—and financially strapped black homeowners failed to maintain their properties. As a result, between 1945 and 1960 racial residential shifts combined with racial discrimination to create a slum-ghetto vastly larger than anything the city had seen before.[3]

A new awareness of the relationship between the creation of slums and racial housing discrimination provided the initial impetus for a fair housing movement in Cincinnati. In the pre–World War II period, Cincinnati housing reform organizations and city planners had encouraged racially and class-segregated residential neighborhoods on the basis of their current understanding of good housing policy. But in the postwar period they attacked involuntary racial residential segregation, first because they had come to believe that it helped create and perpetuate bad housing and slum neighborhoods, and later as a fundamental infringement of the rights of African Americans and poor people to freedom of choice in place of residence. African American activists, for their part, had concentrated before the war on gaining access to an equitable portion of newly built public housing for their constituencies while acquiescing in racial segregation. In the postwar period, they vigorously attacked involuntary racial residential segregation as a fundamental infringement of the right to freedom of choice in housing, while also arguing that segregation was bad housing policy.[4]

Cincinnati's African American leaders were in the forefront of attacking discrimination as a cause of slums after World War II. In 1945, Theodore Berry, a black Cincinnati attorney, testified before the Ohio Urban Redevelopment Commission about the likely impact of racial discrimination on urban renewal. Speaking as president of the Cincinnati Branch of the NAACP and as a representative of the Ohio Conference of NAACP Branches, Berry urged the commission to bar racial discrimination in housing built under Ohio's proposed urban renewal program. Berry argued that the restriction of blacks to limited neighborhoods in Cincinnati and other Ohio cities had contributed to a critical housing shortage for blacks and to slum conditions in black neighborhoods. Failure to end housing discrimination, he argued, would result in the creation of new slums even as the old ones were being leveled. Berry apparently failed in this effort because in June 1953, as a Cincinnati City Council member, he fought for and won the passage of an ordinance requiring that deeds to land cleared by the city under its urban redevelopment program contain a clause banning racial discrimination in their subsequent use.[5]

But the most important attack by Berry and the NAACP on housing discrimination during the 1950s came in the spring of 1954 when they tried to force the integration of a proposed private housing development in northern Hamilton County. This time they argued primarily on the grounds of freedom of choice in housing. Berry argued that the city of Cincinnati should block the supply of water to the development unless its developers promised an open housing market. Since Cincinnati owned the waterworks that supplied most of Hamilton County, the project's developers, the Warner-Kanter Corporation, had to contract with Cincinnati for its water supply. Berry and the NAACP concluded that for the city to cooperate with Warner-Kanter constituted government assistance in creating a new racially segregated community. This, they argued, was fundamentally unfair to African Americans.[6]

For their part, the Cincinnati city administration and the not-for-profit Cincinnati Community Development Corporation (CCDC), which had initiated the plans for the development, believed that the city desperately needed the project to relieve serious overcrowding in Cincinnati's slums so that demolition could begin for proposed West End urban renewal projects. The city and CCDC hoped to fill the proposed eleven thousand housing units in the development, which eventually became the city of Forest Park, with white, middle-income city dwellers. The city housing vacated would then become available to moderate-income residents of slum clearance sites, while public and private low-income housing projects would take care of those unable to compete for market-rate housing.[7]

The NAACP acknowledged that the development had the potential for "relieving the housing stresses among the entire population of the City of Cincinnati," but argued that "a municipality concerned with the welfare of all the elements of its population" would negotiate for a nondiscrimination clause. In addition, the NAACP asserted that the absence of such a clause would violate democratic principles and "give further ammunition to those who claim that American democracy is a democracy in words . . . but a fraud in practice."[8]

Ultimately, the council amended the proposed water contract with Warner-Kanter to include a clause that bound the developer to a nondiscriminatory policy "if, as, and when" the general city-county water contract then under negotiation between the council and the Hamilton County commissioners included such a clause. But on December 15, 1954, the council voted to approve a thirty-year water contract with Hamilton County without a nondiscrimination clause. That action rendered the nondiscrimination clause in the Forest Park contract void, a result that the council, no doubt, had fully expected.[9]

Others joined Berry and the Cincinnati NAACP in their attack on housing discrimination during the 1950s, including the Better Housing League (BHL), the Mayor's Friendly Relations Committee (MFRC), the Cincinnati Metropolitan Housing Authority (CMHA), and residents of several racially changing neighborhoods.[10] The activities of the BHL and the CMHA provide a dramatic reminder of how much attitudes toward the volatile mix of race and housing had changed. Prior to the end of World War II, the BHL had been an active ally of the Cincinnati city administration and the CMHA in creating racially segregated neighborhoods and public housing projects. Starting in the mid-1950s, however, members of the BHL began to quietly express concern about the effect of housing discrimination on the city's slum housing problem. By the late 1950s, the BHL publicly advocated a racially open housing market. The BHL had concluded that opening white residential communities throughout the metropolitan area to blacks was the only way to empty decaying residential areas slated for redevelopment without contributing to the overcrowding and excessive housing costs that helped create new slums in black neighborhoods.[11]

The CMHA also broke with its earlier support of segregated housing and began in the 1950s to seek ways to integrate its projects. Ramsey Findlater, head of the CMHA, promised as early as 1951 that the housing authority would no longer draw the color line. Indeed, during the first half of the 1950s, the CMHA sought to build small projects of three hundred to six hundred units integrated into existing neighborhoods scattered throughout the metropolitan area. Instead, it found itself repeatedly blocked by whites who feared the mostly black West End residents who would likely fill these projects as urban renewal destroyed the old ghetto. Because of these defeats, the CMHA was forced to build mostly large-scale projects on land it already owned close to or adjacent to projects it already operated.[12]

Despite the defeat of its scatter-site efforts, the CMHA attempted to integrate three of its projects during the 1950s. It opened its new Millvale project to both whites and blacks during 1954 and 1955, but found few whites willing to move in even when they were allowed to occupy the second phase of the project before blacks. In 1955, the CMHA also tried to integrate the white section of its prewar Laurel Homes project. Faced with the high demand for housing among low-income blacks and vacancies in the white section, the CMHA opened all of the project to blacks. Many white families moved out soon afterward, and within three years few remained.[13]

In 1958, the CMHA again attempted to integrate a new project, Findlater Gardens. It hoped that with help from the MFRC, the Urban League, and other organizations it could finally create a stable racially integrated project. This attempt was particularly important to the CMHA. In 1943, at the completion of its World War II–era project building, CMHA projects held equal numbers of blacks and whites in segregated locations. But with the exodus of whites from Laurel Homes and the almost complete occupation of Millvale by blacks, only its Winton Terrace and English Woods projects had white tenants. CMHA officials worried that if Findlater filled with blacks it might lead to an exodus of whites from the adjacent Winton Terrace. That situation, CMHA officials feared, would confirm the perception of white Cincinnatians that public housing was for blacks only, and as a result voter approval for funding for desperately needed additional projects would disappear.[14]

The CMHA faced grave problems. Slum clearance had recently begun in the West End, and applications for Findlater Gardens ran "10 to 1 colored" four months before the first units would be completed. Moreover, low-income whites displaced from slum clearance sites were finding housing with relative ease. As a result, rather than merely dropping the color bar to Findlater, the CMHA moved white residents in first, kept blacks in the minority of project residents, and assigned them apartments in scattered locations. For a time the presence of a few black families in Findlater Gardens had little effect on the white residents of either Findlater or Winton Terrace. However, by 1970 few white residents remained in either project.[15]

The Mayor's Friendly Relations Committee during the 1950s intervened several times in attempts to encourage peaceful neighborhood transitions to stable racial residential integration. Perhaps the most volatile situation developed in the spring of 1953 in the city's Avon View neighborhood adjacent to the expanding ghetto after an anxious white home-owner decided to sell to an African American family. Soon real estate agents induced panic selling by warning residents that if they did not sell their houses quickly their property values would drop precipitously. At the request of Avon View residents, the MFRC led a neighborhood meeting intended to "help quiet the hysteria and dispel stereotypes." In addition, the MFRC helped form a racially mixed community council. Nevertheless, some blacks moving into the area needed police protection, and the neighborhood became virtually all black soon after.[16]

A mile away and six years later, the Crescent Civic Association (CCA) also failed to keep its neighborhood racially mixed. In 1959, that group organized residents of a four- or five-block area that previously had been almost all white and largely middle class. Many of the new, mostly middle-class black families who began to move into the area in early 1959 joined with a number of the remaining white families to protect their neighborhood from deteriorating, as had some nearby areas that had undergone nearly complete racial transition. The CCA used two complementary tactics. It successfully lobbied the city of Cincinnati to upgrade the zoning of the area to allow only one- and two-family housing units. It hoped that this would keep the large homes that dominated the area from being chopped up into multiunit apartments and rooming houses. It also sponsored a "not for sale" sign campaign to fight against panic selling by whites. Despite these efforts, the association survived for less than a year and failed to preserve its area as both racially mixed and middle class.[17]

Park Town Cooperative homes, opened in 1961, provided the most widely publicized contemporary example of the failure of integration in Cincinnati. As such it illustrated the host of problems facing any integrated neighborhood in this period and the limits to the ideal of a "free" housing market held by supporters of integration. Park Town was one of two privately built housing developments on the city's first postwar slum clearance site. City officials, good housing advocates, and civil rights groups hoped that Park Town would become a flagship for the renewal of a portion of the West End as moderate- and middle-income housing attractive to both whites and blacks. Vast areas of slums to the west and north of downtown were slated for redevelopment as good housing and new commercial and industrial areas.[18]

Park Town, however, had little chance of remaining a racially integrated middle-income community. Perhaps the central reason was that racial discrimination in housing had combined with other factors to make the demand for housing among all classes of blacks desperate. These factors included a growing black population, the failure of the city to develop sufficient low-income housing, and the displacement of thousands of black families because of superhighway construction and slum clearance since the mid-1950s. In contrast, new construction on the urban fringe, like Forest Park, open only to whites, made it possible for most whites, including low-income whites, to find housing with relative ease either in these new developments or in formerly middle-class housing. Park Town had the added disadvantage of being surrounded by new and existing public and private housing occupied almost completely by low-income African Americans. Only the most committed white pioneers of racial integration were willing to buy apartments in Park Town, and there was an insufficient number of such pioneers. As vacancies in the new apartments stretched over many months, Park Town's management was forced to refinance the development under a federal program targeted to low- and moderate-income families displaced from slum clearance sites. Although Park Town retained its cooperative ownership scheme, it, like the projects that the CMHA had tried to integrate, soon filled mostly with black residents.[19]

As it became clearer that Park Town's survival as an integrated community was in grave danger, its advocates moved beyond support for a housing market unencumbered by racial restrictions to one where they and government agencies would promote integration through coercion, if necessary. To that end, advocates for Park Town persuaded the city of Cincinnati to try to force the owners of the adjacent Richmond Village low-income development to stop rejecting white applicants—white Park Town advocates had "tested" Richmond Village and been turned away. And advocates sought, unsuccessfully, to persuade the CMHA to punish white applicants for public housing by placing them at the bottom of its waiting list if they refused to accept available space in its new Stanley Rowe Towers project to the north of Park Town. Indeed, whites seeking CMHA housing consistently refused to accept apartments in Rowe Towers or other largely black projects, preferring to wait for space in white projects or to seek housing in the private market.[20]

By the early 1960s, then, efforts to open public housing to blacks on an integrated basis had largely failed, though the results of the Findlater Garden experiment remained in doubt. Moreover, efforts to stabilize racially mixed neighborhoods had failed repeatedly, and the attempt to build a new, middle-income racially integrated community from the ground up seemed doomed to failure. Reflecting this situation, the minutes of the MFRC's October 1959 meeting noted, "Our Committee on Changing Neighborhoods . . . concluded that slowdown in change rate, not permanent integration was the best attainable goal *under present conditions.*"[21]

As a result, a new and more activist approach to attacking racial housing discrimination began to develop in Cincinnati. During the 1950s, most fair housing advocates, except for the NAACP, had not sought to use the law to end discrimination, but rather had attempted to persuade whites to voluntarily accept racial residential integration through public relations campaigns and through mediation between old and new residents of racially changing neighborhoods. Indeed, Park Town had been opened with a fanfare of publicity intended to entice middle-income whites. But it had become clear that most whites would not voluntarily live in integrated neighborhoods. The few whites willing to live in mixed neighborhoods soon found themselves in a very small minority and generally moved to areas with a more even mix of races or abandoned the effort. Faced with this, advocates of fair housing attempted to force the integration of Richmond Village and Stanley Rowe with the few tools they had available to them. These same advocates also began to work for laws that would "give ... democracy meaning" by banning racial housing discrimination, and they attempted to apply the lessons that they had learned to new neighborhoods.[22]

This work became intimately intertwined in Cincinnati's North Avondale neighborhood. The North Avondale Neighborhood Association (NANA), formed in 1960, welcomed "all good neighbors, without prejudice as to race, creed, or color, believing that people can live together harmoniously." NANA's territory encompassed some of the most stately mansions in Cincinnati, but was also in the direct path of the expanding ghetto. Some sections were rapidly becoming all black, increasing in multifamily housing, and becoming home to more moderate-income families. But NANA's leadership believed that simply creating an open housing market in the neighborhood would not assure stability as an integrated community. As long as good housing open to blacks remained limited to a few neighborhoods, North Avondale faced the likelihood that black demand would so overwhelm the neighborhood housing market that it would rapidly become largely black.[23]

NANA attacked this threat to choice in several ways. It sought to maintain racial balance by trying to calm North Avondale homeowners in areas where panic selling seemed imminent, by trying to dissuade real estate agents from activities that might contribute to panic selling, by actively recruiting whites to live in the neighborhood, by trying to dissuade the local newspapers from racial labeling in real estate ads, and by working to maintain the residential values of the neighborhood at the high standards that had attracted middle-class whites before it became racially mixed, including working to upgrade zoning to help preserve the character of much of the neighborhood as one of single-family homes. Moreover, it opposed the placement in the neighborhood of several institutions and businesses that it believed inappropriate because they served blacks almost exclusively.[24]

NANA also worked for fair housing legislation, knowing that North Avondale had little chance of remaining integrated as long as discrimination closed most good neighborhoods to blacks. Theodore Berry, now a resident of North Avondale, and two other NANA members drafted an ordinance in early 1962 that proposed to prohibit real estate brokers from soliciting home-owners to list their houses for sale. Concentrated and repeated "cold canvassing" often resulted in panic and flight by white homeowners and tenants, NANA claimed. As an alternative, city manager C. A. Harrell proposed an ordinance based on one adopted recently in Shaker Heights, Ohio, a Cleveland suburb. This would have made it illegal to "Incite, arouse or refer to neighborhood unrest, community tension or racial, religious or nationality change in a neighborhood ... for the purpose of inducing ... the sale or lease of real property."[25]

Both ordinances faced opposition from a number of sources. The white

Cincinnati Real Estate Board (CREB) and the black Cincinnati Association of Real Estate Brokers (CAREB) opposed the first ordinance on the grounds that it would interfere with the freedom of their members to conduct business. One black broker argued, and BHL director John G. Vaughan agreed, that the second ordinance might lead to problems for black real estate dealers because whites might interpret the mere presence of an African American broker in a neighborhood as "the use of 'scare tactics.'" Others believed that any local ordinance would be ineffective because it would accelerate the movement of white people from the city to the suburbs. This argument led some, at least, to support statewide open housing legislation, but not local legislation. Others argued that public discussion of local fair housing legislation would help prepare the way for broader legislation on both the state and the national level.[26]

As a result of this new activity in support of fair housing legislation, Cincinnati advocates reactivated the Greater Cincinnati Committee on Equal Opportunity in Housing (later renamed Housing Opportunities Made Equal or HOME), which they had founded in 1960. HOME's existence as an active and effective organization dates from the fall of 1962 and its decision to focus on state fair housing legislation through its role as a local unit of the Ohio Committee for Civil Rights Legislation (OCCRL). A November 27, 1962, meeting of HOME brought together representatives from the Urban League, the Jewish Community Relations Committee (JCRC), the Better Housing League, Park Town, the NAACP, the AFL-CIO, the MFRC, and other housing reform and civil rights organizations.[27]

Despite election-year support for the "principle of fair housing legislation" from James A. Rhodes, the successful Republican candidate for governor, prospects for its passage looked grim. After the November 1962 election, Republicans dominated the general assembly. Only two blacks sat in the House and no blacks sat in the state Senate. Moreover, the Republicans had elected conservatives to leadership roles in both the House and Senate, and Rhodes's support seemed cool at best.[28]

Nevertheless, in January 1963, the Ohio Civil Rights Commission released a report based on hearings on housing discrimination in twelve cities, including Cincinnati. The commissioners proposed a strong law with few loopholes and strong enforcement powers. Only two-family dwellings where the owner occupied one unit or rental rooms in single-family homes would be excluded from coverage. Moreover, common pleas courts would be given the power to grant temporary restraining orders for thirty days, subject to extension, to prevent the sale or rental of property where prospective tenants accused owners or their agents of illegal discrimination. In mid-February supporters of fair housing in the Ohio House introduced House Bill 308 with provisions virtually identical to those recommended by the OCRC.[29]

The Ohio Committee on Civil Rights Legislation, led by Theodore Berry and white Cincinnati businessman Charles Judd, provided strong but unsuccessful support for the bill. This support included a Statehouse rally in late May, as it became clear the bill was in trouble, attended by approximately one thousand demonstrators, including a number of Cincinnatians. Further demonstrations followed in mid-June as more than two hundred demonstrators from around the state conducted "chain-ins, lie-ins, and sit-ins" at the Statehouse. Demonstrators remained until June 20, when the House Government Operations Committee killed the bill.[30]

The results of the November 1964 general election sent mixed messages to fair housing advocates planning a second attempt to obtain state open housing legislation. In Akron, voters repealed a fair housing law passed by their city council earlier in the year. But the landslide vote for Lyndon Johnson for president helped sweep enough Democrats into the Ohio General Assembly to weaken Republican control. So on February 22, 1965, three state senators introduced SB 113, a bill that virtually duplicated HB 308. And in March, fair housing advocates received a boost when the Ohio Supreme Court found that a city of Oberlin fair housing law did not violate the Ohio Constitution.[31]

Senate Republican leadership countered with a substantially weaker alternative, SB 189, and then bottled it up in committee from April 1 until mid-June as it maneuvered to force Democrats to accept it. Republican leadership apparently wanted a weak fair housing bill that they could use to appease both black voters and white opponents, and they wanted Democrats to accept the bill so it would appear bipartisan.[32]

Fair housing supporters worked to strengthen the bill through pressure on the legislature. Cincinnati supporters urged city council to go on record in support of SB 113. But the council waffled and voted support for both bills. And on June 9, the OCCRL and the Ohio Council of NAACP Branches sponsored demonstrations at Republican fund-raising meetings in Cleveland, Columbus, Toledo, Youngstown, Canton, Cincinnati, Lima, and Dayton. In Cincinnati, HOME, the NAACP, CORE, the Catholic Interracial Council, and the Council of Churches sponsored a demonstration and called for "as many people as possible to show Cincinnati is in favor of Fair Housing."[33]

Despite a handful of strengthening amendments, the bill, which passed both houses in late July, remained critically weak. It failed to include large numbers of real estate transactions by exempting the sale, rental, or leasing of owner-occupied one- and two-family housing, a situation that included most sales. But its fundamental weakness lay in its enforcement procedures. It required that only bona fide home-seekers could file complaints, a provision that ruled out complaints by advocates who had no intention of actually renting or buying. In addition, the bill required that complainants post "sufficient bond" before a court could issue a temporary injunction or restraining order against a defendant, and it required that the OCRC determine that a complainant "acted with intention of fulfilling any contracts or agreements he was seeking" before holding hearings on a case. Both of these clauses seemed designed to discourage all but the most determined complainants. Moreover, the law imposed no time limits on the Civil Rights Commission in reaching conclusions in cases before it. Indeed, as efforts by HOME and others would show, it was virtually unenforceable.[34]

After the passage of the bill, HOME transformed itself from an organization devoted largely to legislative advocacy to one intended primarily to serve a mostly black clientele seeking housing outside of traditional African American areas. In the fall of 1966, a year after the effective date of the new state fair housing law, HOME began its attempt to obtain enforcement under its first paid director—Martha Smudski, a white woman and former member of the Mayor's Friendly Relations Committee. In planning its program of enforcement, HOME reaffirmed its belief in an open housing market: "The opportunity to compete for housing of one's choice is crucial to both equality and freedom. No one can be said to be really free unless he can freely choose where he will live—limited only by his own personal preferences and financial ability."[35]

This commitment to choice is critical to understanding HOME's program over the next several years. Indeed, a HOME proposal for a low-income housing plan prepared about this time stated explicitly that HOME was "not committed to the principle of 'wiping out the ghetto.'"[36] Rather, HOME committed itself to developing programs designed to increase choice, rather than to promote pro-integrative moves. This meant providing information, moral support, and legal assistance when blacks, primarily middle-income blacks, chose to look for housing in white neighborhoods. In these largely individual investigations, white members worked as "checkers" to test whether rental and sales agents practiced racial discrimination. Members also assisted blacks seeking housing outside African American neighborhoods by providing information on how to find and obtain housing and acting as escorts into white neighborhoods. Smudski coordinated these activities and helped to pursue cases of discrimination with the Ohio Civil Rights Commission.[37]

HOME first tested the law when Smudski went to the OCRC in late 1966 about an illegal apartment rental ad in the *Cincinnati Enquirer*. The ad stated that the rental was available to "colored" tenants. Despite the clear violation of the law, the commission informed Smudski that she had no standing to file a complaint because she was not herself seeking the apartment. Smudski persisted with her work, and by March 1967, HOME had helped clients file four cases with the OCRC, although with little result.[38]

Smudski's notes on one such case revealed both clear racial discrimination by the landlord and the ineffectiveness of local OCRC employees whose job it was to investigate. In that incident, on Tuesday, February 21, 1967, a landlord refused to show an apartment advertised in a local newspaper to a "Miss P." The landlord told her that there were no vacancies and that he would allow no African Americans to live there. She immediately complained to Sanford Wright at the Cincinnati NAACP office. When Wright called about the apartment, he was told that vacancies existed, but when he arrived in person he was told there were none and that he might find an apartment at an address in a mostly black neighborhood.[39]

Wright then enlisted Smudski's help. Smudski assigned one of HOME's volunteer checkers to the case. He went to the apartments, inspected two of them, and placed a deposit. He reported that when he gave the landlord his current address, the landlord said, "Oh, they have colored and white over there, but we don't mix them here." With that information Smudski called Arthur E. Layman, director of the local OCRC office, to see what action could be taken. Layman spoke with Miss P. and then informed Smudski that he would have an investigator, Perry Brunson, on the case Thursday morning.[40]

On Thursday evening, Smudski found Miss P. had failed to sign a complaint because she was confused and overwhelmed. Brunson had warned her that he could not handle her case if she was merely testing for violations of the law. In addition, he warned that she needed to be prepared to move into the apartment immediately, despite the fact that she had never seen it and had no basis on which to make the decision. Smudski, however, reassured Miss P., who signed the complaint late on Friday afternoon, February 24. By February 28, however, the OCRC had made no attempt to confront the landlord or to settle the case. This delay occurred despite a new directive from the OCRC central office in Columbus instructing local OCRC offices to contact landlords within forty-eight hours after filing a signed complaint.[41]

HOME's records fail to reveal the outcome of this case or the other three filed in this period. But in early 1968 HOME complained that with regard to cases it had helped file, "One charge filed in January 1967 has just been scheduled for public hearing on February 29, 1968. In the only other charge which went to public hearing on Nov. 21, 1967, the findings of the hearing examiner have not yet been submitted to the Commission as of [Feb. 12, 1968]."[42]

Because of the difficulties of enforcing the Ohio fair housing law, HOME turned to challenging housing discrimination under the federal Civil Rights Act of 1968 and the Supreme Court finding in *Jones v. Meyer* (1968) that the Civil Rights Act of 1866 outlawed racial discrimination in housing. And experience apparently proved helpful to HOME, because it won several cases against housing discrimination in the late 1960s. Nevertheless, it is clear that only the most tenacious person could effectively fight the evasions and delays perpetrated by discriminatory landlords and inept or indifferent public officials. Indeed, the level of racial residential segregation in Cincinnati decreased little between 1960 and 1980.[43]

The failure of the battle against racial housing discrimination coincided with the emergence in Cincinnati of a huge and economically segregated

African American ghetto. Prior to World War II, public policy and racial antipathy largely confined blacks in Cincinnati to two relatively small geographic areas, the West End and Walnut Hills-South Avondale. In 1940 these two areas accounted for 80 percent of Cincinnati's black population. Although good housing existed in both of these communities, their small geographic extent made it difficult for blacks who could afford quality housing to escape close proximity to slum conditions. By 1970 a sharper stratification on the basis of income had developed in the now vastly larger "second ghetto." Relatively high incomes and fair housing laws allowed some African Americans to move outside the areas of heaviest black concentration. Nine of the twenty-two census tracts with black median family annual incomes over $6,500 (the median for the city's African American families) and a black population over four hundred lay outside those areas greater than 50 percent black. In addition, all but one West End census tract had a black median family income below the citywide median for black families. All eleven census tracts in Hamilton County outside the city with more than four hundred blacks had median family incomes above $6,870, the median for Hamilton County African American families, and only two had greater than 50 percent black population. Tracts with high black incomes generally clustered together, as did tracts with low black incomes. But higher incomes enabled few blacks to escape racial residential segregation. Indeed, calculations of the degree of segregation in the Cincinnati Standard Metropolitan Statistical Area at the 1980 census showed that middle- and high-income Cincinnatians were only slightly less residentially segregated on the basis of race than were low-income Cincinnatians.[44]

The fair housers failed to create substantial housing choice for African Americans and to disperse the ghetto in the 1960s and 1970s for several reasons, including the low incomes of many blacks, racial antipathy between blacks and whites, and racially discriminatory sales practices by real estate agents. A report prepared in late 1964 makes clear the financial difficulties facing the black Cincinnati home-buyer. It observed that in 1959 only sixty-six hundred black families earned enough to compete in the housing market, even if all racial restriction ceased to exist. Moreover, in addition to overt discriminatory practices that a law might ban and commitment to existing housing that many could be expected to have, the report argued that the racial attitudes of both blacks and whites would restrict the growth of integrated neighborhoods—many of both races would simply decide that living with the other race was not worth the trouble.[45]

But open housing legislation largely failed even for blacks with adequate incomes and the fortitude to seek housing in white areas. HOME found in the 1980s and 1990s that real estate agents still steered prospective buyers to housing in neighborhoods with residents predominantly of the same race as the prospective buyer, that they listed school districts in real estate advertisements as codes for the racial characteristics of neighborhoods, and that the city of Cincinnati continued to site low-income housing in low-income, especially black, neighborhoods. Moreover, government at all levels failed to enforce fair housing laws, leaving that up to HOME and individual African Americans who chose to bring charges against those who discriminated against them.[46]

Despite its early allegiance to an ideology of equal opportunity and individual choice, HOME's leadership came to recognize that tactics based on these ideas had not worked as they hoped. While not abandoning the ideal of a free housing market, HOME began to espouse a variety of affirmative action programs intended to tilt the playing field in favor of racial residential integration and toward dispersing the black populations of racially segregated neighborhoods throughout the metropolitan area.[47] As Charles Judd, a founding member, noted in 1990, "For many of us in the civil rights struggle over the years, freedom of choice with no restrictions based on race, color, creed, sex, age or national origin has been our goal, even if neighborhoods or institutions became or remain de facto segregated. . . . I would like to argue that even though both [choice and integration] are terribly important for a free society, integration is the more important for our future."[48]

Judd's conclusions speak to an important dilemma in the struggle for racial equity and suggest a largely overlooked reason for the failure of efforts to create housing choices unencumbered by race. Since the mid-1950s the idea of community control of self-defined neighborhoods has emerged as a powerful ideal that has appealed to Americans across racial and class lines. This idea is one of several contradictory and competing tendencies in American social thought, all of which fall under the rubric of support for individual choice and which reflect the widespread desire of many groups in American society for self-determination. The idea of community self-determination attained such widespread legitimacy that in the mid-1960s Lyndon Johnson's Model Cities program incorporated it as a central goal. And in the early 1970s one Cincinnati African American neighborhood activist defended the right of a working-class white neighborhood to oppose the siting there of public housing that would be largely filled by blacks. He did so on the grounds that whites had the right to control the nature of their communities.[49]

For their part, wealthier white neighborhoods effectively camouflaged race and class concerns by also invoking the notion of community control when they opposed subsidized housing for their neighborhoods. Indeed, among the most bitterly fought battles caused by conflicts between the perceived needs of black communities and white communities was the siting of low-income subsidized housing that would be occupied largely by blacks. Black neighborhoods often rejected such developments because they increased the concentration of poor people in already overcrowded and overly poor communities, while whites rejected them on the grounds that they lowered property values, increased the likelihood of crime, and changed the nature of their communities unacceptably. The question became which community ought to have control over such planning. Too often the wealthier and more powerful white neighborhoods were the ones with the control.[50]

Given this set of circumstances, a stalemate now exists in the attempt to help poor blacks move out of unsafe and decaying neighborhoods and to give middle- and upper-income blacks significant choices about where they might live. This situation sends a powerful message to all African Americans. Even if against the odds they manage to do what mainstream society asks—get a good education, find a job, raise a family, and partici-pate constructively in the social and civic life of the wider community—the quintessential American reward of decent housing in the neighbor-hood of their choice may still be denied to them. The frustration of this promise can be expected to embitter middle-class and prosperous blacks and to corrode the will of impoverished African Americans to break out of poverty on their own or to take advantage of programs intended to increase their economic opportunities. It may also help in the maintenance and growth of an alienated black underclass as numbers of African Ameri-can youth of all classes reject the values of a society that denies them access to one of its most treasured goals.

Notes

I wish to acknowledge the support of the Graduate School of Arts and Sciences of the University of Cincinnati, which provided me with a Graduate Summer Research Fellowship, an Advanced Taft Fellowship, and a University Dean's Distinguished Dissertation Fellowship. This support enabled me to complete the dissertation from which this chapter is drawn. I also appreciate the gener-ous leave policies of the Children's Defense Fund, which provided me with the time to complete this essay.

1. Douglas S. Massey and Nancy A. Denton, *American Apartheid: Segregation and the Making of the Underclass* (Cambridge: Harvard University Press, 1993), esp. pp. 186–216.

2. Zane L. Miller, *Boss Cox's Cincinnati: Urban Politics in the Progressive Era* (New York: Oxford University Press, 1968), pp. 14–15, 28, 30–31, and 251 n. 8; United States Department of Commerce, Bureau of the Census, *Thirteenth Cen-sus of the United States Taken in the Year 1910* (Washington, D.C., 1913), vol. 3, pp. 426–27; *Sixteenth Census of the United States: Population and Housing: 1940, Statistics for Census Tracts, Cincinnati, Ohio, and Adjacent Area* (Washington, D.C., 1942), p. 4; United States Department of Commerce, Bureau of the Cen-sus, *United States Census of Population and Housing: 1960, Census Tracts, Cincin-nati, Ohio-Ky* (Washington, D.C.), pp. 15, 70.

3. Charles F. Casey-Leininger, "Creating Democracy in Housing: Civil Rights and Housing Policy in Cincinnati, 1945–1980" (Ph.D. dissertation, University of Cincinnati, 1993), especially chaps. 2, 3, and 4, and "Making the Second Ghetto in Cincinnati: Avondale, 1925–1970," in *Race and the City: Work, Community, Housing, and Protest in Cincinnati, 1820–1970,* Henry Louis Taylor Jr., ed. (Urbana: University of Illinois Press, 1993).

4. See Robert B. Fairbanks, *Making Better Citizens: Housing Reform and the Community Development Strategy in Cincinnati, 1890–1960* (Urbana: University of Illinois Press, 1988), for a discussion of prewar housing policy in Cincinnati and the African American response to it.

5. "Race Segregation Ban is Urged in Housing Jams," *Cincinnati Post,* Dec. 6, 1945; City of Cincinnati, Ordinance No. 318–1953, July 1, 1953.

6. Cincinnati Community Development Co. and Warner-Kanter Co. to Council of the City of Cincinnati, Feb. 17, 1954, Theodore M. Berry Collection, mss782, box 6, file 9, Cincinnati Historical Society; "Warner-Kanter—Suggestions Re: Water Contract," Berry Collection, box 6, file 9.

7. Zane L. Miller, *Suburb: Neighborhood and Community in Forest Park, Ohio, 1935–1976* (Knoxville: University of Tennessee Press, 1981), chap. 2.

8. Cincinnati NAACP, "Statement to Cincinnati City Council of position of the Cincinnati branch of the National Association for the Advancement of Colored People on the proposed Greenhills Development," Apr. 20, 1954, Berry Collection, box 6, file 9; City of Cincinnati, *City Bulletin* 28 (Apr. 27, 1954), p. 2; James W. Farrell Jr. to "Hon. Members of Council," May 21, 1954, Berry Collection, box 6, file 9; "Says Withdraw City Aid From Jimcrow Units," *Cleveland Call and Post,* May 1, 1954.

9. *City Bulletin* 28 (June 1, 1954), p. 3; *City Bulletin* 28 (Dec. 21, 1954), p. 2; Miller, *Suburb,* p. 42.

10. Founded in 1943 in the wake of the Detroit race riots, the Mayor's Friendly Relations Committee sought to reduce racial tensions by mediating between African American organizations and the city administration and between blacks and whites as they came into contact in the workplace and in their neighborhoods. In 1964 it became the Cincinnati Human Relations Commission. See Robert A. Burnham, "The Mayor's Friendly Relations Committee: Cultural Pluralism and the Struggle for Black Advancement," in *Race and the City: Work, Community, Housing, and Protest in Cincinnati, 1820–1970,* Henry Louis Taylor Jr., ed. (Urbana: University of Illinois Press, 1993). The Better Housing League was founded in 1916 by housing reformers who sought to attack Cincinnati's growing slum problem. Through at least the 1960s it played an important role in shaping housing policy in Cincinnati. Fairbanks, *Making Better Citizens,* pp. 29–30.

11. Fairbanks, *Making Better Citizens,* chap. 9; Better Housing League Board Minutes, Dec. 16, 1954, Better Housing League Collection, University of Cincinnati Libraries, Department of Archives and Rare Books; Better Housing League, "Page-a-Month," no. 204, June–July 1958, BHL Collection; *Cincinnati Enquirer,* May 20, 1959, p. 8A.

12. Fairbanks, *Making Better Citizens*, pp. 251ff; BHL Minutes, Dec. 20, 1951, Mar. 27, 1951, BHL Collection.

13. Henry L. Reece, "Recapitulation of the Cincinnati Metropolitan Housing Authority's Experience with Racial Integration," Urban League Collection, Cincinnati Historical Society, box 5, file 4; MFRC Annual Report for 1955 [1956], Cincinnati Human Relations Commission (CHRC) Collection, University of Cincinnati Libraries, Department of Archives and Rare Books, S.32, box 1.

14. Reece, "Recapitulation."

15. Ibid.; MFRC Annual Report for 1955, 4; MFRC Board Minutes, Sept. 11, 1958, p. 1; Oct. 9, 1958, pp. 1–2, CHRC Collection; United States Department of Commerce, Bureau of the Census, *1970 Census of Population and Housing, Census Tracts, Cincinnati Standard Metropolitan Statistical Area* (Washington, D.C.: Government Printing Office, 1972).

16. *Cincinnati Enquirer*, classified advertising section, Apr. 4, 18, 25, 1954; MFRC Board Minutes, Apr. 9, 1953, CHRC Collection; Ethel Edwards, *Ringside Seat on Revolution*, (Cincinnati: Psyche Press, 1972), pp. 44–48; MFRC Board Minutes, Apr. 9, 1953, p. 2, May 14, 1953, p. 3, CHRC Collection; MFRC Board Minutes, Feb. 20, 1958, pp. 2–3, CHRC Collection.

17. *Cincinnati Post*, Feb. 4, 1958; MFRC, "Minutes of the Board of Trustees," Feb. 20, 1958, pp. 2–3, CHRC Collection; Gary P. Kocolowski, "The History of North Avondale: A Study of the Effects of Urbanization Upon an Urban Locality" (M.A. thesis, University of Cincinnati, 1971), pp. 47–50; "Cincinnati Residents Fight to Prevent Real Estate Panic," *Cincinnati Post*, May 16, 1959, p. 4–A; George Amick, "'Crescents' Stand Fast," *Cincinnati Enquirer*, May 18, 1959, p. 1–A.

18. Charles F. Casey-Leininger, "Park Town Cooperative Homes, Urban Redevelopment, and the Search for Residential Integration in Cincinnati, 1955–1965," *Queen City Heritage* 52 (Fall 1994): 36–40.

19. Casey-Leininger, "Park Town," pp. 40–43.

20. Ibid., pp. 43–45.

21. MFRC Board Minutes, Oct. 29, 1959, CHRC Collection.

22. See Barbara Hadden to author, interview, Oct. 17, 1984, for an example of a white woman committed to racial integration. Hadden moved in 1959 from one area that was rapidly becoming all black to another area that she helped to become stably racially integrated. Cincinnati NAACP, "News release," n.d., National Association for the Advancement of Colored People, Cincinnati Branch Collection, Cincinnati Historical Society, box 61, file 31.

23. "Bylaws" [1961], North Avondale Neighborhood Association Papers, North Avondale Neighborhood Association Offices, bylaws folder.

24. Helen Ehoodin to author, tape-recorded interview, Oct. 30, 1984; Kocolowski, "History of North Avondale," pp. 59–60, 63.

25. "Proposed Ordinance to Prohibit Certain Types of Solicitation by Real Estate Agents," 1962, Urban League Collection, box 56, file 5; MFRC Minutes, Mar. 28, 1962, CHRC Collection, pp. 1–2; MFRC Minutes, May 16, 1962, CHRC Collection; "An Ordinance . . . Prohibiting Certain Practices Regarding the Sale

of Real Estate . . . ," attached to C. A. Harrell, City Manager, to City Council, Apr. 11, 1962, NAACP Collection, box 31, file 2.

26. *City Bulletin*, Apr. 17, 1962, pp. 1–2; MFRC Minutes, Feb. 28 and May 16, 1962, CHRC Collection; BHL Minutes, Apr. 19 and May 18, 1962, BHL Collection; John Vaughan, *Housing for Negroes in Cincinnati, 1962* (Cincinnati, 1962), pp. 1–2, BHL Collection, US-75–18, box 8, file 93.

27. "Cincinnati Committee for Equal Opportunity in Housing," 1960, typescript with hand-written date "6/15/60" and initials "MB," CHRC Collection, S.32/H3.15; Cincinnati Committee for Equal Opportunity in Housing, Minutes, Nov. 27, 1962, NAACP Collection, box 5, file 31.

28. John B. Combs, "Ohio Capital Comments," *Cleveland Call and Post*, city ed., Oct. 6, 1962, p. 3C; MFRC Minutes, Jan. 23, 1963, CHRC Collection; "Rhodes to Support Fair Housing Bill," *Cleveland Call and Post*, city ed., Nov. 24, 1962, p. 1a; John B. Combs, "Capital Comments," *Cleveland Call and Post*, city ed., Dec. 1, 1962, p. 3C.

29. Ohio Civil Rights Commission, *A Survey of Discrimination in Housing in Ohio*, Urban League Collection, box 34, file 1, pp. 48–49; "Digest of the Fair Housing Bill, attached to "Chas. M. Judd, Chairman, Lois Conyers, Secretary to _____, draft" and "Chas. M. Judd to _____, draft, 1963," HOME Collection, US-82–5, box 1, file 89.

30. "Cincinnatians Lead Civil Rights March," *Cincinnati Enquirer*, May 23, 1963; John Combs, "1,000 Stage March for Fair Housing," *Cleveland Call and Post*, city ed., June 1, 1963, p. 12A; Jesse R. Shaffer, "Columbus: Fair Housing Bill Dies as Committee Fails to Approve," *Cincinnati Enquirer*, June, 23, 1963, Cincinnati Municipal Reference Library Clipping File, xa31; John B. Combs, "Capital Comments," *Cleveland Call and Post*, city ed., June 29, 1963, p. 3C.

31. "Akronites Repeal Fair Housing Legislation," *Cleveland Call and Post*, city ed., Nov. 7, 1964, p. 1A; John B. Combs, "Ohio Capital Comments," *Cleveland Call and Post*, city ed., Nov. 14, 1964, 3C; Casey-Leininger, "Creating Democracy in Housing," pp. 278–87.

32. Casey-Leininger, "Creating Democracy in Housing," pp. 282–87; John B. Combs, "Ohio Senate Passes Fair Housing Bill," *Cleveland Call and Post*, city ed., June 26, 1965, p. 1A; Combs, "Ohio Capital Comments," *Cleveland Call and Post*, city ed., June 26, 1965, p. 9B; Dr. Bruce Green and William E. Garnes, NAACP press release, June 23, 1965, NAACP Collection, box 60, file 34.

33. Abraham Citron, "Housing Bill Sponsors React to City Council Resolution," May 10, 1965, NAACP Collection, box 57, file 9; Nathaniel Lee, Warren Pate, and Harold Strickland, "Memorandum," June 1, 1965, NAACP Collection, box 58, file 4; Charles Judd to Marshall Bragdon, June 4, 1965, CHRC Collection, S.32/H/1.18.

34. State of Ohio, *Legislative Acts*, vol. 131, Ohio Revised Code, sec. 4112.01–.08 (1965), pp. 980–90; "Summary of Ohio Fair Housing Law," CHRC Collection, box 58, file 24; Ohio Association of Real Estate Boards, "Memorandum Analysis of Amended Substitute Senate Bill 189," 1965, NAACP Collection, box 6, file 31;

George L. Marder, "Negroes Lagging in Quest for Housing Equality," *Cincinnati Post and Times-Star,* Dec. 13, 1965, p. 16.

35. "The Need for an Open Housing Market," HOME Collection, US-82–5, box 1, file 20.

36. HOME, "Low-Income Housing Plan" [1967], CHRC Collection, S.32, box 59, file 17.

37. Ibid.

38. HOME Board Minutes, Dec. 12, 1966, HOME Collection, US-82–5, box 1, file 19; HOME, "Minutes of 'brainstorming' committee—Feb. 28, 1967," HOME Collection, US-82–5, box 1, file 20, p. 1; "Case 4, Notes of M. Smudski, HOME," Feb. 21–28, 1967, p. 1, HOME Collection, US-82–5, box 1, file 20.

39. HOME Board Minutes, Dec. 12, 1966, HOME Collection, US-82–5, box 1, file 19; HOME, "Minutes of 'brainstorming' committee"; "Case 4, Notes of M. Smudski, HOME."

40. Ibid.

41. Ibid.

42. "H.O.M.E.'s Observations Re: Housing Since the Riots," HOME Collection, US-82–5, box 1, file 77, p. 3.

43. HOME, "Annual Report, 1969," HOME Collection, US-82–5, box 1, file 3; Douglas S. Massey and Nancy A. Denton, *American Apartheid: Segregation and the Making of the Underclass* (Cambridge: Harvard University Press, 1993), p. 47; Gerald David Jaynes and Robin M. Williams Jr., *A Common Destiny: Blacks and American Society* (Washington, D.C.: National Academy Press, 1989), p. 79.

44. Bureau of the Census, 1970; U.S. Department of Commerce, Bureau of the Census, *Census of Population and Housing, 1980: Summary Tape File 3C* (Washington, D.C.: Bureau of the Census, 1982); Massey and Denton, *American Apartheid,* p. 86.

45. George Schermer, "A Background Paper for the Greater Cincinnati Conference on Equal Opportunity in Housing" (Cincinnati: President's Committee on Equal Opportunity in Housing, 1964), pp. 8–10.

46. See, for example, "Open Housing Agency Charges Apartment with Discrimination," *Cincinnati Enquirer,* June 7, 1984, p. 3D; HOME, "Realtor Use of School District Citations in Newspaper Advertising," draft, Jan. 1986; HOME, "Annual Report, 1990–1991," pp. 5–6; HOME, "Over-the-Rhine: A Permanent Ghetto," July 1, 1991.

47. See, for example, NAACP Collection, box 56, file 12, which documents a program involving HOME, the Cincinnati branch of the NAACP, and the Cincinnati Board of Realtors that sought to market housing outside of African American neighborhoods to blacks.

48. "Notes by Chas. M. Judd about 'scattered sites,'" March 1990, copy in author's possession.

49. Don Lenz to author, interview, December 1991.

50. For more on this, see Charles F. Casey-Leininger, "Planning, Community Control, and the Persistent Ghetto in Cincinnati, 1956–1980, *Planning History Studies* 2, no. 1 (1997): 31–37.

Postscript

The Queen City and Its Historian

ROGER W. LOTCHIN

This festschrift represents a fitting tribute to Zane L. Miller's long and distinguished career as an urban historian. Miller's publication record stretches
back to his days in graduate school, when he published a piece on Nathaniel
Macon, and has continued to the present in undiminished volume. His
books run to many and his articles, at last count, to fifty-eight. Most historians are egotistical enough to think that everything they do is suitable for
publication. However, it speaks especially well of Miller that a broad spectrum of editors of publications ranging from the *Journal of American History*
to the *North Carolina Historical Review* to the *Reviews in American History* to
the *Journal of Urban History* to the *Journal of Community Psychology* to the
American Jewish Archives have also thought that his output was worthy of
publication. Their collective judgment is a high compliment to Miller.

However important the quantitative dimension of Miller's work, the
qualitative dimension of this corpus is more so. It began with his first major
book, *Boss Cox's Cincinnati: Urban Politics in the Progressive Era*, published
in 1968 by Oxford University Press as a part of the Urban Life in America
series, edited by Richard Wade. American urban history was just entering
its second phase at this time, triggered by Wade's *Urban Frontier* and *Slav-
ery in the Cities* and Sam Bass Warner's *Streetcar Suburbs*. Beginning in the
mid-sixties, a number of historians and political scientists authored outstanding books on various phases of city political history. It was a seminal
period to which Miller's book was an important addition. However, *Boss
Cox's Cincinnati* was more than just a component of this burst of creativity;
it was a unique part.

Although moving in many other directions today, urban history in its
purest form is an attempt to study what is urban, not race, class, gender,
ethnicity, culture, or economics. All these aspects are important, but initially, the study of urban history was the attempt to get at something quin-
tessentially urban that was critical to the best practitioners of the craft. Historians asked what difference does or did the city make; what is the urban

core of this subject? Of all the early books on city political history, Miller's stands near the top in its insistence on the importance of city. Kenneth Jackson's *Ku Klux Klan in the City, 1915–1930* comes closest among the literature that I am familiar with to doing the same thing. Jackson argued that city Klansmen became so out of their experience in the urban "zone of emergence," a fault line where the plates of urban residence collided and produced upheavals such as the Klan. Lyle Dorsett (1968) and Bruce Stave were interested in the connection between city politics and national struggles for power, especially the Skeffington riddle of whether the machines declined because of the emergence of better welfare and security systems provided by the New Deal or took a fresh start from them. Several other excellent books looked at the ethnic groups within cities, especially those by Edward Levine, *The Irish and Irish Politicians* (1966); John Allswang, *A House for All People* (1971); Charles Trout, *Boston, The Great Depression and the New Deal* (1977); Ronald Bayor, *Neighbors in Conflict* (1978); John Stack, *International Conflict in an American City: Boston's Irish, Italians, and Jews* (1979), and, of course, Nathan Glazer and Daniel Moynihan, *Beyond the Melting Pot* (1963). Melvin Holli, in *Reform in Detroit: Hazen S. Pingree and Urban Politics* (1969), took on the task of typing city reformers between structural and social. And many authors attacked the question of the difference between boss and reform. Alexander Callow (1963), Joel Tarr (1971), Alex Gottfried (1962), Lawrence Larsen and Nancy Hulston (1997), and many others outlined the essential nature of the machine and its contrast to reform. More recently, scholars have been investigating the influence of class on city politics, as has Iver Bernstein, *The New York City Draft Riots* (1990), and Glenn Yago, *The Decline of Transit: Urban Transportation in German and US Cities, 1900–1970* (1984). These books have moved our understanding of city politics ahead by a considerable measure.

Miller essentially took on most of these topics in *Boss Cox's Cincinnati*, but in a different way. Instead of singling out one or a couple of perspectives, Miller sought to handle all of them and more, evolving in what he termed the "New City." As he described it, the New City in Cincinnati was one increasingly divided by class, space, ethnicity, and geography. It was the problems of this New City that led the metropolis into both machine and reform. Someone had to hold together the centrifugal forces exploding the New City, and the boss became that someone. This analysis was particularly closely tied to the evolving economic and social geography of Cincinnati. The examination of economic geography was especially useful to scholars and particularly comprehensive. And, of course, for those who really want to descend to the pulsating pavements of the New City, one can consult the three-volume dissertation from which the book is drawn in much abbreviated form. In either form, Miller's study is especially significant. The decline of the "walking city" has been studied from every angle—from urban transit to class—and seems to be central to our notion of what happened to nineteenth-century cities. No discussion is more comprehensive and topically integrated than that found in Miller's description of the New City.

Many scholars have been concerned with this problem of holding the New City together while it was simultaneously fragmenting. Seymour Mandelbaum's city was held together by political communication; Robert Fogelson's, by mass and interurban transit; Harold Platt's, by the electric grid; and Gunther Barth's, by transit and a new city culture. Miller's was held together by the social, governmental, and public works of its machine. The machine arose as a response to riots, police problems, residential flux, ethnocultural change, and so forth. This was one of Boss Cox's contributions to city politics; a second contribution was to pave the way for reform. Miller disputes many of his colleagues' claims that machines and reform were different. He saw a continuity between them, which has been borne out by the subsequent history of machine and reform, whether that written by professional historians such as Joel Shwartz (1993), amateurs such as Robert Caro (1974), political scientists such as Edward Banfield (1961), or practicing politicians such as Ed Koch (1984) and Jane Byrne (1992). From Banfield's *Political Influence* (1961) onward, observers have validated the same evolving merger of reform and machine political styles in other American cities that Miller found in Cincinnati.

Just as he employed a centripetal model of urban society to suggest a novel approach to understanding city politics, Miller also developed a centrifugal model to explain the intellectual changes accompanying urbanization and urbanism. A number of historians and commentators have wrestled with the "idea" of the city. As the New City emerged in the second half of the nineteenth century, social critics pounced upon it, declaring its deficiencies to the heavens—and to any mortals willing to listen. This anti-urban tradition has been developed in works dating back to Morton and Lucia White (1961) and down to the present. Thomas Bender was not certain that the host of intellectuals that the Whites paraded across the pages of history were so much against the city as they were adjusting to it. Again, Miller took a different tack.

In a book on the Forest Park suburb of Cincinnati, Miller turned the tables on the traditional interpretation of the idea of the city. Instead of looking at the way in which cities drove various thinkers to either desperation or accommodation, Miller studied the way in which the evolution of the idea of community shaped both the form and function of the city. Cities change, he argued, because our ideas about them change. The challenge and response is exactly the reverse of what we have usually assumed. That interpretation in itself is a welcome transition from the emphasis on the supposedly overwhelming material and social forces that shape urban history and at the same time are a challenge to them. *Suburb: Neighborhood and Community in Forest Park, Ohio, 1935–1976* (1981) makes it clear that the mental is more important than the material. Suburbs were guided into being and changed by the mental constructs in the minds of their planners, politicians, and publics. As these transmuted, so did suburb and city. Others have interposed this idea into the debate over suburbia, but usually later and only in part. Still others, such as Kenneth Jackson, Robert Fogelson, and Robert Fishman, have described in commendable detail the way in which ideas about the family, religion, nature, rural life, and other matters shaped city and suburb, but do not so fully concentrate on the idea of the city.

While pioneering these new ideas, Miller also contributed one of the first modern scholarly studies of suburbia, which would be followed by others written by Kenneth Jackson (1985), Robert Fishman (1987), Henry Binford (1985), Carol O'Conner (1983), and Ann Durkin Keating (1988), and preceded only by Jon Teaford (1979). In the process, Miller offered both a new chronological paradigm for studying city and suburb and a challenge to those who believed, and stated as much in a vast literature of alienation, that city and suburb were different entities, one superior, the other inferior. Miller believed them to be part of the same continually evolving community. He found that the story of Forest Park began "when a mode of thought about cities and suburbs prevailed which took the metropolis as the basic unit of society" (p. xxii). This idea then shifted to a community "of autonomous individuals as the basic units of society," individuals with a limited liability. These individuals had a partial allegiance to urban community, but also an allegiance to other entities. That idea of community in turn was replaced by a community of advocacy, in which liberated individuals were the basic units of society and acknowledged not even "a partial commitment to civic participation for the sake of community welfare" (p. xxvi). Each alteration "in the taxonomy of reality" (p. xvi) produced different ideas about how city and suburb should be organized, planned, spatially shaped, and struggled over. That process, in turn, was "symptomatic" of what was happening all over the United States.

Miller's career has also been outstanding in another way. He has spent most of it studying one city. To be sure, his scholarship has ventured beyond the confines of Cincinnati to investigate matters like general American urbanism or race in Southern cities. However, most of his professional life has been devoted to uncovering the past of Cincinnati. Others have been loyal to one locale, Roger Lane to Philadelphia and William Issel and Robert Cherny to San Francisco—but their numbers are few. This constancy has allowed Miller to bring coherence of purpose and outcome to the study of one of America's still insufficiently well known places. At a time when urban history is exploding even more than the fragmented metropolis itself, Miller has clung to the urban area centered on the Reds' and Bengals' stadium and the Roebling Bridge and to his ideas, to his own taxonomy of reality and to what it has been all about. Both his own works and those of his students reflect this unfailing interest in Cincinnati and, do we dare say it, love of place.

Of course, this output has been of more than just sentimental purpose. Since the time of Emile Durkheim, Ferdinand Tonnies, Oswald Spengler, and their colleagues, scholars have bemoaned the loss of community in cities. Miller's work has tended in the other direction. Communities cannot exist without some shared experience, and if people do not work in the same ways, share the same religion, cherish the same ethnocultural heritage, or watch the same television programs, they can at least partake of the same history. Miller's work is not written in a chauvinistic way to claim pride of urban place, but to provide a resource that high school teachers, planners, politicians, media personnel, conservatives, liberals, rabbis, racemen, and reformers can draw on and be challenged by. Thus the histories of medicine and health, neighborhoods, the music hall, redevelopment areas, and suburbs have laid the foundations of community by giving people who share only the space of the metropolis a share in its story as well.

Much of Miller's thinking about Cincinnati, community, and civic affairs in cities is expressed in *Changing Plans for America's Inner Cities: Cincinnati's Over-the-Rhine and Twentieth-Century Urbanism* (with Bruce Tucker, 1998). The neighborhood north of Cincinnati's central business district has become a rundown slum or inner-city area. Once the center of German life in the city, it is now a neighborhood of poor whites from Appalachia and poor blacks from the South. Miller explores the consequences triggered by the changing social trends of this area and the changing view of the city. As in *Suburb,* the story of this inner-city neighborhood alters as the thinking of planners and others does.

Not to let the history of a slum and a suburb stand for the history of the whole city, as many historians have, Miller, in conjunction with Henry Shapiro, also wrote *Clifton: Neighborhood and Community in an Urban Setting: A Brief History.* Clifton is one of those old, charming city neighborhoods that has not gone downhill, been deserted in the process of white flight, or lost viability in some other way—as indicated by the residence there of the author, his wife, and their cat. It is also one of the most diverse and complex architectural treasures in any American city.

In these three books, Miller and his collaborators, Bruce Tucker and Henry Shapiro, have done intensive studies of Cincinnati neighborhoods, running from the center to the periphery.

Cincinnati's Music Hall (with George Roth) complements the history of Cincinnati and the taxonomy of reality of these volumes perfectly. Miller wrote the largest portion of this volume, and it plays an important role in his intellectual history of the city. Rather than telling the story of a neighborhood or a mental construct, *Cincinnati's Music Hall* concentrates on a key component of the artistic and architectural heritage of the Queen City. Although the book is not the kind that will win the Bancroft Prize, it is perfectly suited to the task of creating a sense of community in a city that reveres same. The Music Hall is symbolic both of the city's artistic and architectural tradition and of its general quest for prominence. Created in the nineteenth century, it was a crucial part of the Queen City's drive to dominate its own portion of mid-America by outdoing St. Louis, Chicago, and New Orleans and by cutting into the lead of New York City. Starting from a general idea of what a city was all about, its builders believed that just as a city needed commerce and industry, so also it needed culture. The University of Cincinnati was one outcome of this conviction; the park system was another, and the Music Hall, a third. Opened in 1878, the Music Hall played host to varied events over many years. These ranged from opera to orchestral music to saengerfests to music festivals to jazz. Miller integrated his narrative with the story of neighborhood, city culture, race, and recreation, so that the book is not just about the Music Hall, but about much else as well. It is also integrated into his paradigm of urban change. Its history illustrates the evolution of thought—from an organic mode of thought to a community-of-limited-liability type of thought. As each mode of thought changed into another, the purpose of the Music Hall did too. And as Cincinnati scaled back its hopes for urban dominance to an ever decreasing area, the purpose of the Music Hall changed in response.

And where Miller left off, his students have continued the narrative and analysis. Twelve of the seventeen Ph.D. dissertations he has supervised cover Cincinnati subjects. Like the planning studies in the Urban Life and Urban Landscape series, these seem particularly well calculated to cover a subject comprehensively. Despite his own overarching interest in planning, Miller has led his students to a wide variety of topics, each of crucial importance to a city and community. Studies of the Cincinnati Symphony Orchestra, education, the Archdiocese of Cincinnati, women's benevolent activities, metropolitan fragmentation, the rise of city services, housing, social welfare planning, city government (comparatively treated), politics, and civil rights do not quite exhaust the subject of Cincinnati history, but they have created a broad base for other historians to build on and other community leaders to draw upon. This body of scholarship has made Cincinnati one of the most thoroughly studied cities in the country. And his students and others would agree that Miller's orchestration of this ouevre has been nurturant in the extreme.

Miller designed much of his output to be used by professionals and activists who want to improve the city. Fully twelve of the thirty-two volumes in the Urban Life and Urban Landscape series, edited by Miller and Henry Shapiro, are about planning or related topics. These include books on design, suburbs, downtowns, neighborhoods, government, redevelopment, services, the environment, and region, a relatively comprehensive coverage of the subject. His own *Suburb* and *Changing Plans* are heavily devoted to the problem of planning the metropolis. Thus Miller's edited volume with Paula Dubeck, *Urban Professionals and the Future of the Metropolis*, is, in a sense, a continuation of his thinking about city planning, but on a broader scale. Miller has always prided himself on being where the action of city politics is, and the books on planning have helped keep him there. *Urban Professionals* collared several prominent historians to assess the "issues of the role of urban professionals" in formulating and implementing a national urban policy. A series of symposia, inspired by the urban crisis and held at the University of Cincinnati, concluded that the role of the urban professional in the urban crisis had been based on "mechanistic" thinking instead of a new view of what the future city should be. This thinking accounted for the failure of urban professionals to effect the kinds of changes that would be viable in the future and led the scholars at the conference to question the appropriateness of the large role that urban professionals play in shaping urban policy and outcome. Miller must have given the group a thought message because they agreed with him that the reconceptualization of the metropolis was the key to changing it. The urban professionals had assumed that the urban community was a community of limited liability, and a viable metropolis must become more than that.

The contributors to the volume each address the role of the urban professional, past and present, in dealing with the urban dilemma. And Miller and Dubeck, historian and sociologist, end with an especially compelling argument against the kind of history and sociology that deny the value of neighborhood, city, and metropolis as valid units of study. In fact, the discussion of Miller's notion of community is more clearly explained here than anywhere else. His idea that neighborhood, city, and metropolis are valid fields of inquiry seems more preeminently sensible than looking only at family and individual.

Nor has Miller's dedication to neighborhood, city, and metropolis been limited to verbal exhortation and intellectual constructs. He has heavily invested his own life in these things as well. The list of his local activities reads like that of a grassroots organizer. There is no dedication to a community of advocacy here, or even to a community of limited liability. Miller's engagement with his community has been the total, civic kind.

To sum up, what has been Zane Miller's contribution to urban history? He has offered scholars of city politics a novel paradigm for studying big city machines; he has produced a new periodization of urban history, which at the same time amounts to a reconceptualization of the idea of urban community; he has undertaken a scholarly assault on the history of Cincinnati, both in his own works and by his direction of many graduate student investigations of that urban area; he has aimed his scholarship toward the revitalization of planning thought and planning practice; he has led and nurtured the scholarship of others about cities through his mentorship and book series; and he has demonstrated that the ideas that people hold about cities matter and, indeed, are more important than material realities. These things together constitute a major intellectual heritage. In the understated, self-deprecating midwestern language that I grew up with, it would be said that in making sense of the city, one could easily do a lot worse.

Contributors

ROBERT A. BURNHAM is an associate professor in the Division of Social Sciences at Macon State College in Georgia. His publications include "Reform, Politics, and Race in Cincinnati: Proportional Representation and the City Charter Committee, 1927–1957," *Journal of Urban History* 23 (1997), and "The Mayor's Friendly Relations Committee: Cultural Pluralism and the Struggle for Black Advancement," in *Race and the City: Work, Community, Housing, and Protest in Cincinnati, 1820–1970,* ed. Henry Louis Taylor Jr.

CHARLES F. CASEY-LEININGER is an adjunct assistant professor at the University of Cincinnati, where he teaches urban African American history and the history of the civil rights movement in the College of Evening and Continuing Education. He is a research analyst focusing on policy issues in welfare, child care, and child health for the Children's Defense Fund-Greater Cincinnati Project. His publications include "Planning, Community Control, and the Persistent Ghetto in Cincinnati, 1956–1980," in *Planning History Studies* (1997), and "Making the Second Ghetto in Cincinnati: Avondale, 1925–1970," in *Race and the City: Work, Community, Housing, and Protest in Cincinnati, 1820–1970,* ed. Henry Louis Taylor Jr.

BRADLEY D. CROSS is an assistant professor of history at St. Thomas University in Fredericton, New Brunswick. He has written on early-twentieth-century American city planning and is completing a book on twentieth-century conceptions of garden city ideas in Great Britain, Canada, and the United States. His recent publications include "John Nolen, City Planner (1869-1937)" and "Mariemont, Ohio, Model Garden City, " both in *American Cities and Suburbs: An Encyclopedia,* ed. Neil Larry Shumsky. Cross also is interested in how current movements in planning have tried to adapt past models to contemporary problems. Future projects include a study of divergent conceptions of urban and rural.

ROBERT B. FAIRBANKS is a professor of history at the University of Texas at Arlington. He is editor for the Americas for *Planning Perspectives* and is the author of *For the City as a Whole: Planning, Politics, and the Public Interest in Dallas, Texas, 1900–1965* and *Making Better Citizens: Housing Reform and the Community Development Strategy in Cincinnati, 1890-1960.* He is currently writing a book on the history of public housing in the Southwest.

ANDREA TUTTLE KORNBLUH is an associate professor of history at the University of Cincinnati. She is interested in how programs of municipal public recreation in the 1920s, '30s, and '40s trained citizens in the values of liberal democracy. Her published essays examine the interactions among race, ethnicity, gender, and American cities during the first half of the twentieth century. Her publications include "James Hathaway Robinson and the Origins of Professional Social Work in the Black Community," in *Race and the City: Work, Community, Housing, and Protest in Cincinnati, 1820-1970*, ed. Henry Louis Taylor Jr., and *Lighting the Way: The Woman's City Club of Cincinnati, 1915–1965*. She has been the research director for numerous documentaries, including *Degrees of Shame: Adjunct Faculty, Migrant Workers of the Information Economy*, produced and directed by Barbara Wolf.

ROGER W. LOTCHIN is professor of history at the University of North Carolina at Chapel Hill. His books include *Fortress California, 1910–1961: From Warfare to Welfare; San Francisco, 1846-1856: From Hamlet to City; The Martial Metropolis: American Cities in Peace and War, 1900–1970;* and *The Way We Really Were: The Golden State in the Second Great War.* He is working on a book on the impact of World War II on California cities.

ALAN I MARCUS is professor of history and director of the Center for Historical Studies of Technology and Science at Iowa State University. He is the author or editor of ten books. Recent publications include *Cancer from Beef: DES, Federal Food Regulation, and Consumer Confidence* and *Plague of Strangers: Social Groups and the Origin of City Services in Cincinnati, 1819–1870.* He is currently studying the history of management theories and practices in the twentieth century, with particular attention to Total Quality Management.

PATRICIA MOONEY-MELVIN is associate professor of history and director of the public history program at Loyola University Chicago. Her publications include "Professional Historians and the Challenge of Redefinition," in *Public History: Essays from the Field*, ed. James B. Gardner and Peter LaPaglia; *Reading Your Neighborhood: A Brief History of East Rogers Park;* and *The Organic City: Urban Definition and Neighborhood Organization, 1880–1920.* She is currently working on a study of the memorial landscape of Chicago.

JUDITH SPRAUL-SCHMIDT is visiting assistant professor at the University of Cincinnati and former membership secretary of the Urban History Association. She serves as vice chairman of the Historic Conservation Board of the city of Cincinnati and has been a member of the Cincinnati Public Schools Facilities Master Plan Advising Committee. Her publications include "The Ohio Mechanic's Institute: The Challenge of Incivility in the Democratic Republic," in *Technical Knowledge in American Culture: Science, Technology, and Medicine since the Early 1800s*, ed. Alan Marcus, David M. Katzman, and Hamilton Cravens, and "Designing the Late Nineteenth Century Suburban Landscape: The Cincinnati Zoological Garden," in *Queen City Heritage* (1993).

Index

Urban Life and Urban Landscape Series

Zane L. Miller, General Editor

The series examines the history of urban life and the development of the urban landscape through works that place social, economic, and political issues in the intellectual and cultural context of their times.

www.ingramcontent.com/pod-product-compliance
Lightning Source LLC
Chambersburg PA
CBHW020704270326
41928CB00005B/252